ICON READERS' GUIDES

The Plays of

Tom Stoppard

for Stage, Radio, TV and Film

EDITED BY TERRY HODGSON

Consultant editor: Nicolas Tredell

ICON BOOKS

Published in 2001 by Icon Books Ltd.,
Grange Road, Duxford, Cambridge CB2 4QF
e-mail: info@iconbooks.co.uk
www.iconbooks.co.uk

Sold in the UK, Europe, South Africa and Asia by Faber & Faber Ltd.,
3 Queen Square, London WC1N 3AU or their agents

Distributed in the UK, Europe, South Africa and Asia by Macmillan
Distribution Ltd., Houndmills, Basingstoke RG21 6XS

Published in Australia in 2001 by Allen & Unwin Pty. Ltd.,
PO Box 8500, 83 Alexander Street, Crows Nest, NSW 2065

Distributed in Canada by Penguin Books Canada, 10 Alcorn Avenue,
Suite 300, Toronto, Ontario M4V 3B2

Consultant editor: Nicolas Tredell
Managing editor: Duncan Heath
Series devised by: Christopher Cox
Cover design: Simon Flynn
Typesetting: Wayzgoose

ISBN 1 84046 241 8

Printed and bound in Great Britain by
Biddles Ltd., Guildford and King's Lynn

Contents

Preface

THIS BOOK attempts to give an overview of the plays of Tom Stoppard and critical responses to him. Stoppard has written fiction, radio plays, TV and film scripts, as well as for the theatre. This constitutes a considerable body of work, but one cannot chronicle broad shifts of critical response to it, as one can with Readers' Guides to a single book or play written a century or several centuries ago. We are too close and critical responses are mixed. Stoppard himself, however, has contributed many illuminating interviews over the last four decades which comment particularly on the experience of writing plays and emphasise, as one would expect, that theatre is written to be performed. Much academic criticism analyses theme and content, but pays less attention to the varied dramatic forms Stoppard handles. It also focuses on three of the 35 plays so far adapted or written (*Rosencrantz and Guildenstern Are Dead*, *Travesties* and *Jumpers*), so that many 'smaller' works have been, often unjustly, neglected. This book therefore pays attention to the theatricality of the work and provides a roughly chronological and individual commentary on all the published plays, whilst including the observations of the author himself and a number of academic perspectives. This is followed by a general survey of responses to Stoppard's work and some final observations on fundamental questions concerning characterisation and dramatic structure.

CHAPTER ONE

The Background and the Work

A PLAY EMERGES from a transaction between an author's talent and the historical, linguistic and material theatre conditions of his time in a way (as Stoppard acknowledges) not always apparent to the author himself. It is a product of 'temperament' (Stoppard's word); of personal and social background; the historical events he has witnessed or experienced; and the literature and drama available to him, especially at the important moment of a choice of career. This chapter will therefore focus on the transaction between temperament and background, biography and art.

The outlines of Stoppard's biography have been detailed in a number of books (for example, *Tom Stoppard, A Casebook*, edited by John Harty III, 1988). Stoppard was born Tomas Straussler on 3 July 1937 in Zlin, Czechoslavakia, the second son of a doctor working for the Bata shoe company which transferred the Jewish family to Singapore in 1939 in order to save them from Hitler. The Japanese invaded and mother and children found their way to India. The father remained behind and was killed when the Japanese sank the ship on which he was sailing to Australia. In 1945, the mother remarried a major in the British Army and moved to England where Stoppard attended Pocklington Grammar, a minor public school in Yorkshire. In 1954, he left to spend six years as a news reporter, theatre critic and feature writer in Bristol, before he resigned to write plays and fiction. He published some short stories in 1963 and in that year a play, *Walk on Water*, was transmitted by ITV. Another play, *The Gamblers*, was performed by an amateur group at the University of Bristol (see Ronald Hayman's early book, pp. 28–31). In 1965, *Rosencrantz and Guildenstern Are Dead* was noticed by Ronald Bryden at the Edinburgh Fringe and triumphantly produced by the National Theatre at the Old Vic in 1966, eclipsing his novel, *Lord Malquist and Mr Moon*, published in the same year. Since then, he has produced long plays every three or four years, most of them to great applause, and written fairly extensively for radio, television and film, as well as adapting plays by foreign playwrights such as Schnitzler and Nestroy. His contribution to the script of the film *Shakespeare in Love* (1999) was his most recent success.

Stoppard is not a directly biographical writer and until recently he was reticent about his private life. On 10 October 1999, however, a memoir by Stoppard appeared in the *Sunday Telegraph Magazine* which contains moving details about his Czech mother and his Jewish background and a more detached section describing his relations with his stepfather 'Ken'. The article emphasises his early lack of a sense of his European roots, provides some explanation for his growing interest in eastern European writers and their political background (as in the TV play *Professional Foul*), but ultimately declares: 'Englishness had won and Czechoslavakia had lost'. This seems to imply that his gradual growth of awareness of his Jewish and Czech origins came too late to make him a different kind of writer. England and the English language had provided him with places and discourses within which he says he feels entirely at home.

No writer, however, can detach himself from the history of his own time. It is true that one or two of Stoppard's characters, such as John Brown in *A Separate Peace* (1966), may be projections of an understandable writer's desire to evade the outside world and live within a closed room, but Stoppard spent several years in the very public world of journalism. His characters who live in their own imaginations – George Riley is another example in *Enter a Free Man* (1960) – are counterbalanced by characters such as the active journalists in *Night and Day* (1978). Stoppard makes dramatic use of a double need to participate and withdraw.

The personal and private travails of childhood are not always easy to detect in a writer's work. They may appear in indirect ways, as the experience of fictional characters or filtered subtly through invented dramatic structures. They may be incorporated into forms he appropriates from other writers, ancient and modern. Stoppard, in early interviews, suggested that his work was not personal and that his writing emerged from external ideas and reading. But all writers combine observation and study of the outside world with personal experience, even though they may not recognise it at the time. The biographical article in the *Sunday Telegraph* describes his very early Czech childhood: his mother and stepfather; his discovery of his Czech family destroyed in the holocaust; the scanty knowledge of his real father drowned in the strait between Sumatra and the island of Bangka; his early life in India; his lack of awareness of his Jewishness. It is dangerous to find a causal relation between Stoppard's 'extraterritoriality' (George Steiner's word) and the plays. Stoppard resists the idea, though there may be an oblique relation with past and possible future work.

To identify biographical material does few favours for the artist, though it may create an alternative text of some interest for the reader. This book will not indulge in such speculations, except to remark that concern with human relations, love, private angst, game-playing, language, dreams, freedom and the nature of history, the creative process itself in the face of death, Stoppardian themes all, must have some relation to the man and artist, whilst at the same time much has doubtless been drawn from the experience of others.

What may be said is that historical and social material is bound to be present in the mind of a former professional journalist. He knows about the media and problems of free expression, about the processes of image building and the difficulties of transmitting events and activities to a reader and audience. Memories of war and cold war amalgamate with reading about it. Reading about the Russian Revolution, about spying, about life behind the Iron Curtain, about African states, about India, mingles with buried memories, with chance remarks and random experience and with theories about the origins of the natural world, the nature of language and of art.

Reading is an important source for Stoppard. A voracious appetite for knowledge sends him into philosophy, science, mathematics, theories of literature and visual art, as well as into the riches of English drama, poetry and fiction. The reading suggests an idea for a play and prompts further reading which, in a mysterious and apparently chaotic manner, mingles with other material, often visual. Thus Hamlet and the Players mingle in Stoppard's *Rosencrantz and Guildenstern Are Dead* with Beckett's image in *Waiting for Godot* of 'two guys who don't know why'. In *Travesties*, reading about Tristan Tzara and the Dada movement fuses with *Memories of Lenin* by Lenin's wife, with James Joyce's *Ulysses* and much else. The unlikely origin of the semi-historical Henry Carr and his role in Joyce's production of Oscar Wilde's *The Importance of Being Earnest* is recounted in Stoppard's preface.

Stoppard frequently refers to T.S. Eliot and particularly 'The Love Song of J. Alfred Prufrock'; E.M. Forster's *A Passage to India* and ideas of Indian art feed into his play *Indian Ink*. *The Invention of Love* is about the dual character of A.E. Housman, poet and scholar, and various Victorian Oxford scholars appear on stage with Housman (and are poled across the Styx by Charon). Stoppard owes a special debt to early twentieth- and late nineteenth-century 'modernist' literature, but he also feeds on contemporary philosophy and science. In Arcadia, 'chaos theory' combines with an interest in the pastoral, a reading of Byron and the landscapists Humphrey Repton and Capability Brown. Wittgenstein's *Philosophical Investigations* figure among the strongest literary influences on *Jumpers* and prompt the language games in *Dogg's Hamlet* and Cahoot's *Macbeth*. Stoppard's reading is part of his work, though he may not know exactly where such reading will take him.

A writer, then, is fed by roots both personal and impersonal and the vocal and visual 'theatre language' he employs (which involves the nature of the casting, the actor's use of voice, the relationships between actors, between actor and director, the director's choice of pace, the designer's set, the lighting and costume design) is not entirely his. Theatre is in the public and commercial domain and a play arises from a collaboration with material conditions. Shakespeare was constrained by the talents and gender of the actors at his disposal and could not write many parts for women because women could not appear on stage. Similarly a modern dramatist takes into account not only what his temperament and background prompt him to write, but also what is acceptable at a particular moment to a particular institution, a particular director, a particular audience. A series of compromises or negotiations with directors, designers and actors is inevitable. At the same time, producers, theatres and audiences exert strong pressures. The author is not the only person responsible for his work.

In film and television the pressure to change a submitted script is especially great. Stoppard's description in his introduction (p. 9) of the evolution of *Squaring the Circle* (1984) is illuminating. The play is a kind of documentary and therefore an ostensibly 'objective' account of what happened during the Polish 'Solidarity' movement. It seeks to examine the roles of Lech Walesa, General Jaruzelski and others, but there are problems. Who *was* Jaruzelski, or Walesa for that matter? What did Walesa not say in recorded interviews? And what were his private thoughts? Evidently creative choices and an element of subjective speculation play a part in all histories and documentaries of this kind. These leave an author open to accusations of bias.

Stoppard experienced problems that were creative, technical, financial and cultural. It was difficult to find a director. Mike Hodges was number eight and 'worth waiting for'. There were problems of choosing a location or studio, of casting, of finding investment, of meeting the demands of Metromedia, the American sponsor. He who pays the piper wants to call the tune and the length of programme and inclusion of commercial slots, the apparent ideology of the script and the shape of the film were all argued over. Metromedia considered they 'had bought the right to alter *Squaring the Circle* in any way they liked' says Stoppard in the published introduction (p. 15). With a cast list of 50 named characters, Metromedia's desire for control was as understandable as the director's and author's desire to retain it. With pressures such as these, Stoppard's preference for the live theatre is not surprising. There he has mainly acquired the power to choose actors and directors who are in sympathy with his work and his scripts are less likely to be warped by commercial and technological pressures.

The origins of Stoppard's scripts are worth further comment. Sometimes a particular actor is in his mind when writing a play. John Wood, who played Henry Carr in *Travesties*, is a case in point and Stoppard acknowledges his creative debts in rehearsal and performance to other actors and directors. Many plays, however, spring in the first place from ideas and images. Stoppard's account in another interview with Mel Gussow (*Conversations*, pp. 89–91) reveals the way his creative mind worked on perhaps the finest of his plays: *Arcadia*.

■ *M.G.*: To return to *Arcadia*, where did it begin? With the book *Chaos*? [a challenging book by James Gleick about a range of new scientific ideas]

T.S.: I think so. On the other hand, I must have been reading *Chaos* because of something else I read, maybe in a magazine or a newspaper. It's like a river with more than one source. There's no 'where' about it. You just mentioned the *Chaos* mathematics book. At the same time, I was thinking about Romanticism and Classicism as opposites in style, taste, temperament, art . . . You and I tend to talk about all this as if it really works like that, as if there's this acorn that you find somewhere and put manure around and water, and hope it grows into some kind of sapling . . . it doesn't seem to me to be that kind of orderly natural development.

M.G.: No single acorn?

T.S.: It's more than that. I have the feeling that you throw the acorn away at some point . . . an alternative way of making a picture of the process would be to say that it's something that starts you up, like a motor gets started up, like a cranking handle. Then you throw the handle away, and drive off down the road somewhere and see where the road goes. (pp. 89–90) □

Leisure reading is 'subconsciously purposeful'. A particular scientific book, picked up out of general interest, mingles with ideas about classical and romantic temperaments, which generate characters that demand their own voice. The original source is no longer primary and early concerns may disappear as the work develops. It behoves critics to be careful with identifying origins.

If this is true of the evolution of a particular play, a commentator should also be wary of defining the development of Stoppard's whole career. Certain tendencies are visible – towards a greater naturalism, a deeper concern with human (and female) experience, a stronger involvement in political drama, as well as a sense of time passing and a greater confidence in the value of art, literature and particularly, poetry. At the same time there seems to be a movement away from dazzling exhibitions of wit and formal parody. But Stoppard's future work may well confound the academic tracer of patterns. In interview he consistently warns us against it.

CHAPTER TWO

Early Stage Plays: Playing Games

Enter a Free Man and *Rosencrantz and Guildenstern Are Dead*

Enter a Free Man

Stoppard resigned from the *Bristol Evening World* in 1960 in order to complete his first play, entitled *A Walk on the Water*. It was transmitted by Rediffusion in November 1963, received its first stage production in Hamburg and was televised in 1964 as *The Preservation of George Riley*. In a version Stoppard claims was substantially the same as the original, it became *Enter a Free Man*, first performed in London at the St Martin's Theatre on 28 March 1968.

■ The first play I wrote was very much in the mode of *Flowering Cherry* [by Robert Bolt]. Or *Death of a Salesman*, but not in the class of either. It was a naturalistic play about people I had never met. (Gussow, p. 115) □

The play has not received a good press, probably because it lacks the originality of form that marks Stoppard's subsequent major plays. It opens with a complicated split stage and the action switches between 'a slightly old-fashioned, unfashionable pub in what is probably a seedy urban suburb' and the overdecorated but neat home of George Riley, dreamer, inventor and parasite, who accepts spending money from his nineteen-year-old daughter Linda and is looked after by his wife Constance. George invents, among other things, an envelope that can be used twice. But like all his inventions, it turns out to be useless and he discovers that the 'partner' he had been leaving home to set up business with has been pulling his leg. He returns to his understanding wife and daughter.

The play is naturalistic, apart from initial cross-cutting between the two locations and a later fade into a spotlit soliloquy. It is reminiscent of the late-50s urban and kitchen-sink settings of Osborne, Pinter and Wesker, and has a flavour of Henrik Ibsen's masterpiece *The Wild Duck*, as well as Arthur Miller's *Death of a Salesman*. Both of these are much concerned with failed dreamers. Stoppard's treatment, however, owes more to stand-up television comedy.

There is little commentary on the play. Ronald Hayman finds the construction neat and the dialogue generally convincing:

■ The dialogue is at its worst when trying to explain relationships and at its best when demonstrating a lack of contact between two people who are having a conversation. George Riley finds his only appreciative audience in the pub where Carmen, the barman, sympathizes without listening and Able, the gormless sailor, admires without understanding, while Harry, who lives on his bets and his wits, mocks at Riley with an irony he fails to notice:

> *Harry*: Don't you think George here is a clever bloke?
> *Able*: Course he's a clever bloke. He's an inventor isn't he?
> *Harry*: My very point. An inventor. That's your job. Amazing. I don't know if you've ever thought George, but if you took away everything in the world that had to be invented, there'd be nothing left except a lot of people getting rained on . . . (Hayman, pp. 15–16) □

Another failed invention – an indoor watering system – is responsible for George being rained on as the play ends.

Hayman feels the play communicates some pathos through the isolation of its characters. Anthony Jenkins, in *The Theatre of Tom Stoppard*, sees the play as farce and feels the play ceases to work when the characters start to interact emotionally:

■ As motivated individuals, rather than cartoon figures who move through a series of stock situations, the characters of *A Free Man* wobble disconcertingly . . . After he [George] leaves, Persephone, whom we have seen two-dimensionally, is suddenly given a brain and a heart as she appeals to Linda's sympathy:

> *Linda*: It costs him – every time he comes back he loses a little face and he's lost a lot of face – to you he's lost all of it . . .

If we are to take this seriously beneath the card-board cut-out housewife, we must wonder how she can accept her daughter's escapade with her latest motor-cycling knight . . . (Jenkins, pp. 5–6) □

Stoppard, himself, talks rather disparagingly of the play, but it is not negligible, even if ultimately it seems derivative, and the farce rides uneasily with the naturalistic elements. It is a thoroughly professional piece of work and, although at this stage Stoppard described himself as a professional writer who writes for a market, the play has qualities that raise it well above run-of-the mill TV. Behind the problems Jenkins identifies may be found some of the ambitions and serious concerns of the later and better known plays. One of these is dualism of character:

■ *Persephone*: Well, why shouldn't he go to the pub? At least he meets people.
Linda: How do you know? I bet he's just another lonely feller having a quiet drink. The point is, what's he like? I mean when we can't see him. He's got to be different – I mean – you wouldn't even know me if you could see me –
(*Able enters as before . . .*)
Persephone (leaving): Come on Linda.
Linda: And that goes for everyone. There's two of everyone you see –
(*Brown enters as before*)
And if the two of him's the same, I mean, if he's the same in the pub as he is with us, then he's had it.
(*Riley enters as before*)
Riley: Enter a free man! (pp. 53–4) □

Here in relatively direct form is the question of dual personality that continues to fascinate Stoppard. In *Enter a Free Man* characters are seen as double, but are not necessarily so. Riley and Brown enter on Linda's lines to query or exemplify Linda's statement that everyone is dual. Brown seems not to be dual. George Riley thinks he is an industrial spy, but the duality exists in George's imagination. Brown is just another lonely feller having a quiet drink and probably just the same at home. Riley, too, remains the same in two places – a romantic who fails to connect his dreams with the practical world. His duality consists in the discrepancy between what he is and what he imagines he might become.

But even at this early stage, Stoppard's characterisation is developing complexity. Persephone (real name Constance) has imagination enough to identify the way George's mind works and to encourage it (rather like Relling, the doctor in Ibsen's *The Wild Duck* who provides dreams for ordinary men to live by). Constance/Persephone is only double insofar as she is given a second name, but her daughter Linda wants to see George as double and is herself something of a dual personality. Like George, she is not fully grown up and her dreams come from the Hollywood dream factory. This makes her, like George, vulnerable and more attractive, indeed more dramatic, than the realists who are no longer children and no longer dream. But she is a realist about George, whose imagination she deplores, yet for whom she still has a strong affection, as does Constance. This mix of realism and romanticism lends Stoppard's characters a self-awareness that takes them out of the category of stereotypical dreamers and fool figures. Even George eventually realises he should compromise with reality and go to the labour exchange whilst waiting for an invention to be taken up.

Enter a Free Man heralds Stoppard's concern with a number of issues. One is imagination and creativity. Another is the related question of individual freedom. George Riley quotes Rousseau's *Social Contract*, chapter 1: 'A man is born free and everywhere he is in chains. Who said that?' George imagines he is free, but desperately holds on to childhood, reading children's books, chained by dreams which keep him happy. Yet he condemns dreams in others, in his daughter, in gamblers:

■ *Riley*: Gambling. The opiate of the common herd . . . Dreams, diversions to keep the mob happy. It's the Government you see.
Harry: I always suspected it.
Riley: It's the truth. The government's taking a tip from the Romans. When the place was declining and falling around their ears, you know what the Romans did?
Harry: No?
Riley: Bread and circuses. To take the mob's mind off it. Same thing now, only it's football . . . (pp. 13–14) □

Stoppard will continue to examine the question of freedom and control in the political plays. Even Riley's farcical conviction that the inoffensive Brown is an industrial spy anticipates Stoppard's interest in the Le Carré thriller and in espionage as a weapon of power.

Other philosophical questions are raised. The nature of time (and Englishness) is hinted at in Riley's invention of a clock (a continuing leitmotif in Stoppard) which plays *Rule Britannia* instead of striking twelve. Behind the joking is the question of time passing. George Riley is determined to remain young and does not want to hear the clock strike or England to change. Occasional inflated lines such as: 'People will see this once uncharted, untrod path and say . . . George Riley walked this way' (p. 32) and 'When a man's past outweighs his future, then he's a man standing in his own shadow' (p. 33) have an element of seriousness. The question of using time instead of letting time use you and the need to achieve recognition would not be unknown to an ambitious playwright. Stoppard's early experience of trying to launch his career must have contributed to this and it may well relate to Riley's image of a confined boat which recurs in that play:

■ *Riley*: Odd thing is . . . I sometimes think of myself as a sailor, in a way . . . with home as a little boat, anchored in the middle of a big calm sea, never going anywhere, just sitting, far from land, life, everything . . . (p. 75) □

The idea of waiting, aware of time passing, which is at the heart of Beckett, is in Stoppard too, linked with a form of poetry beneath the jokes that will emerge more clearly in the playwright's work.

Anthony Jenkins may be right to point out that *Enter a Free Man* does not successfully combine farce with a more naturalistic and sympathetic human concern. Stoppard half agrees:

■ *Enter a Free Man* looks as though it's about people as real – at least in terms of art – as the people in *Coronation Street*. But to me the whole thing is a bit phoney, because they're only real because I've seen them in other people's plays. I haven't actually met any of them myself. It's about upper working-class families. They had to be a bit upper because I kept giving them extremely well-constructed speeches to speak at a high rate of knots . . . (Hayman 'First Interview', p. 6) □

Stoppard, however, went beyond the flat figures of TV comedy. He is already overlapping genres and raising complex questions. *Enter a Free Man* anticipates many of the playwright's future concerns.

Rosencrantz and Guildenstern Are Dead

Stoppard tells us of another apprentice play, written in 1960 and performed by Bristol University undergraduates in 1965: ' . . . And then I wrote a *Waiting for Godot* type play called *The Gamblers*. God knows whether a text of that exists or not . . . ' (Gussow, p. 115). '*Waiting for Godot* in the death cell – I'm sure you can imagine the rest', Stoppard told Ken Tynan (*Show People*, p. 60). It may have fed into a one-act play entitled *Rosencrantz and Guildenstern Meet King Lear*, which Stoppard began in 1964. Of this early venture Charles Marowitz says:

■ Mr Stoppard's excerpt concerned two minor characters from . . . *Hamlet* who spend a lot of time tossing coins in the air, and receiving a visit from a hoary old self-denigrating gent called King Lear. It struck me, and most everyone else, as a lot of academic twaddle and I remember thinking that Stoppard, who I knew was a journalist, would probably be more gainfully employed exercising his critical faculties in the columns of some London journal. (*Confessions of a Counterfeit Critic*, p. 123) □

This one-acter, however, formed the basis of the stage play that became the most famous and the most discussed of Stoppard's plays, establishing his reputation and providing financial security. It was, of course, *Rosencrantz and Guildenstern Are Dead*. The RSC took an option on it in 1965, but the option expired and the play was first produced at the

Edinburgh Festival on 24 August 1966 by an amateur group. To his great credit, Ronald Bryden noticed it and reviewed it with acclaim when The National Theatre produced it in 1967 at the Old Vic. John Stride played Rosencrantz, Edward Petherbridge Guildenstern, John McEnery Hamlet and Graham Crowden the powerful role of the Player. A New York production opened on 16 October. It gained Stoppard various British and American awards, including 'Best Play' and 'Most Promising Playwright'.

Charles Marowitz, who had slated the early version, applauded the new:

■ I lacerated my palms expressing my enthusiasm. I had a disturbing little flashback to the tiny Berlin stage where I had seen the play gestate, and downgrading my powers of perception by several points, I marvelled at the miracles that could be wrought by a rewrite and a playwright's conviction that he had something in his bag . . . The glory of our early spring is Tom Stoppard's *Rosencrantz and Guildenstern Are Dead*. (Marowitz, p.124) □

Stoppard explains, in a well-known *Theatre Quarterly* interview, how the 'miracle' occurred:

■ . . . what I wrote in Germany, if I remember – and I'm trying to forget – was just a sort of Shakespearean pastiche . . . what I do remember is that the transition from one play to the other was an attempt to find a solution to a practical problem – that if you write a play about Rosencrantz and Guildenstern in England you can't count on people knowing who they are or how they got there. So one tended to get back into the end of *Hamlet* a bit. But the explanations were always partial and ambiguous, so one went back a bit further into the plot, and as soon as I started doing this I totally lost interest in England . . . I was not in the least interested in doing any sort of pastiche . . . or in doing a criticism of *Hamlet* – that was simply one of the by-products. The chief interest and objective was to exploit a situation which seemed to me to have enormous dramatic and comic potential – of these two guys who in Shakespeare's context, don't really know what they're doing. The little they are told is mainly lies, and there is no reason to suppose they find out why they are killed. And probably more in the early 1960s than at any other time, that would strike a young playwright as being a pretty good thing to explore. I mean it has the right combination of specificity and vague generality which was interesting at that time to (it seemed) eight out of ten playwrights. That's why when the play appeared, it got subjected to so many different kinds of interpretation, all of them plausible, but none of them calculated. . . .

What was actually calculated was to entertain a roomful of people with the situation of Rosencrantz and Guildenstern at Elsinore. The chief thing that added one line to another line was that the combination of the two should retain an audience's interest in some way. I tend to write through a series of small, large and microscopic ambushes – which might consist of a body falling out of a cupboard, or simply an unexpected word in a sentence. But my preoccupation as a writer, which possibly betokens a degree of insecurity, takes the form of contriving to inject some sort of interest and colour into every line . . .

So really Rosencrantz and Guildenstern *doesn't embody any particular philosophy but is a process of solving craft problems?*

That's absolutely the case on a conscious level, but one is a victim and beneficiary of one's subconscious all the time . . . (Delaney, pp. 57–8) ☐

Stoppard is always at pains to emphasise the difference between creating a play and critical analysis. Students ask him what his plays 'mean' and seem to expect simple answers. He proposes in defence a somewhat suspect relativism: 'I personally think that anybody's set of ideas which grows out of the play has its own validity' – a validity for the interpreter, but not necessarily for the play, one imagines. It is important, however, to remember that for Stoppard theatrical craftsmanship is primary and academic questions are secondary. The first and second rules of the theatre, he remarks, are to keep people in their seats. This he did by placing on the forestage his two attendant lords and enacting their imagined words and thoughts whilst they waited to be called on by Shakespeare's major characters, or when they met the travelling players on their way to Elsinore.

The play is famously a conflation and extension of Shakespeare's *Hamlet* and Beckett's *Waiting for Godot*. The image of Beckett's two waiting tramps, Gogo and Didi, itself developed from a music hall double act, as did the travelling Pozzo and Lucky double image of ringmaster and clown (or Irish landowner and peasant or God and man, etc.) who interrupt the tramps' dialogue in each act. These pairings fused with the idea of two minor Shakespeare figures waiting in the wings for orders from above. The onstage Rosencrantz and Guildenstern in *Hamlet* speak when they are spoken to and do not reveal their thoughts either to the audience or to each other. Their untold story becomes the centre of Stoppard's inquiry. What do they do and of what do they speak offstage? In Stoppard's play, Hamlet and the court disappear into the wings and the minor figures whom the King has commanded to spy on Hamlet become the heroes of the drama. Figures lower down the social scale, previously considered the subject of comedy (see Erich Auerbach's study *Mimesis*, English translation 1953), now achieve tragicomic status.

The play has many concerns. It is about the nature of theatre, game-playing and human identity. It is about freedom and control, about memory and consciousness, about time and death, about the rules that govern human events and the possibility that there may be none. All these induce in the characters a constant desire for security.

Critics have written variously and usually thematically about these and other topics. Responses to the London and New York productions of the play and later academic analyses have different emphases. Many reviewers praise the theatricality of the piece and define its strengths and weaknesses; some attack the general content. Academic articles usually interpret the philosophical 'meaning' and may challenge what they see as Stoppard's attitudes and beliefs. Ronald Bryden's *Observer* article saw the Edinburgh production as 'the most brilliant debut by a young playwright since John Arden's' (28 August 1966). Harold Hobson in *The Sunday Times* went further and declared it to be 'the best first London-produced play written by a British author since Harold Pinter's *The Birthday Party* in 1958' (16 April 1967). Hilary Spurling felt that the play's greatest strength 'comes to a fine point in Graham Crowden's Player King' (*The Spectator*, 21 April 1967, p. 465). Albert Bermel agreed and picked on the play's Pirandellian, self-referential quality when reviewing the New York production:

■ The part [of the Player] . . . stands for the whole drama. It observes itself and simultaneously reports back; it is a display of acting and commenting on that acting as it comes to life. The Player is also Stoppard's instrument for expounding the play's theme: that an artificial death on stage looks more real, is easier to believe in, than a death in real life. (*New Leader*, 6 November 1967, pp. 29–30) □

Bermel's use of the word 'believe' may be queried. A feigned death paradoxically can be 'believed' because we know it is unreal. In life it is harder to imagine, perhaps because we know there will be no reappearance.

Reviews praise the fusion of languages in the play. Frank Marcus affirms: 'The play's great achievement is in its use of idiom . . . which . . . blends quite naturally with the excerpts from *Hamlet*' (*London Magazine*, July 1967, p. 76). Charles Marowitz defines this further, picking up the theme of dual personality which has already been broached in *Enter a Free Man*:

■ Stoppard vividly suggests the two languages which are native to us all. One, our own carping, unbridled tongue with which we question our existence and bitch at our circumstance; the other, the formal and politic language with which we conduct our business in society. (Marowitz, pp. 125–6) □

Walter Kerr, in *Thirty Plays Hath November*, feels that Stoppard's presence is too insistent, that he encroaches on the freedom of his characters:

■ Stoppard himself is watching too closely, is too much with us. His two principal characters are not baffled and lost in their own ways. They are baffled and lost in his, speaking his words for him, placarding his thoughts . . . The effect is to remove Rosencrantz and Guildenstern not only from the fevered life that is rumoured about them but also from the arbitrary play that is surely going to execute them. They stand outside both, ignorant and omniscient at once, intellectualizing for their author. What this ultimately suggests is a Presence in the wings after all. A designer, a dictator, a listening God of some sort – and it tends to undercut the play's own premises. (Kerr, p. 51) □

Stoppard might in part agree with this. He has affirmed that, at least in his early plays, he lends his characters his own modes of speech, but he would, I think, point out that in performance actors bring their own presence and voice to a part; Graham Crowden's Player is a case in point. He was very much taller and bigger than the role Stoppard envisaged and his voice much louder. If performance is what counts, then the actor takes over the dialogue and distances the author. As for Kerr's comment on the play's 'premises', which implies that the play is close to *Waiting for Godot* and makes a statement about the absence of God, Stoppard is less likely to concur. On occasions, as in *Jumpers*, he has seemed to suggest at least the possibility of a Presence in the wings.

A debate about fundamental premises leads into the question of genre – of how far the play is comedy, tragedy, farce or parody and the use Stoppard is making of his Shakespeare and Beckett sources. The play has been claimed as 'existentialist' – arguably a descendant of the tragic tradition – and it was assigned to the so-called 'absurdist' school, strongly associated with the black and grotesque comedy (or comi-tragedy) of Beckett, Ionesco, Genet and other (including Czech) writers. It was defined by Martin Esslin in his influential book, *The Theatre of the Absurd* (1961):

■ The plays of Tom Stoppard clearly show the impact of the Theatre of the Absurd, in spite of the obvious difference in other aspects of their approach, and the tradition – that of English high comedy – which they represent. *Rosencrantz and Guildenstern Are Dead* (1966) uses standard elements of *Waiting for Godot* (1953) . . . (pp. 433–4) □

Esslin goes on to suggest that Stoppard is among the absurdist writers who 'have naturally and smoothly reintegrated themselves into the main stream of the tradition'. (This point is expanded in chapter twenty-one.)

In the case of *Rosencrantz and Guildenstern*, other critics have taken a different view of the relation. Roger Sales, in his book on the play, *Rosencrantz and Guildenstern Are Dead* (1988) argues that despite similarities with Beckett's play, Stoppard's is fundamentally parody:

■ Ros and Guil, like Vladimir and Estragon, fill up the empty theatrical spaces by improvising, and then repeating, a number of language games. Both pairs then seize upon other kinds of play in order to pass the time: the attendant lords play with coins while the tramps improvise a routine with their hats. There are also a number of more specific instances of similarities between the two plays. For instance, Estragon loses his trousers at the end of *Godot* and Ros also inadvertently lets his slip when he takes off his belt during the game of hide and seek with Hamlet. It is, however, more important to stress the differences between the two plays . . . Stoppard gentles *Godot* in much the same way as he domesticates *Hamlet* . . . Beckett uses theatricality as a way of posing questions about politics and religion. This heightens the confrontational nature of his dialogue with the audience. Unlike Stoppard, Beckett uses grotesque characters to confront the audience with its own (possibly meaningless) quest for meaning. It is therefore dangerous to suggest that Stoppard was one of Beckett's disciples when he wrote Rosencrantz. It makes more sense to see the play as an exercise in parody . . . minimalism was never his favourite mode. (Sales, pp. 149–50) □

The question of the nature of parody and pastiche is complex and relates also to a discussion of *Travesties*. Meanwhile, let it be said that Sales's interpretation is a long way from that of William Grüber in his article '"Wheels within Wheels etc."' (in Harty's *Tom Stoppard: A Casebook*). Like Sales, Grüber sees the play as 'rejecting much of the absurdist canon', but argues that the effect of the play is that of classical tragedy:

■ It testifies to the informing aesthetic power, even today, of a tragic dramatic force far older than the Elizabethan play which inspired it. *Rosencrantz and Guildenstern Are Dead* offers its audience the vision of two characters caught in the agony of moral choice. At a moment when they least expect it, and in a place they had never foreseen, they must decide the shape of their lives. To be sure, the information upon which they must base their decision comes to them in the form of riddles, half-truths, things only partly known; but when has it ever been otherwise? Like other tragic protagonists before them, Ros and Guil must choose, and they choose in error . . . for his theme, Stoppard offers a version of justice: all the characters get what they deserve. So simple, so moving, so regrettable, but, finally, so consoling: what in the end could be more like classical tragedy than that? (Harty, pp. 42–3) □

This is well said, but Grüber seems to incorporate the sense of the absurd, waiting for us unexpectedly just around the corner, and the idea of existential choice in a world where values are created by man, into his definition. What makes classical tragedy different from its modern descendants is the sense of the presence of the Gods. Absurdism, in the definition of the French existentialists Camus and Sartre, asserts that God is a hole in the sky and, as such, deaf (French *'sourd'*, Latin *'surdus'*) to our pleas. Stoppard's play can certainly be felt to be 'tragic', but perhaps more a sceptical modern tragedy than a classical one.

Grüber's account is to a degree corroborated by one of the best critics of Stoppard, Anthony Jenkins in *The Theatre of Tom Stoppard*. He, too, sees the play as offering its heroes (or anti-heroes?) a choice: 'Doomed as they are, the pair still seem free to choose, and their refusal to seize that opportunity is never so clear as when they read the letter condemning them to death' (pp. 48–9). Stoppard's universe, suggests Jenkins, is 'not the mechanistic one' of the absurdists. For him, the possibility of choice and the failure to choose makes Act III powerful and moving. Other critics find it less so and ultimately the choice between those who prefer to see the play as parody and fundamentally comic, and those who respond to the movement into tragedy with the death, or rather disappearance, of Rosencrantz and Guildenstern, is a question of the power of a particular performance and the response to it of particular critical temperaments. As Ionesco pointed out: *'le comique est tragique'*. There is a black side to any farce, which can flip when the coin is spun. Its characters are at the mercy of a mechanical fate, and in their frenetic attempts to achieve their desire they assume the possibility of escape. Stoppard's play is double-edged and, its author would suggest, so are we all.

A less sombre view than Jenkins's might see the play as a comment on its own processes. In *Rosencrantz and Guildenstern Are Dead*, both in the drama and very interestingly in the much later screen version, Stoppard causes his characters to play games. They are in the grip of forces, constrained by the power and purposes of the King and the powerful personality of the Prince. They are also 'tied' (a Beckettian word) to the written script and to one another. The play resembles a famous Stanislavsky rehearsal exercise in which actors improvise what is referred to or implied by the story but not contained in the onstage action or plot. In this way Stanislavsky meant to give actors a greater sense of the fullness of their roles.

Stoppard's dramatic structure emerges from a Stanislavsky improvisation and his characters play games in order to control the constraints the situation places upon them. They want to find out what game the

King is playing, what game Hamlet is playing and what game they are to play in the world and the drama they inhabit. They are, like Gogo and Didi, 'two guys who don't know why' and play is a way of trying to find out. Is the King, is Hamlet, is God, is Nature playing with them? What are the rules of the bigger games within which they play their smaller ones?

They spin coins as the play opens, filling in time. The game raises questions for the loser, Guildenstern. What rules govern the behaviour of a coin that keeps on coming down heads?

- *Guil*: And if you'd lost? If they'd come down against you, eighty-five times, one after another, just like that?
  Ros: Eighty-five in a row. *Tails?*
  Guil: Yes. What would you think?
  Ros (*doubtfully*): Well . . . (*jocularly*) Well, I'd have a good look at your coins for a start!
  Guil (*retiring*): I'm relieved. At least we can still count on self-interest as a predictable factor. (p. 9) □

Guildenstern is looking for security – the security of rules, a Law of Probability, or less comfortingly, of Diminishing Returns. He seeks the comfort of a script that has been written – by other characters, by the dramatist, by Nature or by God. 'We are entitled to some direction . . . I would have thought', says Guildenstern. The word 'direction' is important and frequently played upon. Sure enough, on Guildenstern's words a band is faintly heard off stage. The author is directing in the Players.

In an improvisation, when the performers are in danger of drying up, the director injects dramatic interest by sending in another character. Enter the Players who, it soon appears: ' . . . do onstage the things that are supposed to happen off. Which is a kind of integrity, if you look on every exit being an entrance somewhere else' (p. 20).

Stanislavsky insisted that, to create a full environment around the play, every entrance must be considered an exit *from* somewhere else. Stoppard turns the concept upside down, parodying the Russian director while copying him, creating an unseen Danish countryside, then an unseen Elsinore around the visible stage. However, the castle lacks consistent entrances. Shakespearean characters – Ophelia, Claudius and Gertrude, Hamlet – enter at unexpected moments and from unexpected 'directions'. Rosencrantz and Guildenstern face in one direction. Rosencrantz says: 'I forbid anyone to enter!', and a procession enters behind them (p. 52). This disconcerts the pair as much as not knowing where they came from or where they are going:

- *Ros* (*an anguished cry*): Consistency is all I ask!
  Guil (*low, wry, rhetoric*): Give us this day our daily mask.

> *Ros (a dying fall)*: I want to go home. (*Moves*) Which way did we come in? I've lost my sense of direction. (p. 28) □

The two characters, of course, are spectators, like ourselves unsure of what will happen next (unless we know the play). A known script provides greater security than a chancy future.

An audience also offers the security of a known environment. In the theatre, some actors say, 'at least you know who you are supposed to be'. Thus Rosencrantz and Guildenstern offer security to the Players by acting as an audience. However, when the pair depart in the middle of the performance and the Players slowly find they are playing to nobody, they are: 'tricked out of the single assumption which makes our existence viable – that somebody is watching . . .' (p. 45). *Esse est percipi*. Beckett quotes the philosopher Berkeley's suggestion that to exist we need to be perceived. Yet to be perceived engenders fear as well as security. When, like Beckett's characters, Rosencrantz and Guildenstern face the audience from the footlights, they see 'an appalling prospect'. Audience and characters offer each other a distorting mirror.

The theatre space does not offer security. Nor does the notion of time. Future prospects are not very promising and, in an attempt to control the future, the pair improvise an encounter with Hamlet in which Guildenstern takes Hamlet's part. The 'improv' doesn't help. To anticipate Hamlet's words and actions they would have to *be* Hamlet. But he is unpredictable, like the direction they have forgotten they came from or the direction of the wind or compass point they frequently ask about. Is the wind southerly? And isn't the compass erratic 'this far north'?

The pair see in the arrival of the Players at Elsinore a chance to establish superiority and a measure of control: 'You may have no doubt whom to thank for your performance at court' (p. 46), they tell the Player. But the Player assures them: 'I know which way the wind is blowing' and 'Uncertainty is the normal state. You're nobody special' (p. 47). The pair left the Players alone, needing an audience to confirm their identity. The Player describes and dramatises his sense of isolation before the audience who left them:

■ No one came forward. No one shouted at us. The silence was unbreakable, it imposed itself upon us; it was obscene. We took off our crowns and swords and cloth of gold and moved silent on the road to Elsinore. (*Silence. Then Guildenstern claps with slow measured irony.*) (p. 46) □

But the tables have been turned. The Player re-establishes control over his recaptured audience. He is the one who has an entry to Elsinore 'and always has had'. He is now at home while Rosencrantz and Guildenstern still seek (in 'bad faith', Sartre would say) to ease their anguish, to find why they are there, who they are, who Hamlet is, for Hamlet is 'not himself'. For confirmation they need something more than a Godot or a Pozzo, an impersonator of God.

'A step in the right direction' (p. 63) comes when Claudius gives them the job of seeking out Hamlet and bringing the body of Polonius to the chapel, but they do not know what direction to go in, and whether to go separately or alone. In the end they do not move and the act is done for them.

Finally in Act III we find them on a boat, going with Hamlet to England. On a boat they are 'free': 'Free to move, speak, extemporise, and yet. We have not been cut loose . . . ' (p. 73). Indeed they have not, and they prefer the security of not being free, obeying orders, following the script and the rules of the game. They will not become dramatic loose ends, free to go at the play's end when they have delivered the letter to the English king. On a boat they can go where they like 'without restriction' but 'Within limits of course' (p. 84), since 'Other wheels are turning'. Those limits are the script and the will of others within it. Or is it 'fate' or some more abstract form of 'direction'?

They have, perhaps, one moment of choice when they discover what is in Claudius's letter to the English king, but they decide to keep to the script and they disappear to deaths which are both less and more convincing than the death which Guildenstern thinks he has encompassed by stabbing the Player with the Player's own (stage) dagger.

Stoppard's first hit is meta-theatre in the tradition of Pirandello and Beckett. It displays impressive knowledge of complex theatre processes. In 1990, when he came to direct the play as a film, Stoppard extended the observations on creative games. The slow Rosencrantz scores over the logical, contemptuous and analytical Guildenstern by teetering on the edge of making world-shaking discoveries. An apple falls on his head. He drops a light and heavy article together to see if they fall at the same speed. He plays with paper aeroplanes. He sits in a bath and watches curiously as the water rises and falls when he moves up and down. Galileo, Newton, Leonardo and Archimedes preside over his half-perceptions. Alack, the logical training and scholarly discipline are missing. Otherwise the little games he plays might have enabled him to make the jump of genius between apparently unrelated fields that Koestler named (in *The Act of Creation*) the 'Archimedes Principle'. Imagination, as with George Riley, might then have become a reality.

CHAPTER THREE

Early Radio Plays

The Dissolution of Dominic Boot; 'M' is for Moon Among Other Things; If You're Glad, I'll be Frank; Albert's Bridge; Where Are They Now?

In the same year (1964) that *Walk on the Water* had its first stage present-ation and Stoppard was experimenting with the Rosencrantz and Guildenstern story, he also wrote two short 15-minute plays for BBC Radio: *The Dissolution of Dominic Boot* and *'M' is for Moon Among Other Things*. In the 60s, radio was an attractive medium for the aspiring writer, since the low cost of production allowed the BBC to produce hundreds of new plays every year. The radio writer needs a good ear, a talent for dramatic struc-ture and skill in the use of sound effect and dialogue, since he can move very rapidly from scene to scene and dramatise extraordinary events such as disjointed dream sequences (as in Dylan Thomas's *Under Milk Wood*). It is not surprising that so-called absurdist writers were drawn to radio. They included Stoppard's forerunners, Beckett (*All That Fall*, 1956) and Pinter, both of whom Stoppard studied and admired.

Between 1964 and 1991 Stoppard wrote eight plays for radio of increasing sophistication and power. Although there is a ten-year gap between the last three, Stoppard's enthusiasm for the medium has not waned. It is rather the greater appeal of the stage than the decline in radio opportunities during the 1970s that accounts for his intermittent contribution. Radio language appeals particularly to the poet in Stoppard and it made its appeal early.

The poetic and emotive potential of radio was not something Stoppard chose to stress when asked by Mel Gussow whether his one-act radio plays 'counted'. He replied: 'They do count. They don't count in the same way. It's not that the plays are short, it's that they are funda-mentally jokes. They're musical boxes, mechanical contrivances. They're not plays about characters.' (Gussow, p.24). 'Jokes' are usually at the expense of flat characters and Stoppard's use of names confirms a penchant for apparent stereotypes: 'I can't help it if the names keep turning out to be Moon or Boot', he says in an interview published in the programme of the National Theatre production of *Jumpers*, 'I keep writing about the same double-act . . . the chief characters in *Jumpers* are masquerading under false names. Moon and Boot is what they are really called'. John Bailey, in an article entitled 'The Ironist', quotes an interview with the *Observer* drama critic, Robert Cushman:

■ Whereas the name Boot is derived from Evelyn Waugh's novel *Scoop*, Moon comes . . . from the name of the victim in the Paul Newman film *The Left-Handed Gun*. Cushman therefore maintains that there is no lunar significance to the name in Stoppard . . . But that is surely an oversimplification. In conversation with Cushman, Stoppard has said, "Moon is a person to whom things happen. Boot is rather more aggressive". One might add that Moon is more articulate and less successful with women than Boot. Not all the principal male characters in Stoppard's plays come into this category – Rosencrantz and Guildenstern come to mind in this regard . . . (Bloom, p. 38) □

The names certainly indicate a repetitive pattern, but Stoppard's comment that the short plays are not about character should be taken with a pinch of salt. Dominant characters and their victims are frequently found among farce stereotypes, but when an author moves beyond the genre, as Stoppard does, even in his one-acters, the pathos which comes from seeing characters as human and suffering begins to be felt. The handling of language and the bizarre situations in *Albert's Bridge* and *If You're Glad, I'll be Frank* differentiate them from the more conventional *The Dissolution of Dominic Boot, 'M' is for Moon* and *Where Are They Now?*, but even these 'jokes' convey a similar pathos analogous to that which exists (for some) in *Enter a Free Man*.

The Dissolution of Dominic Boot

The Dissolution of Dominic Boot was written in 1964, together with *'M' is for Moon*, for the BBC series *Just Before Midnight*. The former – 'I think I wrote it in a day', Stoppard tells us – is a well-crafted, professional piece of radio which shows the writer in full control of a conventional form. It is about an increasingly desperate, vulnerable, exploited little man with a bank account £43 in the red who takes a taxi from place to place, trying to get money from banks, his fiancée, the gas meter, parents and colleagues, to pay the taxi driver his ever increasing fare. Intermittently, he is castigated for excessive expenditure by those for whose benefit he takes the taxi. The play is a kind of striptease, a process of asset stripping that is not unknown in tragedy. At the end, all Dominic has to pay the driver with is a pair of wet pyjamas. Anthony Jenkins remarks:

■ Throughout its fifteen minutes, the comedy is kept aloft by the breezy energy of Stoppard's narrative, and to find weighty significance in the fact that Dominic is defeated by machines (the banks, the junk shop, paper-work at the office) would overload things. The play stretches a single ridiculous idea to the ultimate or, in Stoppardese, it is about a man who is always being encouraged to pull his socks up and who can usually manage to pull the wool over other people's eyes until he is bereft of footwear. (Jenkins, p. 11) □

Jenkins suggests one should not exaggerate the pathos. It is a clever idea about a downtrodden fool figure who is less lucky than his namesake, Evelyn Waugh's comic foreign correspondent. Dominic does not live up to his masterful name and rather than give others the boot, he himself gets it. For Jenkins he is more 'pathetic' than sympathetic.

Stoppard seems more concerned with exploring the medium than character and makes splendid, if conventional, use of sound effects. Rapid cross-cutting is effected by traffic noise, taxi doors shutting, clinking coins, a smashed gas meter and rain falling. Boot gets progressively wetter, having given his fiancée the umbrella she claims she bought for *him*. All the characters are oblivious of Dominic's plight. The play is short, simple and funny even if, behind the laughter, a certain desperation communicates itself. The farce diffuses the anxiety of listeners who may at times dream that like Dominic they are little men, caught in a trap, alone in an indifferent world. Yet behind farce, chaos and cruelty threaten. Mid-century absurdists like Ionesco and Beckett reminded us of this and so in his own way does Stoppard.

'M' is for Moon Among Other Things

This play was broadcast on 6 April 1964, about six weeks later than 'Boot'. It originated as a short story and probably for that reason does not explore the radio medium to the same degree. It has only two characters, no changes of location, more dialogue and fewer sound effects. Alfred, an irascible middle-aged man, reads the paper, while his wife, Millie, slowly digests an encyclopaedia that she receives in monthly instalments. She is a downtrodden figure wishing to fill her life with meaning. Her name suggests *milieu*, a woman of 42 in the middle of her life. She recites words beginning with M as the play begins and is just about to move from M to N in the middle of the alphabet. What is your name, M or N?, the catechism asks. Millie is her middle name, her favourite till she goes over at 17 to her first name, Constance, which suits the kind of constancy she has exhibited to Alfred for 25 years. In half an hour, Millie/

Constance will be 42 *and a half.* Halves are important to her and the M halfway through the alphabet is important in the play. Constance has spent half of half a lifetime as a Mrs in Marriage, not wanting the Moon, she tells Alfred, but seeking a Meaning as the Menopause approaches and she works Mechanically through an encyclopaedia that lacks such entries as Marilyn Monroe, whose death to Alfred's horror is announced on the radio. Other M words – Mollusc, for example – have an unspecified relevance. A mollusc is invertebrate – like Millie metaphorically? Mandragora appears to have no connection. But it is taken from *Othello* (Act III, iii, 335–8) and is a narcotic:

■ Not poppy nor mandragora/Nor all the drowsy syrups of the world Shall ever medicine thee to that sweet sleep/Which thou owed yesterday ... □

The word parodies Millie, who swallows pills to make her sleep. Shakespeare's *Macbeth* is the first word of dialogue in the play, suggestive perhaps of Murder and Madness, both preoccupations of the playwright – like Memory, another Stoppard motif, for Alfred like Rosencrantz finds it hard to reconstitute the past:

■ Alfred ... what time were you born? I can't remember. (p. 16) □

As in *'Boot'*, a comic angst hovers behind this light-hearted drama. Stoppard plays games with the letter 'M' and emphasises the couple's mutual isolation by contrasting their reading matter. In Constance's dogged march through her encyclopaedia, she will soon reach the word 'Nausea', which suggests Sartre's novel of that name. In it a sad character called 'the autodidact' also works his way through encyclopaedias. The motif reappears in Stoppard's *Travesties* (1974). This play of motifs and discourses tempts one to carry them further, e.g., 'A is for Alfred and he comes first'. But apart from its jokiness, the play drops hints about serious questions of time and consciousness. Minds and lives acquire habits and routines framed by the mechanical ticking of a clock. They divide past and present – and less securely the future – into fixed, discrete bundles. Henri Bergson's famous definition of comedy as 'the mechanical encrusted upon the living' comes easily to mind. So do Beckett's habit-ridden characters and William James's apposite remarks in his chapter on time and consciousness in his classical *Principles of Psychology* (1890). A period of life, says James, which drags tediously when lived through, seems in memory very short, whereas a period when life was exciting, and there was no consciousness of time passing, leaves a memory that is rich and full. The comic poignancy of Millie resides in her wanting to fill her life with something more than an awareness of time passing. The reading of entries in an encyclopaedia is no real substitute for living.

Stoppard has fun with words and motifs, mocking banal speech and the journalistic clichés that are Alfred's favourite reading. The marriage is encrusted with habit, yet Stoppard's laughter is not entirely cruel. Paradoxically, the listener's sympathy is aroused by a failure of communication that the characters do not notice. When the bedtime routines are completed, Alfred murmurs: 'Poor old thing', but Constance does not realise that he is thinking of Marilyn Monroe and replies touchingly: 'Oh, you mustn't worry about me, Alfred'. Behind the commonplace language of marital monologues lie problems that lend some depth to this piece of radio fun. Constance thinks constantly of time passing. She would like to tie time down. Letters, when she was a child, stood for one thing. A was for Apple (not Alfred). But M now stands for other things – disparate, dislocated, related in space, but not causally or experientially in consciousness. The clock of her life has become a succession of ticks and Millie continues ticking off the letters and subjects – Marshmallow, which is soft, Mickey Mouse, which is not serious, Mule, which is rigid and obstinate, Meat, which she served to the boss's Catholic wife on a Friday. Less humorously, *Dial M for Murder* is a radio programme just finishing and perhaps a thought that Alfred harbours. The word Mother reminds us that Constance is childless – perhaps one of the entries she is 'skipping madly', along with Madness and Memory which Alfred says always betrays her. Millie would be good material for one of Alan Bennett's poignant *Talking Heads*.

Anthony Jenkins, one of the few critics to take these plays seriously, finds more substance in *'M' is for Moon* than in *Dominic Boot*:

■ In *'M' is for Moon*, Stoppard's structure and style carry, and are intrinsic to, his theme. The interior threnodies of Constance and Alfred supply separate perspectives which dictate the way the pair react to Marilyn's suicide. By allowing the listener to participate in both these worlds, and to measure them more objectively against the details surrounding the actress's death, Stoppard creates a third perspective so that we experience for ourselves the fact that meaning depends upon point of view. Compressed into fifteen fleeting minutes, this multilayered structure may not be completely apprehensible and it is not surprising that the idea originated as a short story. Yet, as a listening experience, the play offers more than a gentle comedy of manners. From the outset, Stoppard makes us cast about for our bearings. Whether we are totally aware of it or not, we search for a frame of reference, a way of measuring events and investing them with meaning. And something of Stoppard's own way of looking at things seems to have found a clear focus within the limited and limiting format of this brief radio play. (Jenkins, p. 14) □

If You're Glad, I'll be Frank

In this play Stoppard demonstrates an original and developing handling of the radio medium. It has 14 scenes and 12 characters. Gladys, the main character, is the 'time-clock girl' who prompts Stoppard's fascination with time. She is a kind of parody Greek chorus with two voices. A rhythmical, semi-poetic interior monologue alternates with a mechanical monotone announcing the time. These are intercut by episodes during which Frank, her bus driver husband, who identifies her voice and wishes to rescue her, stops at the Head Post Office on his bus route (to the dismay of Ivy his conductress) to grapple with the strict hierarchy of officials, from the porters to the new secretary of the 'First Lord', which bars his way.

In a BBC radio broadcast on 10 November 1972, Stoppard was interviewed by Richard Mayne who quoted a section from the play:

■ . . . the lady who is playing TIM, that is, giving the time signals on the telephone, says "and they count for nothing measured against the moment in which a glacier forms and melts. Which does not stop them from trying to compete; they synchronize their watches, count the beats, to get the most out of the little they've got, clocking in, and out, and speeding up, keeping to their time-tables to keep up their speed." This seems to me a very profound statement and a . . . it's the sort of area of your work which made me ask you the first question, you know, is it tragedy? (Delaney, p. 35) □

Stoppard avoided a solemn discussion of tragedy:

■ . . . the great wheeze was to talk about a time-clock girl, just that instant appeal was where the idea originated . . . the play is not the result of any obsession with time. The obsession is the result of the play. (Delaney, p. 36) □

The author emphasises as usual that his plays find their source in a concrete idea, not in an abstraction. And Stoppard has fun with the way these characters address each other – as Sir, or Mr, by surname, or first name, or Sir John, or My Lord, or Lord Coot, or, when familiarity breaks through the pecking order, Cooty, or even 'darling', which Myrtle, a secretary of long standing, who no doubt takes up other less vertical positions, addresses to two of her superiors. The officials are flat comic stereotypes, but Frank, the bus driver, acquires humanity in the desperation of his search and his readiness to stretch the regulations in order to find his wife. The play, which begins as a gag, becomes something more than a wheeze.

The seriousness behind the absurdity is to be found in Gladys's frustration with her role. A machine has her in its grip, as was the case with Dominic Boot and Constance/Millie. Her interior self examines the situation, then almost breaks down. But time has trapped her as it traps Frank in his schedule. Frank lives *inside* time, however; whereas Gladys is conscious of it, *outside* time, looking down as if from the moon, therefore more alive, more individuated, more isolated and more pathetic. She has seen the beginning and seen infinity. Can she return, and return Frank's love? She'd be in the middle of things if she did and the attraction of being out of things, serene, in a nunnery or a private room, is one she strongly feels: 'it was the serenity I was after' – another Stoppard motif.

For a moment the sense of the world's smallness, and of human lives lived in a flicker, breaks into the play. Better to assume one is the centre of life than reflect on the vast sweeps of time and space. Frank is close to life. Gladys is far off, though she moves nearer and towards the end of the farce echoes Joyce's Mollie Bloom: 'yes, I will, yes', she says. The voice of Eliot's 'Hurry up please it's time' (in *The Waste Land*) is heard. Is it a call to use time before it uses *you*, or a call to repent? If it is a call for love, love is what makes the machine break down, and Gladys very nearly does. But the First Lord steadies her, puts her back on track. The relation with Frank is doomed because the couple have different concepts of time. Time wins in the person of the First Lord. 'He thinks he's God', says Gladys. And, indeed, he is responsible for the words sent to those who dial GOD and hear the equivalent of TIM announce through the phone: 'In the beginning was the Heaven and the Earth' (p. 40). Gladys has seen the beginning and the end. She looks *at* time, cannot live *through* it, cannot move back inside time and 'normality'.

Such a description of the play's content exaggerates the anxiety, and the fear of chaos that lies behind the pattern of farce, at the expense of the comedy and laughter that disperse the anxiety. In this play, concern with what used to be called 'universals' is distanced by the absurdity of the basic idea. Yet the concept as well as the passage of time is disturbing, and Stoppard makes us feel it, even while he has his usual fun with the idea: 'Silence is the sound of time passing' (p. 36), says Gladys. Stoppard has been reading modernist writers. The leaden circles of Big Ben that cut across the consciousness of Virginia Woolf's Mrs Dalloway come to mind. And the voice of Eliot – 'Caught by the wind, blown into the crevasse' (p. 38) – can also be heard in Gladys's (semi-parodic?) lines.

The tragicomic aspect of the play finds different responses in the critics. Richard Corballis, in his book *Stoppard, The Mystery and the Clockwork*, places the stress, as one would expect from his title, on the dramatic tension between the mechanical and the living – an idea which relates very closely to Bergson's definition of comedy in *Le Rire* (*Laughter*, 1900). Gladys and Frank, the bus driver in *If You're Glad*, tire, as do characters in other plays, of the clockwork nature of their lives and either break out of it or break down:

■ Frank . . . recognizes Gladys' voice. He decides to save her. At first he tries to do this while keeping his own 'clockwork' intact . . . he soon finds he needs more time, however, and so he throws caution to the winds and abandons his timetable – and his bus, and presumably his job.

Gladys clearly wants to be saved; she is starting to crack under the strain, thinking thoughts which are hilariously at odds with what she is saying. When she countenances an obscene outburst to put "the fear of God into their alarm-setting, train-catching, coffee-breaking faith in an uncomprehended clockwork" we are reminded of Guildenstern with his dagger, Moon with his bomb. [In the novel, *Lord Malquist and Mr Moon*] (Corballis, p.161) □

Anthony Jenkins emphasises the tension between mechanical and free speech, the growing psychological concern with duality of character and the relation between time and consciousness. The distinction Stoppard makes between time as flow and time as a set of chronological ticks anticipates a similar concern with the dual nature of light in *Hapgood*, which (as both wave and particles) becomes a metaphor for dual personality. Jenkins observes:

■ Gladys has seen that nine today is not the same as nine tomorrow. Time flows on and reduces man to a minuscule part of that flow. Yet from a human perspective, time is divisible into ticks and tocks which give our lives importance. Through Gladys, Stoppard makes us see that Frank's slavish obedience to his timetable is not simply a funny joke but absurdly sad as he drives around in circles, and the satire on departmental bureaucracy widens and deepens when we are made to recognize Lord Coot's ludicrous concern for efficiency as a magnifica- tion of every man's belief that he is time's master.

But what makes Gladys crack is neither the physical effort of her job, nor her feeling that it is pointless to divide time into units of ten seconds. Her position has become absurd because she feels compelled to keep on, despite her knowledge . . . she has seen the void, and "if you can't look away/you go mad". (p.51)

The struggle against madness stands as the common denominator between the two centres of the play's action. Stoppard marries farce to the play of ideas by making both Gladys and Frank the puppets of circumstance . . . (Jenkins, pp.17–18) □

The dizzy frenetic panic of farce, which affects both figures, is thus scrutinised within a structure of important philosophical and psychological ideas, which relate the play both to tragedy and – Jenkins uses the word twice – to the tragicomic theatre of the absurd. Or should one not say that the containing structure is farce? Bernard Levin puts it thus:

■ It is a dazzling piece of work, real theatrical Fabergé, juggling excellent but straightforward jokes . . . with a constant stream of time-metaphors turned inside out, all spinning round the still centre of Gladys . . . all controlled by the inexorable pips. (*Sunday Times*, 28 November 1976) □

Albert's Bridge

The next radio play was broadcast in 1967 on the Third Programme about 18 months later and won the *Prix Italia*. Its central character, Albert, opts to spend his life on the mechanical task of painting and repainting a bridge – with semi-comic consequences. The play employs 12 characters and has 14 scenes. It experiments with sound and the creation of space and height. The microphone is hung next to Albert, a philosophy student doing a holiday job. Below him at different points on the bridge are three full-time painters for whom keeping the bridge from perpetually going rusty is just a way of making a living. For the older man, the work blocks the life he might have had: 'I could have made my mark', he reiterates. Younger and older voices speak at different distances from the mike, creating a sensation of great height as Albert croons tunelessly into it, still absorbed in his job, while the others are knocking off and climbing down. The sound of feet on metal, then gravel as they reach the ground, the gradual levelling of strength of voice as the speakers close on one another, supports the creation of scene by dialogue – 'Mind your head, Dad', as the painters abandon their work and avoid the fresh paint of the one directly below. Later, we are told, the bridge has a characteristic sound. Its key is B flat, but its music ends in a brilliant cacophony when 1,799 painters singing 'Colonel Bogey', who have been employed to finish the painting in one day, march from land onto metal (a splendid effect) and set up vibrations that collapse the structure and Albert with it. (This is a clear spoof of the film *Bridge on the River Kwai*, which becomes more than a spoof if one remembers that the Alec Guinness character succumbs to the mechanical nature of his military training. It is also worth remarking that the iron Albert Bridge across the Thames in London still bears a small notice which says: All Ranks Break Step.) The creative opportunities Stoppard imaginatively provides for the sound engineer and director are irresistible. Stoppard has followed his own advice to writers 'to create a play they cannot afford to turn down'.

Early in the play, Albert drifts into marriage. His wife has a child, but its cries and its rattle are not, to him, as musical as his airy environment on the bridge. (Albert's tuneless crooning and the key of B flat hint ironically that Albert is not entirely in tune with the world.) The women's voices – those of Albert's mother and his wife Kate – lighten the tone of the predominantly male cast. We hear the clipped voice of an accountant, Fitch, which is persuading a provincial committee to sack three painters in order to save money. With new durable paint one workman can do the job, even if it will take him eight years instead of two. Albert, the only painter whose mind is attuned to painting a bridge in perpetuity, gets the job. The catch, of course, is that in two years Albert can cover only one quarter of the bridge and the old paint begins to rust. An army of painters is therefore hired for one day to cover the unpainted remainder. Unfortunately, no one tells the army to break step to counter the vibrations of marching feet and the bridge collapses. The clever accountant has forgotten two things that undermine his logic and cause the catastrophe.

Apart from Albert, the characters are mostly stereotypes. The father assumes his son will go into the business. His keynote is that he 'started from the bottom' (where Albert does not want to be). The committee member Dave says no more than 'Hear, hear', which is welcomed or ignored as the case demands. The Chairman tramples on opposition. George, another committee member, emerges from the stereotype. He is sensible, but cannot make his common sense heard. The painters are stereotypes, occasionally humanised. 'Dad' has laid ten coats of paint on the bridge: 'In five minutes I could scratch down to the iron, I could scratch down to my prime' (p. 55). The first coat – a primer? – represents his youth; since then his life has been routine and repetition.

A certain sympathy for those trapped in routine also goes out to Kate the wife, who is good-hearted but lonely and finally leaves Albert. She and George and Dad are little people, like Fitch the accountant. A last character, Fraser, compulsively climbs the bridge to commit suicide and changes his mind, to Albert's disgust and irritation, when he gets up there. He is a counterpart to Albert and the only other semi-complex character. Fraser decides not to jump off the bridge because people seem little when seen from above. Height places human problems and irritations in perspective.

This also applies to Albert, but Albert gains a sensation of power within his 'giant frame'. Life acquires a certain beauty when the people are diminished to dots and a sensation of infinity makes its appeal. There is a paradox here and psychological acuity. Albert chooses routine as a substitute for family obligations. He prefers his bridge to following in his father's business footsteps. On the one occasion when he accedes to his wife's desire for a holiday to break the routine, he finds the Eiffel Tower disappointing compared to a bridge. Presumably a bridge gives him a greater sensation of power over people going somewhere, whilst a tower reminds him he is going upwards to infinity. But there is a further irony in the idea of 'somewhere' evoked by the powerful sound of an approaching and disappearing express. The travelling train is also trapped within a timetable.

Albert's university education was not meant to prepare him for a life of painting bridges. And indeed it might have been better if Albert hadn't studied philosophy. It seems to have given him a sense of his own insufficiency from which he needs to escape. Albert therefore creates a sub-poetic vision of infinity: 'The university lying under you like a couple of bricks, full of dots studying philosophy' (p. 62), which leads him to care for no one but himself. It helps to think of other people as tiny: 'I've got me under my skin', he croons, 'Shall I compare me to a summer's day?'

The play's characterisation of little people seems partly to support Albert's view of life. Stoppard is not yet writing with a full sense of a character's pain that will take the plays out of the detachment of laughter. But the ultimate collapse of the bridge that stands as metaphor for Albert's phoney dream, disturbs the listener, like the isolation of Gladys in the previous play. These are not plays in which the little man, in John Arden's definition of comedy, proves indestructible. If comedy is cruel and depends, as Bergson says, on a sense of superiority, on a rejoicing at a downfall (the pot of paint on the ladder, the banana skin), then this is comedy. But not at the expense of the strong, as often in Chaplin when he defeats the big man, the manager, the owner. It is at the expense of the little man and this creates a greater unease.

Anthony Jenkins is as enthusiastic about this play as he is about *If You're Glad*:

■ The play spans its sixty minutes of air time with all the logical simplicity of a (non-collapsed) bridge. Its characters, blinkered or made grandiose by a particular view of things, rigidly pursue their individual ends. Despite its rich texture, the main thread of the plot arcs through the air with none of the diversionary tangents of those plays which set out to snare the audience along the way . . . each ensuing scene is riveted to its neighbour by a linking sound effect or by an abrupt cross-fade so that the play's momentum undulates with a pleasing delicacy. These transitions telescope the time scheme, as Albert flies higher in his pride and Kate [his wife] sinks lower into despair. Within those clear lines of development, Albert has Gladys-like soliloquies whose lyricism, while not so metaphysically complex, is particularly suited to the creation of radio's mind-pictures . . . (Jenkins, p. 64) □

Where Are They Now

Another radio play was written for Schools Radio and was broadcast on the BBC in 1970. In December 1994, Stoppard looked back at this play in a discussion with Mel Gussow about the nature of happiness – a matter for the writer of 'shifting one's weight': 'You receive these moments which might stretch for a day where you think everything's O.K.'. 'That reminds me', says Gussow, 'of the boy in your play, *Where Are They Now?*'. Stoppard responds:

■ *Where Are They Now* is a play I never think about, but it keeps coming up as we talk. There's something in there about the boy, who was unhappy at school, saying as a grown-up, "If there was only some way of telling them it doesn't matter that much, the things that devastate you as a child, the things that spoil the whole term at school." One would like to impart the lesson to one's children that it's really O.K., it's not as bad as you think. (Gussow, pp. 112–13) □

Children become the ethical touchstone of Stoppard's later political plays and elements of Stoppard's life are indirectly assimilated into *Where Are They Now?*. Stoppard tells us in the introduction that he 'dropped a leaky bucket into the well of personal experience'. This gives the play a special edge that goes beyond the experimental concern of his other radio plays. It moves rapidly back and forth in time and space from a school scene to a Reunion Dinner in a hotel, the first taking place in 1945, the second taking place 25 years later in 1969. The same characters appear in each, changed by time (the schoolmaster Dobson speaks to the Old Boys as he did to them as pupils, except that he is now somewhat deaf). The difficulty for the listener and writer consists in keeping the times and locations clear. This Stoppard overcomes, not by the conventional radio technique of fading up and down, but by changing voice and tone as the crossovers between time and place occur. He chooses moments when past and present conversations touch on the same topic, such as salmon for dinner, or when a sound effect allows a transition (such as the caning in one place that cuts to the Headmaster using the gavel in another). The tone of discussion makes clear the place and time.

The comic interest lies in an expatriate called Jenkins who has a pastoral dream of his old school which turns out not to be the one that those around him have attended. He is sitting in the seat of a master of the same name who has just died and ought to be at the reunion on the floor below. This gives rise to the kind of misunderstandings which are the staple diet of conventional farce. But, as usual, Stoppard plays with the convention. The serious interest lies in identifying the characters of the Old Boys with their younger selves. As schoolboys, three Old Boys, now a businessman, cleric and journalist respectively, were dubbed Harpo, Groucho and Chico. It seems fairly evident which characters are which, but Stoppard plays a trick on us. The talkative Old Boy Marks with the apparently happy memories was the silent and tearful Harpo and not the silent Old Boy Gale. The characters have changed. Gale, a journalist of repute, has come to find out if the French teacher Jenkins is really as unpleasant as he remembers him. Jenkins, however, has died and must remain forever the image which Gale forcibly describes, contradicting the sentimental obituary which the Headmaster is simultaneously painting: 'We walked into French like condemned men. We were afraid to learn. All our energy went into ingratiating ourselves and deflecting his sadism onto our friends . . . ' (p. 103).

The sudden realism is shocking after the clichés and conventional dialogue, and a similar shock occurs when the ex-Head Boy Crawford, obsequious among his elders, enacts a scene at school in which the son of Marks is verbally whiplashed and then caned. The sadism beneath the obsequiousness in Crawford, the banal and false recollections of Marks, the acid memories of Gale that he sympathetically wished to verify, make this a memorable piece. Memory, indeed, is the central topic. Jenkins, again, puts it as follows:

■ Our memories colour and are coloured by the persons we are; happiness comes at the most unexpected moments . . . each character views an inescapable fact of life with about as much accuracy as his fellows. In other plays, one character's frantic obsession collides with another's, which can also sometimes represent the daft systems of society, or all the characters hold contradictory ides about a particular event. Like *Rosencrantz*, and, in its minor way, *'M' is for Moon*, this play illumines the human condition. Here though each character seems impelled completely from within. Only once does Stoppard impose a jokey *aperçu* – when he makes Marks giggle after the final Grace, having had the unlikely thought (for him) that after thanking the Lord three times a day at school "We lost touch . . . where is he now?" (137). A small masterpiece, this script implicates the listener beyond the momentary trap created by the boy's identities. Its tricks of memory resonate against the truth of our own experience to remind us that we too are the victims of perspective. (Jenkins, p. 71) □

Jenkins acutely identifies the differences between these plays. Stoppard does not repeat himself and he shifts his weight according to the situation explored. Yet there are similarities, too. Again, a short play with strong elements of farce moves towards naturalism and raises important questions about identity. The play makes fun of caricatural characters, but it also raises questions about how and why people deny the past and make caricatures of themselves. Gale looks to verify the past as a way of remaining more fully human – by doing justice to a master he may have demonised. Stereotyping is seen as a suspect process. Farce and its complex relations with anxiety, pride and prejudice are held up for scrutiny and comedy becomes satire.

CHAPTER FOUR

Early TV Plays

A Separate Peace; Teeth; Another Moon Called Earth; Neutral Ground

Writing for radio and TV attracted Stoppard in the sixties, though he still regarded them as 'stepping stones towards getting a play on the boards' (Stoppard Introduction: *The Television Plays*, 1993). 'Bliss was it to be performed, but to be *staged* was very heaven.' Even during the earlier apprentice stage of 'professional writing', he sought to go beyond the limitations of craftsmanship and break the conventional rules – as had Dylan Thomas and Samuel Beckett before him. His plays are innovative, constantly changing form and pattern. The pressures of television, however, made innovation more difficult.

A Separate Peace

Over the early period, when Stoppard was writing for radio, he wrote a number of TV plays, four of them between 1965 and 1967. The first, *A Separate Peace*, was transmitted by the BBC in August 1966 and is, like *Albert's Bridge*, about a man who tries to escape from the world, but this time he enters a private hospital. It comprised one half of an hour-long programme alongside a documentary about chess, though how the play relates to chess is unclear. Stoppard interestingly says in his 1993 introduction: 'I now doubt that chess and the desire to escape from the world are good metaphors for each other'. In 1966 he seems to have felt that playing games, whether it was chess or writing plays, was escapist: 'I actually had to think up some kind of play which was about exclusion, about disappearing into oneself, about finding a substitute for reality. As you can see, it's quite a loose analogy . . . ' (Delaney, p. 72). Now he may feel that chess, playwriting and play-acting are metaphors for what happens *in*, rather than out of, the social and political world.

There is little commentary on the play. Jenkins says it makes few demands upon the viewer: ' . . . neither the dialogue nor the cutting jolts our expectations nor forces us to participate by experiencing a character's dilemma in ourselves. We are not disoriented as we are by the radio scripts and later stage plays . . . ' (Jenkins, p. 20). Ronald Hayman agrees about the relative conventionality of *A Separate Peace*, describes the plot, and relates it to Beckett:

■ Beckett's early fiction is full of heroes whose only ambition is to withdraw into isolation and inactivity . . . Beckett's Belacqua wants "to break not so much the flow of people and things to him, as the ebb of him to people and things. It was his instinct to make himself captive . . .". In the novel *Murphy* (1938) the hero's favourite occupation is to lock the door of his room and tie himself naked to a rocking chair. (Hayman, p. 60) □

A Separate Peace is about John Brown, a would-be escapee from the world, who takes refuge in a hospital after arriving as an 'emergency' in the middle of the night. It has 19 scenes and it cross-cuts, cleverly and rapidly, but without much variation, between two conventional sets – a private hospital office and a private ward. Most of the office scenes are phone conversations in which the doctor ponders ways of getting a perfectly healthy man out of bed and back into 'society'. This proves difficult, for John Brown has covered his tracks.

The ward scenes are more varied than the office scenes, but still unsurprising. We see Brown eating breakfast, having his temperature taken, engaging in basketwork to please matron, then engaged more interestingly in painting pastoral scenes on the walls of the room, though it seems he prefers to do nothing – a subject not, until Beckett, seen as dramatic. But Stoppard extracts a half-hour play from a joke situation that reverses conventional expectations. Healthy men don't want to go to hospital, but this one does. The unconventionality is in the joke, rather than the dramatic form.

Innovation for a previously untried TV writer is not easy. He or she is not likely to be trusted with more than a low budget, two studio sets, a half-hour slot and a small cast. Stoppard was lucky to have Peter Jeffrey as Brown. TV, in any case, is a narrower medium than cinema. It excels at close-ups, monologues and duologues and the small cast TV film can make do with as few as three cameras, one for the 'two shot', with each of the other two focused on a different actor. Variation is achieved by editing camera angles and distances. Large public scenes, as any TV representation of Shakespeare shows, are hard to control within the narrow camera field. This early play makes no great demands on the medium. Its freshness derives from unconventional dialogue and a surprising situation rather than from formal experimentation.

John Brown is surrounded by minor characters who cannot compre-hend why he wants to live in a hospital:

■ *Matron*: Now what's your problem Mr Brown?
Brown: No problem.
Matron: Your complaint?
Brown: I have no complaints either. Full marks.
Matron: Most people who come here have something the *matter* with them.
Brown: That must give you a lot of extra work. (p. 10) ☐

The exchanges of Morecambe and Wise linger in the ear. Brown plays the innocent fool figure; the matron, doctor and nurse play the feed. Reality, however, soon enters. Brown remarks that his money is not limit-less and will only carry him through the summer. What will he do when the holiday ends? Meanwhile, he cocoons himself in a fake reality by painting his room with pastoral scenes: 'Hospital routine in a pastoral setting. That's kind of perfection, really' (p. 18). But Brown is aware his retreat is a fake, for when the matron suggests that he make artificial flowers to fill the time, he replies: 'What on earth for? You've got lots of real ones' (p. 13). The comment could equally be applied to his own murals. 'You could have put your bed in the garden', says the sym-pathetic nurse. And the doctor, whom Brown accuses of meddling, tells him (quoting E. M. Forster):

■ (*pause, not phoney any more*) It's not enough Mr Brown.
You've got to . . . *connect* . . . (p. 21) ☐

The trouble is – connect with what? The doctor is talking about people. And people in Brown's past world seem to have behaved badly enough to justify his withdrawal. The fool figure Brown is playing out an illusion, but it may be preferable to 'reality'. With Stoppard there is always a *pro* and a *contra*. A preference for clockwork routine may have its justifications. Brown has been a prisoner in a concentration camp and has found the routine preferable to the chaos of war during which, as Private Brown, he has painted tanks with pastoral colours to disguise their lethal function.

Such violence is generally excluded from farce (though repetitive murder is used in *Arsenic and Old Lace* and *Kind Hearts and Coronets* to great effect). Here it is only hinted at and the tone of this early play is predom-inantly light. However, in a disturbing ending, Brown leaves the hospital to avoid his relatives. His identity is discovered and he has no second haven. He departs, as he has arrived, by night. Here again, as in the radio plays, the comic innocent ceases at crucial moments to be comic. The joke does not quite last.

Teeth

Stoppard's next TV play was transmitted on BBC 2 on 7 February 1967. It has five speaking parts. John Stride played George, a 'saloon bar Lothario' with dazzling teeth. John Wood, who was to work a great deal with Stoppard, played Harry, a dentist whose teeth are matchingly good. The situation is appositely the conventional story of the 'biter bit'. George has been having an affair with Prudence, the ill-named wife of Harry. George's wife Mary is coincidentally and dentally Harry's assistant. Harry will take his revenge by extracting George's front tooth and colouring another green, destroying his charm and reducing him to the decrepit facial state of the ladies in the waiting room. He also seduces Mary, just off screen, as George's head is clamped to the dentist's chair.

The story is slight, unlikely and hilarious. The topic of ageing and the motive of revenge are kept at a distance by eliminating sympathy for the victim. A fascination with the TV form is apparent, since the story gives ample opportunity for the use of close-ups. The facial expressions when the dentist produces his villainous instruments are of the stuff of farce – which plays on a common anxiety while making it ridiculous. The victim tells increasingly desperate and amusing lies to avoid detection by the verbally sadistic dentist, whose cleverness enlists the viewer's connivance. We have little sympathy for the ignorant victim, who gets his deserving come-uppance at the hands of his knowing tormentor.

Commentators on the play commend its televisual expertise and recount the plot. Hayman observes that the camera

■ . . . can move in on eyes dilated with fear about what is happening in the mouth; our own anxieties about teeth and sexual attractiveness makes us more vulnerable in the privacy of our home . . . the fantasy takes on a dangerous aura of reality. (Hayman, p. 79) □

Jenkins provides a fuller description and comments:

■ All Stoppard's early plots, when they are not evolved from other plays, either build out of joke ideas that are a part of modern folklore, like the human TIM voice, or in this play, the dangers of offending one's dentist, or they centre on a recent event: the first moon landing, the deaths of Marilyn Monroe and Winston Churchill, the Magritte retrospective at the Tate. These ideas seem to trigger a fantasy which divides off into many seemingly contradictory directions, but which finally comes together in the neatest and tightest of knots. (Jenkins, p. 59) □

Another Moon Called Earth

The adultery joke is carried through into the next TV play, which will be considerably expanded in Stoppard's big stage drama *Jumpers* (1972). It was transmitted in June 1967, with John Wood as Bone and Diane Cilento as Penelope, in a cast of four. In this play there is a comic death, that of Penelope's nanny, Pinkerton, who, deriving her name from a famous detective agency, fails to have her own death elucidated. In fact, she is 'given the push' (out of a window) by Penelope, a child/woman who fails to exhibit the same constancy towards her husband as does her famous Greek namesake on Ithaca. The push is reminiscent of André Gide's *'acte gratuit'* (motiveless action), except that it appears to arise from Penelope's childish resentment at the games Pinkerton keeps on winning. Add to this her sense that, since a 'lunanaut' has landed on the moon and returned to earth, the pattern of history assumed by her historian husband, Bone, who prides himself on his logical acuity, no longer exists. She takes to her bed. Everything becomes possible, including murder, an existentialist thought at least as old as Dostoievsky's Ivan Karamazov.

A number of Stoppard motifs are discernible. The husband lives in his own world and does not like to be interrupted by a wife who makes constant demands on his attention. Penelope throws herself like a child into a number of games, parodying the language of war in a game of *Battleships* with her husband. She is daily visited by a handsome young man, who might be a doctor and affects to cure her by playing charades. How to interpret the whole charade is the problem for Bone. His logic does not lead him to very sensible conclusions, for it half persuades him that the so-called doctor's visits are as harmless as they seem.

The logician is weakened by his capacity for seeing things from different perspectives. Logic may be based on assumptions one wants to believe (Bone's is that his wife is not making a fool of him). Fresh viewpoints may be disturbing – such as the one experienced by the lunanaut who sees the earth from the moon instead of vice versa. Unlike the perspective seen by Albert from his bridge, the viewer from a distant moon sees chaos not serenity. May we not rely on reason and causation? 'If it's all random what's the point?', asks Bone. 'What's the point if it's all logical?', replies the doctor/lover. 'No one is safe now', opines Penelope.

There is some visual sophistication. Stoppard mixes documentary with a comic situation whose absurdity disguises interesting issues. The comic exchanges take place alternately in study hall and bedroom, using conventional sets. The outside world is shown on television, a scene of national fervour as the lunanaut parades the streets to great applause. The mix, however, is not entirely successful. The play, suggests Hayman, citing Stoppard, is of its time but does not stand the test of time:

■ "Plays", says Stoppard, "go off like fruit. They're organic things; they're not mineral. They change their composition in relation to the time they exist, or are seen to exist, and in relation to oneself; they start to decompose the moment the word is on the page." Television plays decompose faster than stage plays, and retrospectively the main interest of *Another Moon Called Earth* is as a stepping stone between *Lord Malquist* and *Jumpers*. In all three an attractive girl is confusing her husband between a rich mixture of evidence that suggests adultery and explanations that almost quell his suspicions. Is she as innocent as he hopes or as unscrupulous as he fears? (Hayman, p. 62) □

The reception at the time was not warm. George Melly felt the play was pretentious:

■ Does it really need an astronaut on the moon to destroy a silly vain girl's moral sense? Well, it might, but it made an improbable fable, and the language, and in consequence the acting, had something of the fussy dated quality of Christopher Fry. Come to that, so did the title. (*The Observer*, 2 July 1967, p. 19) □

Stanley Reynolds in *The Guardian* observed that Penelope's 'view that our absolutes are mere tribal customs' was set against her husband's belief in a logical pattern of history: 'Unfortunately, Stoppard's brave new moon stance wasn't argued with enough earthbound tribal logic' (29 June 1967, p. 6).

Discussing the later play *Jumpers* with Mel Gussow, Stoppard avows that

■ My objective has always been to perform a marriage between the play of ideas and a farce . . . as to whether this is a desirable objective I have no idea. It represents two sides of my own personality which can be described as seriousness compromised by my frivolity or . . . frivolity redeemed by my seriousness. (*New York Times*, 23 April 1974) □

One might say that *Another Moon* is the first case and *Jumpers* is the second. But whatever stance one takes, the continuing attempt to mix genres and vary perspectives merits applause. If only as a dry run for the later play, *Another Moon* retains its interest.

Neutral Ground

Neutral Ground is the most ambitious of this group of four TV plays, being three times as long as *Teeth* and *Another Moon Called Earth*. It was written in 1965 for a series of plays based on myths, but was shelved and not transmitted until December 1968 on Thames TV. The central role was played by Patrick Magee, of Beckett fame, but there are eight main characters and over 20 others, not counting a host of supernumeraries in bars, buses and railway stations. The play is based, Stoppard tells us, on Sophocles' *Philoctetes*, in which Odysseus encourages Neoptolemus to persuade Philoctetes to use his magic bow in the war against the Trojans. Without it, according to an oracle, the war will not be won. Philoctetes' bow cannot miss, but he has a stinking wound, which causes Odysseus to leave Philoctetes on the island of Lemnos, thereby incurring his hatred. The cunning Odysseus employs the more trustworthy Neoptolemus to persuade the warrior to return. He does so when Heracles as *deus ex machina* (the god who resolves problems at the end of classical tragedy), convinces Philoctetes that Neoptolemus is telling the truth.

In *Neutral Ground*, as in T. S. Eliot's *The Family Reunion* and *The Cocktail Party*, the underlying Greek myth is unrecognisable, save for the name of the central role, Philo, and the parallels between Odysseus and Otis, a cunning spymaster, and Otis's subordinate spy, Ascherson, and Neoptolemus. Philo has been working for British intelligence in Russia, but he has lost belief in the restoration of independence to his homeland. When the play starts, he is making his way to England across an unnamed frontier. Otis, however, thinks Philo's despatches are suspect. Philo may be a double agent and he prevents him coming in from the cold, leaving him stateless and a likely victim for the KGB to hunt down. Philo is drinking himself to death in 'neutral ground' in the Balkans. His despatches, however, prove to be highly valuable and two years later Otis needs to save his own skin by finding Philo. He concocts a plan whereby Ascherson pretends to meet Philo by 'coincidence' and bring him 'home'. Philo, in disgust, decides to go back to his unnamed home country, which has been assimilated into the Soviet Union and where the KGB will surely find him. Otis's trick is to overcome the human desires of this ageing 'used up' spy who loses belief in the restoration of his lost but loved country but wishes to return 'home'. (In 1965 the revolution of 1989 did not seem possible.) He achieves this by playing on the human sympathy of the disenchanted Philo for Ascherson and his apparent wife.

The play links Sophocles with John Le Carré and George Smiley in *Tinker, Tailor, Soldier, Spy*. The example of Eliot is there, too, but the underlying poetic tension that Eliot hoped to gain by using a free verse form and a haunting parallel subtext is not achieved in *Neutral Ground*. According to the famous essay of Edmund Wilson in *The Wound and the Bow*, Philoctetes, the outsider with an unerring eye, is a symbolic artist figure – and there are moments when Philo rises to a kind of poetry, as, for example, in the long speech in which he describes the market in his native village:

■ . . . I particularly remember the peppers lying around the edges of the square – red, orange, yellow, green, and all shades in between, all

sunset and forest colours lying about the square. What mattered to us then is that they were edible and free . . . (p.123) ☐

Philo is due for a shock on his return home, one imagines, though this irony does not seem to be present in the dialogue, which, unsupported by Eliot's rhythms, is a difficult speech for the actor to render and a point at which, as Stoppard admits, the play is occasionally 'overwritten'. The moment when the character is portrayed at his most sincere seems paradoxically weak and the nostalgia self-indulgent. Anthony Jenkins remarks: 'Nobody who had suffered from the political realities of Europe would indulge in the high-flown sentiment that clothes Philo's reasons for returning' (Jenkins, pp.22–3). In this clever, complex and powerful drama, Philo's sincerity should emerge in stronger contrast to the demeaning role-play of those who are using him. There is a poet in Stoppard attempting to get out. Unfortunately, poetry in a taut TV drama is a dangerous mode to employ.

The presentation of the KGB agents is in a different mode entirely. Laurel and Hardy, a fat and a thin, courteous but sinister pair, derive from Hemingway, Pinter, farce and *film noir*. They are highly entertaining, but they lighten the tone and limit the emotional power of the generally naturalistic treatment. Again Stoppard is trying to mix the genres and break away from the standard TV spy story to which John Russell Taylor still assigned the play: 'It was just a very routine addition to the cycle of downbeat, John Le Carré-type spy dramas' (*Plays and Players*, February 1969, p.12). Taylor is not entirely fair. The pressures of TV towards conventionality are obvious. Jenkins remarks more generously:

■ At this point in his career, Stoppard was probably content to make his script craftsmanly and marketable. An earlier play *This Way Out With Samuel Boot*, from 1964, had been rejected and, in synopsis, appears to have been much more adventurous . . . After that script had been turned down, Stoppard's agent, Kenneth Ewing, advised him to "stick to theatre. Your work can't be contained on television". (Jenkins, p.23) ☐

Stoppard proves Ewing wrong. *Neutral Ground* is a brilliantly plotted spy story that plays confidently with time and space, with flashbacks and flashforwards, darkness and light. The spectator is kept guessing and the visual craftsmanship is of a very high order. It uses exterior and interior locations with great skill. Shots of open country, the village where Philo is holed up and the city nearby, a rich penthouse and seedy rooms alternate with a train compartment, a vet's waiting room and surgery, car interiors, a bar scene with skittles, other bars, a disco, even a church wedding. Animals are (dangerously) used, including a cat, a monkey, a parrot and a menagerie in a seedy flat. Stoppard's visual imagination and capacity to develop plot by intercutting camera shots and varying lenses from long shot to close-up reveals a writer at the top of his profession. Most importantly, the play raises questions about human needs, trust, ageing, duplicity, the question of political ends and means, and the whole process of cold-war spying. The play is more than 'thoroughly workmanlike' (Hayman's description). It is a powerful and successful piece, even if its weaknesses at this stage are due to Stoppard's ambitious attempt to go beyond the conventional form.

CHAPTER FIVE

Detective Stories

The Real Inspector Hound and *After Magritte*

The next stage play, written in 1967, was *The Real Inspector Hound*, first performed at the Criterion Theatre on the 17 June 1968 and revived as part of a double bill many times. The idea originated in Stoppard's experience as a theatre critic in Bristol:

■ I went around for years actually reviewing the kind of play I'm parodying. I started out to be a glamorous foreign correspondent. Reviewing Agatha Christie plays was merely the first step to lying on my stomach in some oriental airport while plate glass was smashed by bazookas. (Gussow, pp. 1–2) □

In the play, Richard Briers and Ronnie Barker played two theatre critics, Moon and Birdboot. A body lies on the floor hidden by a sofa. Who has done the deed? It turns out to be Higgs, the first string reviewer whose place Moon has taken. In Act III, a phone rings. Moon answers it. But it is for Birdboot. The critics step on the stage to become involved in the whodunit and shot by the third string reviewer, disguised as Inspector Hound.

After Magritte closely followed. 'Neither play is about anything grander than itself', said Stoppard, but that has not stopped critics from commenting on profound questions of identity and illusion, art and reality, reason and redemption. Others have endeavoured, with Stoppard's encouragement, not to make the plays more serious than they appear.

The Real Inspector Hound

The play has attracted a strong critical response, both positive and negative. Anthony Jenkins finds its subject insignificant:

■ [It is] . . . the least satisfactory of all Stoppard's plays . . . the theatrical whodunit tends to be transparently banal in the first place, so that to parody its emptiness simply restates the obvious . . . all Stoppard's burlesque does is to underline the banalities in a schoolboy manner. (Jenkins, p. 51) □

This assumes that the play is no more than a parody of *The Mousetrap*. Other critics take the play much more seriously. Weldon B. Durham, for example, quotes a lukewarm comment from C. W. E. Bigsby's book *Tom Stoppard* (1976) in order to take issue with him:

■ Far from stopping "annoyingly short of examining the implications of its central premise", as C. W. E. Bigsby maintains, *The Real Inspector Hound* is wholly and completely responsive to its purgative-redemptive motive. Without denying Stoppard's parodic aims, this essay demonstrates that, in addition to being a barbed satire and a somewhat less successful exposition of a view of a relationship between theatre and life, the play is fully comprehensible as a ritual of riddance. (Harty, p. 102) □

This is close to arguing that the effect of this comedy resembles Aristotle's definition in the *Poetics* of the tragic catharsis or purgation of the emotions 'through pity and fear'. Durham suggests that the 'auditor' identifies during the performance with the human weaknesses of the onstage critics, until their deaths relieve him of the burden of his human guilt. This would make it a very serious play indeed.

Less weighty, but not too far distant from Durham's pronouncement, is Jeffrey D. Mason's perception of the play as an attack on the arrogance of a belief in the predominance of human rationality. The critics in the play are brought down from the lofty seat of judgement and subjected to scrutiny themselves. A similar thing, he points out, happens in *Oedipus Rex* – a comparison which again foregrounds the play's relation to tragedy. Mason then quotes Bigsby on the 'central premise' which Bigsby feels the play comes short of examining:

■ C.W.E. Bigsby identifies the object of mockery in *Hound*:
"... the play which Birdboot and Moon are reviewing is a whodunit, the supreme example of rational art ... a form which rests on the conviction that reality is susceptible of rational analysis, since it turns so clearly on causality".
The detective is the champion of rationalism, the man who claims to solve the problem by building a structure of logically related deductions, and he is therefore the victim of Stoppard's pen. Both Brian M. Crossley and Thomas Whitaker have identified the detective as the philosophical heir of Oedipus, the man who believes confidently that he can resolve a disordered situation but whose investigations lead to

chaos. Oedipus fell from grace because his questions succeeeded too well in revealing a situation that demanded his destruction, but Hound and Foot discover that their very methods are unreliable. . . . they assume a rational order that does not exist. (Harty, pp. 109–10) □

Stoppard would no doubt shy away from questions of cathartic effect as he would from Mason's statement that a rational order does not exist. He is also wary of assigning 'meanings' to plays and suspects the definitions of academic criticism:

■ It's a jokey play.

. . . Do you think critics tend to over-read resonances? [Gussow]

That's absolutely true. When somebody is evaluating a play or a painting, what they think they are doing is recognizing its references and its relevance and from that drawing a value judgement. What really happens is that you have a kind of instant experiential response to a play – and then you justify it. If you don't like it, you justify that; and if you love it, you justify that. (Gussow, p. 2) □

He admits, however: 'I'm the kind of person who embarks on an endless leapfrog down the great moral issues. I put a position, rebut it, refute the rebuttal, and refute the refutation. . . '. It is not surprising, then, that critics find meanings in his play, even if they isolate one of many perspectives at the expense of another. Directors and actors, after all, do the same.

Hound parodies reviewing as well as Agatha Christie's *The Mousetrap* and mocks the critic's game of identifying sources by having one of the reviewers cite nine of them, including Shakespeare, Pirandello, and farce and existential writers with whom Stoppard has been identified, such as Pinero, Beckett, Kafka and Sartre. St Paul is thrown in for good measure with Dorothy L. Sayers (but not Agatha Christie) and the name Birkett, which goes nicely with Beckett, is an invitation to zealous scholars to chase his name in dictionaries of the theatre where he will not be found. Stoppard denies, however, that the play is mainly about critics:

■ I originally conceived a play, exactly the same play, with simply two members of an audience getting involved in the play-within-the-play. But when it comes to actually writing something down which has integral entertainment value, if you like, it very quickly turned out that it would be a lot easier to do it with critics, because you've got something known and defined to parody. So it was never a play *about* drama critics. If one wishes to say that it is a play about something more than that, then it's about the dangers of wish-fulfilment. But as soon as the word's out of my mouth, I think, shit, it's a play about these two guys, and they're going along to this play, and the whole thing is tragic and hilarious, and very, very carefully constructed. (Delaney, p. 60) □

The words 'tragic' and 'wish-fulfilment' suggest a wider human concern than a parody of drama critics. The first, second and third string reviewers represent all who jockey for power and prestige. The word 'hilarious' implies a different perspective, scarcely compatible with tragedy, since it fits Stoppard's description of the play as a 'sort of mechanical toy' (see Bragg, in Delaney, p. 119).

The two onstage critics write in different house styles for different papers. Birdboot is downmarket and his reviews are well used as theatre publicity. Moon, a second string reviewer for a quality paper, has the occasional complimentary word quoted on billboards by theatre management. The play parodies the personal and cultural tension between them, and parodies *The Mousetrap*, which is itself a (probably unintentional) parody of the whodunit genre; thus Stoppard's play is a parody of a parody. One should also remember that Christie takes her title from the play-within-a-play in *Hamlet*, which was partly a parody, partly an allegory conceived by Hamlet to trap a king. Stoppard's play parodies reviewers who take seriously a parody of a parody. His ingenuity and his characters' ingenuousness trigger laughter – at the expense both of those who do and those who don't take the play seriously. Is it 'only' an entertainment? Stoppard himself seems not fully to know and thereby invites you to laugh not only at critics within (and outside) his play, but at the audience, the play itself and its author.

Moon, the upmarket critic, looks for what is 'underneath' the play. Birdboot explodes: 'Underneath?!? It's a whodunit man! – Look at it!' (p. 7). They look. There is a body under a sofa that the characters do not look beneath. We are warned not to look for depth when the play is all surface. Yet the play mocks characters who never look under the furniture. We catch it both ways, whether we take the play seriously or not.

Parody, of course, generally appeals through an interplay of flat characters to a double level of consciousness in the audience. The Christie thriller works through suspense. It employs stereotypes whom we are not meant to see as such. Hence actors often enjoy a Christie play because it provides a frame on which to build characters beyond the dramatist's intentions. Actors, like audiences and critics, like to find subtext. *Hound* is different from *The Mousetrap* in having several parodic layers, but similar in employing stereotypical characters who offer actors an opportunity to create a further layer. In an interview with Melvyn Bragg, Stoppard describes the process:

■ *The Real Inspector Hound* . . . is a sort of mechanical toy; it actually is a play that is built to go: "Brrn, chink, clonk, klump." And it does. And I like it for that. It's about a couple of critics watching a sort of Agatha Christie play and one of them ends up dead. And I wrote the critic, *mea culpa*, without love, you know. He had to . . . parody certain things, he had to get inside the wrong machine and end up dead. And it was an inhuman joke, really. The only thing is . . . the first time it was done, Richard Briers played this critic – I was saved, or scuppered, or whatever, by Richard Briers. When he died, people *cared* about him . . . (Delaney, p. 119) □

That a performance of a play does not always embody an author's intentions could not be clearer. If the play is satire, which depends on dehumanising the object of parody, then the actor's desire to make the audience care about the characters can work against the author's intention and muddy the performance. Stoppard, typically, leaves it to the audience to decide whether they, he, the play or the performance are 'saved' or 'scuppered' by Briers's humanity.

To most spectators the play is a joyful send-up of the thriller genre. No one must leave the isolated house, the fog rolls in and roads lead to it only at low tide. A policeman arrives with pontoons strapped to his feet to enable him to cross the marshes (Christie's inspector has skis). There is a dark secret; a beautiful bride abandoned but true to her loved one; a Mrs Drudge who supplies information and atmosphere at inordinate and ridiculous length.

Christie's *Mousetrap* is formulaic. *Hound* mocks the formula. The play starts with a stage empty of actors except for the corpse. 'You can't start with a pause!', says Birdboot. But Stoppard's play does. It is not a whodunit – it is *about* whodunits and also about the petty jealousies of the second strings, the understudies, the seconds in command and their desire to do away with those who block their way. They watch each other as we watch them. Shakespeare has his audience watching Ophelia watching Hamlet watching Claudius watching the Player King (*Hamlet*, Act III, iii). The barriers between theatre and stage audience dissolve and the distinction between the real and the fictional disappears. In comedy the illusion is usually displayed. Comedy is built, said Yeats in *The Trembling of the Veil*, 'on the dykes that separate man from man'. The blurring between the real and the illusory is in the characters' heads, not in the audience's. Laughter arises from the trick being shown, like the comedian's favourite magician, Tommy Cooper, who gets it all wrong.

However, even in comedy the audience is sometimes tricked by assurances that it is not being tricked. We laugh at the illusionist when his illusions fail. Then suddenly, astonishingly, the trick comes right. We laugh at those who are taken in, then at ourselves because we, too, have been taken in. In *Hound* we need to be very astute to keep up with the trickery. Even in so light a play as this, something draws the audience in. We laugh when the critics' own jealousies and lusts involve them in the stage action, but their inability to get back to their seats because two fictional characters are now occupying them is disturbing. (And perhaps especially if the seats are in the front stalls rather than facing the audience upstage as recommended in the stage directions.) When the crippled half-brother reveals himself as the policeman, killer, lost husband and even more amazingly the third string reviewer, the laughter is not only at the expense of the dying Moon. It is also in appreciation of the trick that has been played on us, the audience.

The main aspect of the play which academic critics have seized on is consequently the question of identity and the relation between audience and actors. June M. Schlueter, in her essay 'Moon and Birdboot', offers the following comments:

■ Stoppard's characters acquire metafictional status by virtue of play within play. In the case of *The Real Inspector Hound*, this "play" is formalized into a structural demand. The characters who are made to function within two structural units, acquire one identity in the frame play – their "real" identities – and quite another in the inner play – their fictive identities. But the distinction between the identities, and, indeed, between the plays, remains less than absolute. As the characters move across the boundary which separates the outer play from the inner one, the line which separates their identities as critics and members of an audience from their identities as actors and participants in the "whodunit" play becomes increasingly fluid, as does the reality which separates the reality of their world as audience and the fiction of the world of Muldoon Manor. In creating first a rigid line of structural demarcation and then violating that line through his protagonists' entrance into the inner play, Stoppard is able to use the play-within-a-play not simply in the traditional way, for enhancing reality, but rather to suggest the nature of role-playing and the power of illusion over reality. . . .

In fact, art emerges in *The Real Inspector Hound* as a force capable of controlling reality . . . In mimetic art, illusion may . . . be giving up its identity, trying to pass for reality. In Stoppard's art, illusion is autonomous . . . illusion imposes itself on reality, in essence destroying the right of reality to be separately defined . . . Nor does the power of illusion stop once it has destroyed the reality of the outer play. It extends to our own reality, which is reflected in the reality of the critics, destroying that as well. And if the mirror which reflected our reality is illusion, then perhaps reality is illusion after all. (Bloom, pp. 76–80) □

Schlueter does not carry this further – into rejection of the possibility of human solidarity which the last line implies and which Marxist-oriented critics, such as Georg Lukács and Raymond Williams, attack in 'modernist' writers (see Williams on Pirandello and Ionesco in *Modern Tragedy*, chapter 4, p.139). Nor do Stoppard's interviews suggest he would agree that reality is an illusion.

There are a number of fuller summaries of the play (by Hayman, Kelly, Whitaker and others), but jokes are spoiled by long explanations and Stoppard warns us not to take *Hound* too seriously. In Beckett's *Act Without Words*, laughter dies when too many tricks are played on the central character. Stoppard, too, can take us to that point. In this play, however, we do not, as in Beckett, wonder why we cease to laugh as the play progresses. Only when the play is over is the critic in danger of becoming serious about it. As Ronald Bryden said at the time:

■ If you liked, you could argue that the play, behind its frivolity, juggled with ideas as serious as the earlier one: that the triple-layered logics Stoppard plays against each other like a multi-dimensional chessmaster stand for the relativist, anthropology-based world-view of Lévi-Strauss and the French structuralists. Myself, I suspect that Stoppard uses them only for the lightning release of humour when logics collide – that, and the comic escape of seeing someone else swallowed up by the universal nightmare of slipping out of ordered experience into chaos. (*The Observer*, 23 June 1968, p.26) □

After Magritte

This play, often performed as a companion piece to *Hound*, was first put on at the Ambiance Lunch Hour Theatre Club and Green Bananas Restaurant on 9 April 1970. It seems an appropriate venue for the spirit of the play in the decade that Stoppard defined as 'simultaneously playful and desperately serious'. Stoppard expresses a strong affection for *After Magritte* – 'a very peculiar and fragile thing' – and prefers it to *Hound* (see Gussow, p.7), although the latter has proved much more popular.

The play has five characters: a husband and wife dance-team; the husband's tuba-playing mother; and two policemen whose job it is to interpret the surreal scene with which the play opens. The mother is lying on her back on an ironing board; the wife on her hands and knees wears a full-length ball-gown; the husband sports thigh-length waders and evening dress and blows into a lampshade; Holmes, a police constable, watches impassively through the window. The tableau closely resembles a painting 'after' – i.e., in imitation of – Magritte (see Keir Elam's remarks below). To complicate the situation, the characters have returned from a Magritte exhibition and are discussing a surreal happening (based on a real event) that has occurred just before their return. The wife has seen a one-legged footballer in a West Bromwich Albion football shirt. The husband says it was a blind man, wearing pyjamas, carrying a tortoise and a white stick. This grotesque spectacle has been reported and is being investigated by Inspector Foot of the Yard, who concocts a criminal explanation that he hopes will advance his career. The family's strange behaviour arouses Foot's suspicions, but it turns out that Foot himself was innocently responsible for the bizarre scene. In the course of the play, all is explained. P. C. Holmes, however, enters as the play ends on a new tableau, even more bizarre, which his superior now finds quite comprehensible. The ignorant constable, who has had access to none of the information, is told: 'Well, Constable, I think you owe us all an explanation'.

■ *The lampshade descends inexorably as the music continues to play; when it touches the table top there is no more light. Alternatively the lampshade could disappear down the horn of the tuba.* □

To make strange, the Russian formalists said, is a function of art. A dream, or an unknown noise in the night, or a Magritte picture, creates anxiety that we seek to disperse by finding an explanation. Or we use invective, which is the mother's response to the Magritte exhibition. Stoppard mocks the false conclusions to which people jump, the vain sleuth who has himself provided the surreal occasion that others misinterpret and on whose false reports he creates a fictional crime whose solution will advance his career. Stoppard explains the origin of the play:

■ I went to see a man who had peacocks. They tend to run away. He was shaving one morning and he looked out of the window and saw a peacock leap over the hedge into the road. Expensive animals, peacocks, so he threw down his razor and ran out and caught his peacock and brought it back home. I had been looking for a short piece and I had some vague idea of what I wanted to do. I didn't write about the man but about two people who just go by, and, boom, they see this man in pyjamas, with bare feet, shaving foam on his face, carrying a peacock. They see this man for five eighths of a second – and that's what I write about. (Gussow, p. 7) □

Stoppard said, on another occasion:

■ I want to demonstrate that I can make serious points by flinging a custard pie around the stage for a couple of hours. In other words, I want to write plays which are just funny enough to do their jobs, but not too funny to obscure them ... (Delaney, p. 95) □

Their 'job', for Stoppard, is to make a serious point and in *After Magritte* the serious point is about the comic way people perceive a situation and jump to false conclusions. Brian M. Crossley argues this case and finds that the play originates in popular forms:

■ **The humour of the plays in question** [*Inspector Hound* and *After Magritte*] **derives mainly from popular forms, such as the *Goon Show* of BBC Radio and the satirical magazine *Private Eye*, the latter being an appropriate title in terms of the plays discussed if ever there was one. Not for Stoppard the black comedy and frightening economy of Pinter's dialogue, nor the "successful conclusion" of the detective form as proclaimed by Ionesco, for all its irony. His reply is to question constantly the notion of the *answer* itself, in a dialogue rich and extravagant with question marks and verbal gymnastics. The figure of the detective is the epitome of the problem-solver *par excellence* who brings order and reassurance because he brings answers. These plays are a mock celebration of such a character, of all who believe in him, and of the concept of drama which defines itself in terms of the enactment of a riddle and its answer.** (Bloom, p. 24) □

Keir Elam approaches the subject of answers more obliquely in an article in *Modern Drama* (Vol. 27, December 1984). He finds the play's sources, not in Stoppard's anecdote or *Private Eye*, but in Magritte, Carroll, Wittgenstein, Aesop, Zeno, Borges, Gilbert Ryle and the author and computer scientist, D. R. Hofstadter. Elam states that Stoppard's major concern and achievement is his engagement with certain of the central aesthetic, philosophical and especially semiological issues of our time and argues that *After Magritte* is a witty pun on the word *after*, which implies not only 'later than' but also 'in (mock) imitation of':

■ **. . . the play's ambiguous title raises explicitly the question of its debts (of whom, as it were, it takes "after"), or of the direct cultural influences on the verbal and visual follies it pursues with such manic energy and rigour. And it is this question of Stoppard's relationship with the cultural patrimony – specifically the non-dramatic patrimony – of our age, his intellectual and intertextual "afterness" or posterity with respect to those figures whose artistic practice or theoretical models are closest to the principles of his theatrical poetics, that is the main concern of this paper . . . since it is in my opinion his success in finding precise and persuasive theatrical coordinates for apparently intractable conceptual material that represents this playwright's major contribution to contemporary dramaturgy . . .**

The "After" of the title has first a simple chronological sense, since the play's controversial central event is witnessed by the Harrises on

their way back from a Magritte exhibition (the implicit suggestion being, naturally, that their very perception of the mysterious figure may have been contaminated by what they saw of Magritte's way of seeing). And second, it has an iconographic sense . . . in that the play's opening configuration appears to be a Magrittean pastiche, both because of its inexplicability as composition or juxtaposition (elder woman on ironing board, younger woman on all fours, semi-naked man in fisherman's waders fixing the light, with a framed policeman looking in), and, as it were, in its component "lexical items," all objects stolen from Magritte's attic: a tuba, a window with a dark menacing figure outside it, a black bowler hat placed on an old lady's body, a screen that might be a canvas *mise en abîme*, and so on. (Bloom, p. 163) □

Stoppard, Elam goes on to say, is concerned with the relations between word, image and object, like Magritte in his famous painting *Ceci n'est pas une pipe*, which shows a picture of a pipe but states beneath it 'This is not a pipe'. The word is not the image, nor is the iconic and naturalistic image of a pipe the same as the image one has of it in one's head or, indeed, the 'real' thing itself. According to Elam, this results, for Magritte, in a closed interplay between signs:

■ there is no way of breaking this interpretational chain or hermeneutic circle so as to arrive finally and reassuringly at the chimeric *"objet réel"*. Magritte's perceptual world is presented as a "mosaic" of adjacent and interdefining forms, rather than an assembly of fixed and autonomous substances. (Bloom, pp. 164–5) □

The process, Elam continues, is reinforced by Magritte's later painting, *The Two Mysteries*, which places the earlier picture within a frame and the 'real thing', i.e., another pipe, outside it, except of course that the second representation of a pipe is not real either. The viewer is trapped in a series of illusions.

Katherine Kelly's *Tom Stoppard and the Craft Of Comedy* (1991) picks up Elam's point, arguing that the common ground between Magritte and Stoppard resides in their targeting 'habitual perception and the habitual response'; but Kelly finds a difference in the implications of their work:

■ the implicit moral judgement by which Foot admits to the folly of his fictional caper – "Bear in mind that my error was merely one of interpretation . . ." (102) distinguishes Stoppard's play from Magritte's insoluble and amoral ambiguities. The play's characters prove finally to be the victims of "their own logical absolutism" (Elam). Or to put it slightly differently, they prove to be entrapped by their interpretative logic, by a single view of a situation that fails to account for them-selves as the seers ...

... Stoppard's parody appropriates Magritte to the Magrittean end of poking fun at the logic of linguistic and visual representations of experience. Magritte's labelling of his painting, "This is not a pipe," might be applied to Stoppard's parody: "This is not a Magritte paint-ing" ... (Kelly, p. 90) □

Kelly argues that in *After Magritte* Stoppard takes a moral view of life and does not see it as a relativistic world of 'insoluble and amoral ambigu-ities'. He escapes from Magritte's circular trap and shows the characters of the play deluded by their own imaginings. In revealing the source of their illusions, Stoppard echoes Lewis Carroll's attack on the false reasoning of Zeno who 'demonstrated' that Achilles could not catch the tortoise. In *Jumpers*, Elam points out, the tortoise is caught when the philosopher, Moore, steps on it. In *After Magritte*, it is the Inspector who is caught and the mystery is explained.

Stoppard's comments on the play are not couched in Elam's struc-turalist terms and locate the appeal of Magritte in the 'reality' of the representation:

■ The absurd and bizarre and incongruous positions in Magritte's art are all placed within an absolutely academic context. He may paint a boulder in the sky but the boulder looks heavy. When he paints an apple in a room, it's an apple you can almost eat. It's that combination I find utterly admirable in Magritte. The play is in a humble way a homage to him. It's not a literary equivalent. The intention is to exhibit the bizarre set of components, but to do so in a mechanism that is closer to Agatha Christie than to Samuel Beckett. (Gussow, p. 7) □

But the Agatha Christie mechanism that supplies an answer at the end is not to be trusted. Nor perhaps are the serious points he raises behind his 'nuts-and-bolts comedy' (Delaney, p. 59).

'Meaning', however, is to be found in the visual impact of *After Magritte*. Stoppard's stage directions invite any director of this play to use his own ingenuity. The disappearance of a lampshade down a tuba would be difficult to engineer. But the visual effect is crucial. Light is shed on the bizarre events, but the play ends in darkness. The visual counterbalances the verbal. We are told the central light is attached to a basket of fruit because the counterweight has broken. The offstage bath-room whose light bulb needs replacing causes Frederick Harris to wear waders over his evening dress (he and his wife are going out dancing). He wishes to avoid electrocution when stepping in the bath. The explan-ation is rational but farcical, raising more questions (why not switch off the mains?). But a more symbolic, even poetic function, is conveyed in the physical impact of alternating light and dark, the centre-stage lamp rising and falling, giving the play a seriousness that the words and situation mock. The serious modes of interpretation and the sheer enjoyment of creating a theatrical vehicle are again counterbalanced in the critical and human responses to *After Magritte*.

CHAPTER SIX

'Thou Shalt Not Kill'

Jumpers

On 2 February 1972 the National Theatre performed *Jumpers* at the Old Vic with Michael Hordern, Diana Rigg and Graham Crowden in the principal roles of George, Dotty and Archie. It received the *Evening Standard Award* and the *Play and Players Award* for the best play of the year. Directed by Peter Wood, who would strike up a fertile partnership with Stoppard, it took advantage of the National Theatre's facilities which, after the success of *Rosencrantz and Guildenstern*, Stoppard felt fairly sure would be offered him:

■ . . . it was on the cards that the National Theatre would do what I wrote, if I didn't completely screw it up, and it has forty, fifty actors on the pay-roll. You can actually write a play for ten gymnasts. (Hayman, p. 4) □

Jumpers seems to have germinated from the unusual visual image of a 'short blunt human pyramid' to which Guildenstern had mysteriously referred five years before.

■ I thought: "How marvellous to have a pyramid of people on a stage, and a rifle shot, and one member of the pyramid just blown out of it, and the others imploding on the hole as he leaves" . . . I didn't know who he was or who had shot him or why or what to do with the body. Absolutely not a clue. So one worked from a curiously anti-literary starting point. (Hayman, p. 4) □

The idea soon acquired an intellectual dimension: '. . . it's the work of a moment to think that there was a metaphor at work between acrobatics, mental acrobatics, and so on' (Hayman, p. 5). Mental acrobatics in a university philosophy department and jumping, or not jumping, to the orders of Sir Archibald Jumper, the Vice-Chancellor, became the main topics. The central figure is a Professor of Ethics called George Moore who is composing a lecture to prove the existence of God and the reality of absolute moral values. Around him the world seems to deny his propositions. A ruthless political regime has just taken over. A lunar landing has shown one astronaut abandoning another on the moon. George's wife, Dottie, a former music hall star who cannot now remember romantic songs about the moon, has had a breakdown and seems to be having an affair with the sinister Vice-Chancellor. The latter may well be the murderer of the man shot in the opening sequence – since the victim, a Professor McFee who was to have lectured, with the VC's approval, on the relativity of moral values, seems to have defected to George's point of view. Alternatively, the murderer could be Dottie or George's silent, unsmiling secretary who was the mistress of McFee before his intellectual defection. Inspector Bones, a fan of Dottie's, investigates the murder, but is caught in a compromising position and persuaded to abandon the case. Sir Archibald's troupe get rid of the corpse, which has hung behind Dottie's door, unbeknown to George, and the VC goes on to get rid of the new Archbishop of Canterbury and to answer George's final pronouncements with a few nonsensical but highly applauded words.

Stoppard devoted two years to *Jumpers*, reading widely in philosophy and reworking material from previous plays, especially *Another Moon Called Earth*. In both plays the wife feels neglected because the husband is absorbed in his academic concerns; she takes to her room and is visited daily by a doctor/lover. Stoppard is more interested in ideas than psychology, but he fills out the stereotype characters of husband and wife, giving them a real poignancy and intelligence. Behind George is the farce type of the absent-minded professor, ignorant for much of the play of what everyone else knows. He misunderstands references to the death of McFee, of which he is slow to learn. Nor does he know of McFee's change of heart to an idealist belief in God or see his corpse as it swings into and out of sight when Dotty's door is opened and closed. George is old hat, a believer in God but not in Archie, the Vice-Chancellor, doctor/lover, politician, psychiatrist, coroner, gymnast and materialist philosopher of the modern British school.

The performance of Michael Hordern, as a professor who was both silly and serious, gained many plaudits. Whitaker quotes Kenneth Tynan:

■ "Hordern", said Tynan, "had the part of his life: quivering with affronted dignity, patrolling the stage like a neurotic sentry, his face infested with tics, his fists plunging furiously into his cardigan pockets, he was matchlessly silly and serious at the same time." (Whitaker, p. 103) □

Hordern patrolled the area between comedy and pathos, acting at the same time as a vehicle for Stoppard's ideas. 'Occasionally', says Stoppard modestly, 'I've got fairly close to a play which works as a funny play and which makes coherent, in terms of theatre, a fairly complicated intellectual argument' (Delaney, p. 59).

Jumpers communicates complex arguments through Stoppard's 'poor professor' and also through vivid stage metaphors, in particular the acrobatic display in George and Dotty's Mayfair home which made a striking and original opening – even more so in the first New York production:

■ In England we had eight actors from the National Theatre. Any one of them could give you an Horatio, but they were not so good at cartwheels or backflips. Here [in New York] we have at least twelve guys who can do marvellous things on trampolines. The pyramid is exactly as I imagined it, which it never was in London. First of all we had four fewer people and secondly you couldn't ask them to do what they do here. The pyramid is eighteen feet high and really quite frightening. In England it was twelve feet high.

Perhaps the critics will say the acrobats are too good.

It's a fair point. Peter Wood quite rightly saw America as the land of opportunity when it comes to gymnastics. Ideally I think they ought to be able to do ineptness brilliantly. Instead of doing ineptness they're just brilliant. Obviously it's a razor's edge. I personally think there's nothing more wonderful than a brilliant juggler playing a bad juggler.

Can you do acrobatics?

I used to be able to stand on my head. I could never do a cartwheel. I was always an intellectual from the word go . . . (Gussow, pp. 18–19) □

In New York, expertise was pre-eminent, though Stoppard would have preferred acrobatics reminiscent of Tommy Cooper bungling a trick.

When the pyramid is complete, the Professor of Logic, Duncan McFee, who half supports one side of the pyramid, is shot, leaving a gap through which the mentally disintegrating Dotty appears before the pyramid crumbles. As in *Macbeth* the female lead is covered in Duncan's blood and utters the famous words: 'What, in our house?'. In Shakespeare's play, however, we know who has done the deed, as we do in *Another Moon Called Earth* where the wife pushed her nanny out of a window. In *Jumpers*, Dotty is only a suspected murderer. She has no motive but was in a position to fire the shot. The murderer might rather be Archie the VC, who has no qualms in killing his appointee, the Archbishop of Canterbury, when, in the coda to the play, the primate evinces, like Thomas à Becket, signs of independence. 'Who will rid me of this turbulent priest?', Archie asks at that point.

There are other suspects – the culprit may be George's silent secretary, Duncan McFee's deserted mistress (who seems to have some understanding with the VC). This becomes a quasi-certainty when she turns her back on the audience and reveals blood on her dress, but the blood turns out to be that of Thumper, George's pet hare, which he hopes to use as a demonstration model, along with his tortoise, in the lecture he is writing to refute Archie's materialism. Certainties – like George's certainty that Dotty has killed the missing Thumper – become less certain. It turns out that George himself has accidentally done the deed. It is as dangerous to jump to conclusions, the play says, as not to jump at Archie's command.

The astonishing visual effect of the play, for which Stoppard gives credit to others, needs to be emphasised as much as the narrative:

■ I write little stage directions which are like little time bombs that go off in the director's hands when he picks them up. In *Jumpers* there is a scene change and it just says, "The bedroom forms around her." Those five words occupied fine brains for five weeks until the bedroom formed around her. It sort of walks in on her. (Gussow, p. 23) □

Film techniques are also employed. Behind the action a moon landing is projected onto an enormous screen. It shows an astronaut called Captain Scott abandoning his subordinate, Oates, to his fate. 'I am going up now. I may be gone for some time', he says, closing the hatch. Dotty, driven to breakdown by the lunar landing, which destroys her ability to sing about blue and harvest moons, is also back-projected onto the screen. Her skin is subjected to Archie's inspection by 'dermatograph' and when seen in unromantic close-up recalls TV shots of the moon's pitted face.

The split set makes a strong statement, switching from Dotty's elaborate bedroom, stage right, where the exhibition of Dotty's beauty is not the least of the visual attractions, to the untidy study of a George in physical decline. A hallway leading downstage, thence to the kitchen, separates the rooms and provides a useful third space. The sinister, unsmiling secretary takes down the lecture that George composes as he looks through a non-existent mirror hung on the fourth wall. Impressive and surprising entrances and exits take place through an upstage door. Here George, his back to the audience, causes a startled policeman, Bones, to recoil as he answers the door, his face covered in shaving foam, carrying a bow and arrow and a tortoise, the props for his intended lecture. George then himself recoils when he sees his own image in the fourth wall mirror. (The idea is, of course, developed from *After Magritte*.)

The visual complexity is well illustrated by the stage directions at the end of Act I when Dotty is swaying and miming 'Sentimental Journey':

■ *. . . The dead jumper is where he fell. The front door opens and ARCHIE enters, and stops inside the front door, almost closing it behind him. He stands listening, an impressive figure, exquisitely dressed: orchid in buttonhole, cigarette in long black holder, and everything which those details suggest. He carefully opens the door of the Study. The secretary looks up. She nods at him, but it is impossible to draw any conclusions from that.*

ARCHIE withdraws closing the door. He comes downstage and looks along the corridor into the Kitchen wing. He returns to the front door and opens it wide.

SEVEN JUMPERS in yellow tracksuits enter smoothly. FOUR of them carry a machine of ambiguous purpose: it might be a television camera. They also carry a couple of lights on tall stands, suitable for filming (these items may be all in one box). SIX enter the Bedroom, ARCHIE opening the door for them.

ONE JUMPER goes downstage to watch the Kitchen exit.

In the bedroom DOTTIE is surprised but pleased by the entry of ARCHIE and the JUMPERS. They put down the 'camera' and the lights. They have come to remove the body.

The song dominates the whole scene. Nothing else can be heard, and its beat infects the business of removing the body, for DOTTY continues to sway and snap her fingers as she moves about welcoming the troops, and the JUMPERS lightly respond, so that the effect is a little simple improvised choreography between the JUMPERS and DOTTY.

ARCHIE moves downstage, facing front, and like a magician about to demonstrate a trick, takes from his pocket a small square of material like a handkerchief, which he unfolds and unfolds and unfolds until it is a large plastic bag, six feet tall, which he gives to TWO JUMPERS. These TWO hold the mouth of the bag open at the door; at the climax of the 'dance' the FOUR JUMPERS throw the body into the bag; bag closes, bedroom door closes, JUMPERS moving smoothly, front door closes, and on the last beat of the song, only ARCHIE and DOTTY are left on stage. □

One can imagine the amount of rehearsal time required to choreograph these directions.

The play employs many powerful sound effects. At her party Dotty tries to sing a song about the moon, but mixes up various well known tunes to the orchestra's distress. The party ends with a blackout and crash of glassware when the drinks waiter backs into the nude secretary swinging on a trapeze. (The blackout and sound effect save the nightly expenditure of glass and avoid danger to actors on stage.) Jet planes, in formation like the acrobats, zoom overhead on the big screen to celebrate the election victory of the totalitarian 'Radical Liberals'. George switches off the screaming sound track in mid-flight, but they return. The most powerful effect occurs accidentally and climactically at the Act II curtain. George has just discovered his pet hare, Thumper, transfixed by the arrow he earlier loosed over the wardrobe when his wife's shout of FIRE! startled him. In dismay he steps backwards onto Pat his pet tortoise – CRRRRRUNCH!!! George becomes a double killer.

This description may suggest that *Jumpers* is no more than a brilliant display of theatrical technique with little serious content. A play whose cast contains a musical star having a breakdown; a Vice-Chancellor who is a psychiatrist, philosopher, gymnast, coroner and doctor; an absent-minded professor trying to prove the existence of God; a murderous secretary who is also a trapeze artist and stripper; a police officer who is a musical comedy fan and eight acrobats who are faculty members of a university does not promise a serious drama, particularly since the characters remain unsurprised, as in farce, by their bizarre situations. Yet George agonises over profound questions and the pyrotechnics are so strange that the play seems to question the responses of the audience and the form that entertains them. Herein lies its seriousness.

George Moore is absorbed in his lecture, but the play mocks all self-absorption and highlights the deadened human response that is a mark of farce and the whodunit. In *Jumpers* egoism and complacency are characteristic of materialist philosophers who do not believe in absolute values, and there seems to be a general moral breakdown. Captain Scott abandons Oates on the moon. The fascist 'Radical Liberals' win the elections. Totalitarian government and the army take over. The police officer, Bones, is blackmailed into dropping charges. George is denied promotion because the VC disagrees with his views. Personal deceit is widespread. Are good and evil no more than social constructs? Are the Ten Commandments only rules that can be changed? Or is George – and, it appears, McFee and the Archbishop of Canterbury in their change of faith – right to think them absolute? Stoppard suggests they are. 'At least my poor professor got that one right', he said in interview (Trussler, p. 66).

In a whodunit, an intellectual game of Find the Murderer is played. A tragedy such as *Macbeth* explores the personal motives of crime and its disastrous consequences. In *Jumpers* we need to laugh to anaesthetise ourselves against criminal events too bizarre to be real. But George steps on the tortoise and stifles our laughter. The commandment, *Thou Shalt Not Kill*, hovers over the play.

From the beginning, the play questions our rejection of what is 'incredible'. Dotty disdainfully dismisses the acrobats because they are not incredible *enough*: 'I can sing better than that. I mean I can sing better than they can jump . . . ' (p. 18). She wants a performance which is 'incredibly' good, not mundane and explicable. As the celebrated Dotty Moore, musical star, she herself incarnates an impossible romantic dream in which her fans (including the police officer) believe. George seeks to prove the existence of God, or at least to mock the state of mind that dismisses mysteries and makes them banal. He wishes to make the jump to infinity, to end an infinite mathematical series, or to jump to the zero from the second term that approaches but never quite reaches it, like the hare trying to overtake the tortoise, or Zeno's paradox about the arrow which never reaches its target. (George's arrow does, but not the one he intended.) *Jumpers* mocks the character and possibly the author here. Yet serious philosophical questions emerge. A. J. Ayer has described the play as one with a central argument:

■ The argument is between those who believe in absolute values, for which they seek a religious sanction, and those, more frequently to be found among contemporary philosophers, who are subjectivists or relativists in morals, utilitarians in politics, and atheists or at least agnostics. (*Sunday Times*, 9 April 1972, p. 16) □

Victor Cahn, in his book *Beyond Absurdity* (1979), picks this up:

■ The specific philosophical problem at the basis of George's inquiry is whether moral judgements are absolute or relative, whether the truth lies in corrspondence with the facts of the world or whether they are merely personal expressions of emotion. Spokesmen for the two primary schools of thought on this issue have been G. E. Moore and A. J. Ayer.
According to Moore, goodness is an actual property possessed by things in the world. Thus if we affirm that some object is good and if in fact the object possesses the property of goodness, then our judgement is actually true. If we affirm that some object is good and the object does not possess the property of goodness, then our judgement is actually false. How is it known whether an object possesses the property of goodness? According to Moore, often referred to as an "ethical intuitionist", moral truths can be known to be true "by intuition", which is to say that their goodness is self-evident. . . . The opposite viewpoint has been defended by Ayer, who has argued that ethical judgements are no more than expressions of emotion:
Thus if I say to someone, "You acted wrongly in stealing that money," I am not saying anything more than if I said "You stole that money." In adding that this action is wrong I am not making any further statement about it. I am simply evincing my moral disapproval of it . . . (Bareham, 1990, pp. 132–3) □

In his interview for *Theatre Quarterly*, 'Ambushes for the Audience', Stoppard comes down on the side of his 'poor professor' George:

■ . . . the play reflects my belief that all political acts have a moral basis to them and are meaningless without it.

Is that disputable?

Absolutely. For a start it goes against Marxist-Leninism in particular, and against all materialistic philosophy. I believe all political acts must be judged in moral terms, in terms of their consequences.

. . . The great irony about Marx was that his impulses were deeply moral while his intellect insisted on a materialistic view of the world . . . (Trussler, p. 66) □

This belief energises Stoppard's subsequent, more obviously political, work and is essential to its comprehension. Behind the modern dispute one seems to hear the words of Shakespeare's Lafew:

■ They say miracles are past; and we have our philosophical persons to make modern and familiar, things supernatural and causeless. Hence is it we make trifles of terrors, ensconcing ourselves into seeming knowledge when we should submit ourselves to an unknown fear. (*All's Well that Ends Well*, Act II, iii, 1–6) □

Shakespeare is much concerned with the question of values and like Stoppard he mingles romance and fantasy with the 'real' – though his plots and genre mixes are scarcely so extraordinary as those essayed by Stoppard in *Jumpers*. What Stoppard has spent two years working on is not only an entertainment, but also a play which asks whether the possibility of disinterested and courageous action, exemplified by Captain Oates in the Scott expedition to the South Pole, is replaceable by a materialist ethic of self-interest and survival. Do absolute values perhaps exist? And what is the value of human relations? The hilarity of a corpse swung into and out of view on a cupboard door asks painful questions about a relationship going dead between the two most human of the characters.

Gabriel Scott Robinson puts it thus. Murder is

■ . . . ultimately associated with the general problem of uncertainty, farcical impotence and a valueless world. These same conditions are part of Scott's betrayal, Moore's anguished questions, and Dotty's disillusionment and despair. Rather than its merely being a heinous crime that goes unsolved, the murder is in fact a symptom of a climate wherein anything is permissible and nothing matters. Once again the thriller is parodied to highlight the opacity of reality, at the same time furnishing a lively and farcical plot. (Harty, p. 135) □

There is a further paradox – Stoppard's long plays always have counter-suggestions. George and Dotty are killers too, if only unintentionally. Dotty kills a goldfish by playing a game of charades (using the bowl to represent a moonman's helmet) and George accidentally kills both the pets for whom his affection is plain. His desolation is poignant as well as funny. The killing of the tortoise and the hare not only allegorises the demolition of Aesop's fable and Zeno's mathematical proof that the tortoise cannot be overtaken. If Dotty forgets to put water in the bath for Archie the goldfish, George is guilty of not knowing what goes on behind his back or behind the cupboard or in the next room. They are both guilty of inadvertence, of ignorance, of obsession, in short of being Everyman and Everywoman – or rather Fool figures at whom we laugh because to cry would be to see them as too close to ourselves. *Jumpers* ends with a paradox which may be a contradiction. Its fun conceals cruelty of various kinds that we are both wise and unwise to ignore.

Most of the criticism of *Jumpers* is interpretative and complimentary. Critics qualify occasional aspects of performance, but are generally very positive. Stanley Kauffmann, however, was enraged by the first New York production (see *Persons of the Drama*, 1976):

■ . . . In style the deliberate circumlocution, lolloping along to a point of heavy comic contrast, is the fake mandarinese of decadent Albee [presumably a reference to the playwright's *Tiny Alice* (1964) which critics found incomprehensible]. If you throw in references to Bertrand Russell and such freshman chestnuts as Zeno's paradox of motion, you reduce the starved theatre audience to quivering cries of gratitude for such profundities, cries mixed with gasps of wonder at a mind that can play so lightly with such deep thoughts. (Bareham, pp. 124–5) □

If Ayer is right, the reviewer of plays is only defining his own emotions. Kauffmann certainly seems to think he is purveying an objective truth. But in responses to this play he is certainly in the minority.

CHAPTER SEVEN

What Did You Do in the Great War?

Artist Descending a Staircase **and** *Travesties*

Artist Descending a Staircase

In November 1972, the BBC broadcast the radio drama, *Artist Descending a Staircase*, which has evident connections with *Jumpers*, produced early in the same year. As one had come to expect, Stoppard continued to experiment in a number of media and to build on his own previous work. Like *Jumpers*, *Artist Descending a Staircase* begins with what might be a murder and asks the inevitable question of who did it, but the construction of the play is very different. Paul Ferris describes the first broadcast:

■ Our old friend Tape Recorder appears at the start, with a recording of the last seconds in the life of Donner, an old painter. Donner shares a flat at the top of a flight of stairs with Martello, an old sculptor, and Beauchamp, an old tape-recorder buff. He is heard to say, "Ah, there you are" before he falls to his death screaming.

Which of the other two did it? Does it matter? Not really, since what we are doing is coasting about in time, listening to the three artists comment, explicitly and implicitly, fluent with epigrams, on another old friend Reality. Their relationship long ago with a blind girl called Sophie, who killed herself by jumping through a window, is what they all cling to. Martello (Stephen Murray) has carved her out of sugar. Donner (Carleton Hobbs) was painting her before he fell downstairs.

Back we go to Paris and the day she died, then back to the day they first met her, then back to a time before they knew her – a stylized but beautifully comic account of a holiday in France in August 1914. Now the play unwinds in the reverse direction – the day of the first meeting, followed by the day she died, followed by the present again. This was as ingenious as poems whose first and last lines rhyme, and so on until the rhymes meet in the middle. It was altogether a marvellous play for those who like ingenuity; less marvellous for those who prefer the mechanism out of sight.

The ending was suitably uncertain. Sophie, we learn, had chosen Beauchamp (Rolf Lefebvre) as her lover because before she went totally blind she fancied one of the three as he stood in front of a particular painting, and later worked out that it must have been Beauchamp. But Martello (fifty years later) tells Donner that she probably mixed up the paintings, which means it was Donner she fancied. Since he has been eating his heart out ever since, perhaps he jumped too, poor chap. (*The Observer*, 19 November 1972, p. 37) □

The two friends of the dead man suspect each other, but as usual in the whodunit, characters and audience reason on false premises and jump to dubious conclusions. Is it murder, suicide or accident?

Artist Descending a Staircase highlights the ambiguities of sound recording and the illusions it creates in the minds of two old men. The first sound is apparently of a man snoring. However, the buzz is not a snore but a fly. Footsteps are heard, but they are not Beauchamp's or Martello's. They are Donner's, alone in his room, as he tracks the fly to kill it. 'Ah! *There you are. . .*' are Donner's words addressed not to Martello (as Beauchamp thinks) or Beauchamp (thinks Martello), but to a fly as he steps forward to strike it and accidentally falls through the balustrade. This, we discover, only at the end from the various hints about a buzzing fly. To use one of Stoppard's favourite words, the listener is 'ambushed' along with the characters, if he or she is not very alert (even an acute critic like Ferris seems to have missed it), for the murder turns out to be accident.

If *Artist Descending* is a variation on *Jumpers*, Stoppard told Nancy Shields Hardin that it was a dry run for *Travesties*. 'It was two bites at the same apple. Sometimes the same bite at the same apple, actually' (*Contemporary Literature*, XXII, Spring 1981, p. 156). This is because *Travesties* even repeats a few lines from the radio play, and both plays are concerned with the nature of art. Sophie has been an art student before going blind and loves the Pre-Raphaelites. This gives rise to debates about 'traditional' and avant-garde painting.

Sophie, in her blindness, gains the artistic licence of the radio listener: 'If I hear hoofbeats I can put a unicorn in a garden and no one can open my eyes against it and say it isn't true' (p. 142). Martello in old age tells Donner that Sophie might have mistaken Beauchamp's picture of black railings against snow for Donner's broad white railings against a black ground. It might have been Donner that she loved. Donner's devastating sense of loss engenders a portrait of Sophie in a garden with a unicorn. Love and regret and accident are sources of true art.

Beauchamp's art, on the other hand, is valueless:

■ (*Beauchamp's 'Master-tape' is a bubbling cauldron of squeaks, gurgles, crackles, and other unharmonious noises. He allows it to run for longer than one would reasonably hope.*)
Beauchamp: Well, what do you think of it, Donner? Take your time, choose your words carefully.
Donner: I think it's rubbish.
Beauchamp: Oh. You mean, a sort of tonal débris, as it were?
Donner: No, rubbish, general rubbish. In the sense of being worthless, without value; rot, nonsense. Rubbish in fact.
Beauchamp: Ah. The detritus of audible existence, a sort of rubbish heap of sound . . .
Donner: I mean rubbish. I'm sorry Beauchamp, but you must come to terms with the fact that our paths have diverged. I very much enjoyed my years in that child's garden of easy victories known as the avant-garde, but I am now engaged in the infinitely more difficult task of painting what the eye sees.
Beauchamp: Well, I've never seen a naked woman sitting about a garden with a unicorn eating the roses.
Donner: Don't split hairs with me, Beauchamp. You don't know what art is. Those tape-recordings of yours are the mechanical expression of a small intellectual idea, the kind of notion that might occur to a man in his bath and be forgotten in the business of drying between his toes. You can call it art if you like, but it is the commonplace of any ironic imagination, and there are thousands of clerks and shop assistants who would be astonished to be called artists on their bath night. (pp. 119–20) □

This exchange contains the gist of what Stoppard is saying. The values are to be found in the blind Sophie and in the dead Donner.

The problem with Beauchamp's art, as also with Martello's, seems to lie in a (commonplace) ironic imagination: 'My brain . . . is so attuned to the ironic tone it has become ironic in repose' (p. 120). Martello resembles Marcel Duchamp, of whom Donner says:

■ I think he had talent under all those jokes. He said to me "There are two ways of becoming an artist. The first way is to do things by which is meant art. The second way is to make art mean the things you do." What a stroke of genius! It made everything possible and everything safe! – safe from criticism, since our art admitted no standards outside itself, safe from comparison since it had no history. (pp. 124–5) □

Real art, the play implies, does not ignore the past. It relates to life and submits to other than aesthetic judgements. Love and a capacity to observe lie behind Donner's work, but the pseudo-artist Martello does not even notice World War I starting all around him. Martello (in his tower) seems aware of his lack of connection when he tells Beauchamp: 'I have achieved nothing but mental acrobatics – *nothing!* – whereas you, however wrongly and for whatever reason, came to grips with life at least this once and killed Donner' (p. 116). He is, of course, mistaken.

Donner believes art must come to grips with life, but not by murder. For him, traditional standards lend art a necessary frame of reference, and he and Sophie speak for Stoppard. According to Sophie, the artist is chosen by his or her talent and skill. A response to art involves a recognition of mastery: 'Part of what there is to celebrate is the capability of the artist', says Sophie and 'The more difficult it is the more there is to wonder at'. She adds: 'It is not the only thing but it is one of the things' (p. 139). Beyond pure skill is the art which emerges when the artist does not choose but is chosen, perhaps by the 'sick apprehension of something irrevocable . . . ' (p. 134).

When he paints Sophie, Donner is attempting to mediate what imagination creates – Sophie in a garden with a unicorn. It may be in Sophie's favourite Pre-Raphaelite style, but it is a product of emotion held in memory and is what Donner 'sees'. Martello is shut in his ironic tower, Beauchamp in his own field. Donner the giver is the one to whom art is given. The pain of loss, a sense of waste and a capacity for enduring love (in both senses) make him the 'real thing'. His friends, innocent of Donner's death, are yet the murderers – for the play closes with Gloucester's famous line from *King Lear*: 'As flies to wanton boys are we to the gods . . . They kill us for their sport'. The fly that Beauchamp kills at the end is the fly which led to Donner's death. Art is a kind of sport – but Stoppard (speaking ironically of his own irony) seems to say that, if art is entirely sport, there is something murderous about it. The dual accidents of Sophie's misapprehension and Donner's death may be the gods' and Beauchamp's (or is it Stoppard's?) sport.

Stoppard's preference for Donner is stated categorically in a Radio Three interview with Richard Mayne before *Artist Descending* was broadcast: 'Donner is me. I'm a very square, conservative and traditional sort of mind. I absolutely think Beauchamp's tapes *are* rubbish and I think that what Donner says about them is absolutely true' (Delaney, p. 37). The quality of art relates to an awareness of tradition and the quality of human feeling that lies behind the artistic attempt.

Donner's sudden devastating (but creative) recognition at a late stage in the play is an effect of the complex time structure. A sense of time passing frames the misunderstanding that determines Sophie's suicide and Donner's wasted life. The play swings from comedy towards tragedy. It is not only a discussion play, Stoppard half-tentatively says: '. . . after exploring the reasons for art, I did want to focus on the different perceptions of it . . . but it's also a love story, isn't it?' (Delaney, p. 232). Perhaps the key line in the play is Sophie's: 'The sick apprehension of something irresistible which I had not chosen' (p. 134).

Travesties

The larger canvas of *Travesties* (1974) aroused considerably more critical response and more fully interrogates a relation between art and history. In the programme to the original production, Stoppard notes:

■ *Travesties* is a work of fiction which makes use, and misuse, of history. Scenes which are self-evidently documentary mingle with others which are just as self-evidently fantastical. People who were hardly aware of each other's existence are made to collide; real people and imaginary people are brought together without ceremony; and events which took place months, and even years, apart are presented as synchronous . . . History rather than imagination places Lenin, Joyce and the Dadaist Tristan Tzara in Zurich at one and the same time. History, too, offers us a new short conversation between Lenin and a Dadaist, recounted in the Motherwell book [*The Dada Painters and Poets*], and also the possibility of a meeting between Lenin and Joyce (though it is hard to imagine what they would have had to say to one another). But for the most part *Travesties* is presented through the fevered imagination of its principal character. □

The whole play is supposedly the projection of one mind – that of Henry Carr – an invalided soldier and consular official who lived in Zurich during World War I at the same time as Lenin, James Joyce and Tristan Tzara. Carr attempts, as an old man, to recount his life in Zurich among men who became famous but were then obscure. The attempt is transmuted by faulty recall, by the linguistic forms Carr employs (he has a gift for limericks), by the rhythms and words of songs of the period and by personal vanity. He takes excessive pride in the role he played as Algy in Joyce's production of *The Importance of Being Earnest* and recalls with fury the (actual) subsequent litigation with Joyce over a question of tickets and trousers. Stoppard, for convenience, imagines them all together in a library in a neutral Switzerland around which rage the appalling events of World War I. Within this enclave foreign exiles write their books, paint their pictures, or work for and against the approaching cataclysm of the Russian Revolution. The subject is highly serious; as ever, the treatment is light and comedic.

The play opens with a mixture of discourses. Tzara pulls poems out of a hat; Joyce dictates a section of *Ulysses*; Lenin writes about imperialism; their folders are accidentally exchanged in a pastiche of Miss Prism's substitution of a manuscript for a baby in *The Importance of Being Earnest*;

papers drop on the floor and are mistakenly appropriated; Joyce and Lenin beg each other's pardon in French, German, Italian and English. Lenin's wife Nadya enters and announces the revolution in Russian. Carr then, as an old man, reminisces about Joyce, Lenin and Tzara, but has difficulty in tying down their identities. Indeed, the characters have several identities, including the ones in Carr's head. Carr writes of Joyce:

■ A prudish, prudent man, Joyce, in no way profligate or vulgar, and yet convivial, without being spendthrift, and yet still without primness towards hard currency in all its transmutable and transferable forms and denominations, of which, however, he demanded only a sufficiency from the world at large, exhibiting a monkish unconcern for worldly and bodily comforts, without at the same time shutting himself off from the richness of human society, whose temptations on the other hand he met with ascetic disregard tempered only by sudden and catastrophic aberrations – in short, a complex personality, an enigma, a contradictory spokesman for the truth, an obsessive litigant and yet an essentially private man who wished his total indifference to public notice to be universally recognised – in short a liar and a hypocrite, a tight-fisted, sponging, fornicating drunk not worth the paper, that's that bit done. (pp. 22–3) □

Joyce, like Lenin and Tzara, goes through various transformations in the next scenes as Carr recasts the conversations between himself and Bennett, who was in fact the British Consul but appears in Carr's memory as the Wildean butler from *The Importance of Being Earnest*. Carr, like Stoppard, like any historical dramatist or novelist, or indeed, Stoppard suggests, like anyone, reshapes the past. His age, memory, personal obsessions and prejudices only make him less reliable than, but not wholly different from, those historians who strive to achieve, without ever quite attaining, an 'objective' account.

Joyce and Lenin write different kinds of history. Joyce strives to recreate the history of a day in Dublin, June 1904, by fusing the *Odyssey* with memories of the personal lives of a variety of Dubliners, transmuted by language and mastery of form. The writings of Lenin impose on the past the semi-mythical pattern of cause and effect which Marx called dialectical materialism. Lenin, however, would see his work as a truthful account of real economic trends. It is also history in the sense that it had a powerful impact on future political action.

In the ensuing debate between the aesthete, the Marxist and the anarchist Dada artist, Tristan Tzara, Stoppard attempts to give dramatic value to each speaker, finding Tzara difficult and notoriously employing several pages of Lenin's own prose to begin Act II:

■ I thought, "Right, we'll have a rollicking first act, and they'll all come back from their gin and tonics thinking, 'Isn't it fun? What a lot of lovely jokes!' And they'll sit down, and this pretty girl will start talking about the theory of Marxism and the theory of capitalism and the theory of value. And the smile, because they're not prepared for it, will atrophy." And that to me was like a joke in itself. But the important thing was that I'd ended the first act with what at the stage was a lengthy exposition of Dada. I wanted to begin the second with a corresponding exposition of how Lenin got to Zurich, not in geographical but political terms. I chose to do that from square one by starting from *Das Kapital* . . . Marxian theory of profit, theory of labour, theory of value, and then to slide into the populist movement, the terrorism, Ulyanov's brother and so on. If I could have brought that off, I'd have been prouder of that than of anything else I had ever written. There wasn't a joke in it but I thought I could get away with it because it was going to be a new set . . . a new character and a new scene after the interval. I overplayed that hand very badly, and at the first preview I realized that the speech had to be about Lenin only . . . and I just blue-pencilled everything up to the mention of Lenin. So now it was one page instead of five. (Delaney, pp. 206–7) □

Stoppard's determination to 'ambush' comfortable expectations is evident here. He admits that it might contain 'a slight sense of sadism towards the audience', but acknowledges that theatrically Tzara and Joyce are more interesting. Though he wished to do equal justice to opposing views, he cut all but Lenin's last paragraph.

This was not the only solution in performance. A French director of the play, although Stoppard warned him against it, wanted to keep the whole speech:

■ So I said "OK, I mean, you do it, and so on, 'sur votre tête be it'"; back he went to Paris. I carried on with my work and they did the play. I heard it went pretty well, and the chap phoned up and said everything was fine, and I said, "How was Cecily's speech at the top of Act Two?" And he said, "Formidable, superbe!" I was thinking, God, this is the sort of audience I deserve. So I went to Paris to see it, and it's fine, and Act Two starts and he was right. She did every word and you could have heard a pin drop. But she was stark naked! He'd altered the equation . . . (Delaney, pp. 206–7) □

Stoppard's anecdote reinforces the argument that an author can never fully control his work. In London, he had tried to solve the problem of Lenin's speech by using the methods of Brecht's political 'epic' theatre (see descriptions of the performance of Brecht's *Mahagonny*). This had not worked in the previews:

■ In my original draft I took the Lenin section out of the play far more radically than in the version you saw. I actually stopped the play and had actors coming down to read that entire section from clipboards or lecterns, because I felt very strongly that one thing I could not do was to integrate the Lenins into the *Importance* scheme. Irving Wardle said he'd have liked to see Lenin as Miss Prism, but that would have killed the play because of the trivialization . . . I wanted the play to stop – to give the audience documentary illustration of what Lenin felt about art and so on. And then carry on with the play. Peter Wood's objection was unarguable: the whole thing is within Carr's memory except this bit. How do you get back people's belief if you interrupt it?

. . . What's altered is the sympathy level you have with Lenin. When you read the words on the page there's a sense in which Lenin keeps convicting himself out of his own mouth. It's absurd. It's full of incredible syllogisms. All the publishing and libraries and bookshops and newspapers must be controlled by the Party. The press will be free . . . (Hayman, pp. 9–10) □

The longer speeches are not only potentially tedious, but also reveal how much Lenin contradicts himself. Lenin's shorter speech creates greater sympathy and provides a better dramatic and aesthetic balance, even if Stoppard's personal preferences are not with Marx or Tristan Tzara, but with Joyce:

■ An artist is the magician put among men to gratify – capriciously – their urge for immortality. The temples are built and brought down around him, continuously and contiguously, from Troy to the fields of Flanders. If there is any meaning in any of it, it is in what survives as art, yes, even in the celebration of tyrants, yes, even in the celebration of nonentities. What now of the Trojan War if it had been passed over by the artist's touch? Dust. A forgotten expedition prompted by Greek merchants looking for new markets. A minor redistribution of broken pots. But it is we who stand enriched, by a tale of heroes, of a golden apple, a wooden horse, a face that launched a thousand ships – and above all, of Ulysses, the wanderer, the most human, the most complete of all heroes – husband, father, son, lover, farmer, soldier, pacifist, politician, inventor and adventurer . . . It is a theme so overwhelming I am almost afraid to treat it. And yet I with my Dublin Odyssey will double that immortality, yes by God *there's* a corpse that will dance for some time yet . . . (*Travesties*, pp. 62–3) □

It is difficult to stop quoting this irresistible speech and Tzara is not given an answer. 'I get emotionally involved in *Travesties*. It disposes of a few private debates of mine', said Stoppard to John Wood and Gussow (Gussow, p. 30).

In later interviews, Stoppard expresses his beliefs more trenchantly than in the early days when he was apt to speak of constant self-refutation. Note, for example, the interview with Ross Wetzsteon in 1975:

■ He wrote the play, Stoppard said, as part of "an ongoing debate with myself over the importance of the artist". It seemed to me that one of the strengths of the play, one of the signs of his maturity, was that he gave equal weight to Joyce, Lenin and Tzara . . . Stoppard only partly agreed. "Equally *just*, I hope, but not equal *weight*. Of course, I don't want to give any of them shallow arguments and then knock them down. No, you have to give the best possible argument for each of them. It's like playing chess with yourself – you have to try to win just as hard with black as you do with white. But while my sympathies may be divided in that sense, I find Joyce infinitely the most important. Are we talking of historical significance or of quality? Tzara's work, for instance, was momentarily interesting but ultimately worthless. Joyce's evolution means more to me than Tzara's revolution." (Delaney, p.82) □

Stoppard clearly defines the difference between historical, dramatic and moral impact. He is aware that a historian would find Lenin of greater 'historical significance' than Joyce. Tzara's fireworks, too, are dramatically very entertaining, but Joyce has his personal sympathy.

Not everyone agrees with Wetzsteon that Stoppard achieves a dramatic balance. Eric Salmon, in an article for *Queen's Quarterly*, reproduced in *Is the Theatre Still Dying* (1985), suggests that

■ The character of Joyce is not really weighty or substantial enough for the burden that it should bear and that of Lenin is too weighty and too explicatory. The device of using *The Importance of Being Earnest*, moreover, though it is brilliantly funny in itself, proves in the long run to be a less than perfect scaffolding for the play because too much of the play has to exist outside it. Carr and Tzara are quite happily accommodated in it; but Joyce has to be dragged in by the hairs of his Irish head and not even Stoppard's ingenuity can get Lenin into it. This gives Tzara too important an advantage over Joyce and Lenin: these three caricatural figures really need to be of equal weight to make the idea of the play work completely: and all three should be on roughly equal footing, dramaturgically speaking, with Carr, who is the catalyst for each of them and the centre of the design for us. (Salmon, pp.218–9) □

The objection is a dramaturgical one, and as a play Salmon prefers *Jumpers*, whose plot is not just a mechanism for bringing the characters together but 'rises to the level of a fable'. A further implied objection might also be that Joyce's speech, though it carries weight, is supposedly contained within the failing memory of Henry Carr, the narrator, and that this framing consciousness trivialises the content either of Joyce or Lenin or both. Stoppard is aware of the charge – he calls it 'eating steak tartare with chocolate sauce': 'Everyone will have to decide for himself . . . whether the seriousness is doomed or redeemed by the frivolity' (Delaney, p. 83).

Opposing views of the nature of history and the function of art, however, emerge in brilliant discussions between the adherents of different schools. The random artist Tzara retains dramatic sympathy independently of whether Stoppard believes in dialectical materialism or that 'all history comes out of a hat', as Tzara claims. Joyce's hat produces a rabbit. His history of a day in Dublin is the product of fact, experience, imagination and magic. Tzara emphasises the part played by chance. The accidental collision in time between Carr's obsession with playing Algy in Wilde's play instead of carrying out his consular duty of stopping Lenin from catching his closed train to the Finland Station (thereby changing the flow of history) is a serious possibility. Thomas Hardy argued in his ghosted autobiography that history is sometimes not a causal flow, but a trickle turned aside by a straw (note Hardy's use of coincidence in, say, *Tess of the D'Urbervilles*). The historian of causes and trends is also a kind of artist who imposes his logic on chance occurrences and makes apparent, but only partly, 'real' sense of the flow of life in retrospect.

A further question arising from the debate about art and history concerns the nature of the artist's, and human, identity. The characters are dual, delivering contradictory discourses. Even offstage characters are double. Hans Arp is also Jean Arp, an Alsatian caught between France and Germany. Joyce is an Irishman as well as a magician who produces a flower out of an empty hat. Lenin, the revolutionary, loves romantic music. We see Joyce through Carr's eyes as a 'joke Irishman'. John William Cooke finds a serious justification for this, quoting Susan Sontag in his essay on 'Perception and Form in Stoppard's *Travesties*' (*Contemporary British Drama, 1970–90*):

■ We have noted in discussing other aspects of *Travesties*, that form asserts an existence of its own, and we perceive the creation of character in the same manner. If form predicates existence [and Cooke has argued that Carr is above all concerned with his personal appearance] then the existence of the individual depends upon clothing. Susan Sontag notes, "Even if one were to define style as the manner of our appearing, this by no means necessarily entails an opposition between a style that one assumes and one's 'true' being. In fact, such a disjunction is extremely rare. In almost every case, our manner of appearing is our manner of being".

Character, then, is a collection of scraps (clothing) formally
arranged . . . [it is] thus a concept of our image progressing through
time [says Cooke, and quotes Arendt]: "Nothing and nobody exists on
this planet whose very being does not presuppose a *spectator*. In other
words, nothing that is, insofar as it appears, exists in the singular:
everything that is, is meant to be perceived by somebody". (Zeifman,
pp.211–12) ☐

Cooke justifies *Travesties* as a play of scraps, finding the organising principle, not, as Eric Salmon wishes to, in the text, but in the audience's
capacity to piece the scraps together, as identity is pieced together by
reconciling different aspects of a person, thereby creating his identity.
Esse est percipi: 'To be is to be perceived', is an idea which has been around
since Bishop Berkeley (1685–1753) and appears in the twentieth century
in the plays of Pirandello and Beckett. Stoppard emphasises the different
sides to his *dramatis personae* and the fun and strength of *Travesties* arise
out of the demands made on the audience to reconcile the pastiche with
the characters' due weight and identity as existents in history.

Other critics refuse to fall back on the unifying principle in the audience. Their emphasis falls on the 'statement' of the play. Gabrielle Scott
Robinson argues: 'In this play the farce tends to render innocuous the
terror of war – which "merely ruined several pairs of trousers"'(Harty,
p.77). And Anthony Jenkins says that Carr's 'egocentric and barren
version of history eventually trivializes the central idea that the artist's
independent vision and humanity turns fact into spiritual gold' (Jenkins,
p. 124). A much less sympathetic Ruby Cohn states, 'Stoppard belabours
ideas . . . until they resemble funeral baked meats that coldly furnish
forth the marriage tables of farce' (*Contemporary English Drama*, p.120).

Thomas Whitaker, on the other hand, praises Henry Carr, and the
performer John Wood, as 'the living centre of the play':

■ Perhaps *Travesties* asks us above all to enjoy – and through that
enjoyment to purge ourselves of – a Henry Carr who seems to be each
of us, at least in our more pretentious and evasive moments, as we try
to make meaning out of our lives. (Whitaker, p. 129) ☐

The dazzling intellectual display may submerge the serious questions
Stoppard's play raises. Stoppard does not, of course, create a feeling of
what it was like to be *in* the war, to be actively affected as man or artist
by the revolution. His experience is not that of Pasternak and other
Soviet writers. His outsider's view allows the words and the fun to flow,
though the sombre realities loom in the near distance. In his enclave
within the chaos, Stoppard's commitment emerges in the words of Joyce:
'What now of the Trojan war if it had been passed over by the artist's

touch? Dust. A forgotten expedition . . . ' (p. 62). It is for the audience, Stoppard remarks, to choose whether the fun and the claim is justified. For Bernard Crick, as a member of that audience, the play is a profound demonstration of freedom. Stoppard is saying:

■ . . . be socialist by all means . . . but don't think the theory must explain everything – particularly art, which is the very badge of freedom and spontaneity among men and women; for if you think that it must, when it so plainly doesn't, then you end up coercing people to fit the facts . . . Stoppard attacks the Leninist theory of art with gusto, seeming madness, jolly obscenity, frantic word play, punishing puns, and incredible imaginative and irrelevant invention of plots all exemplary of how free we could all be just by trying. (*Times Higher Educational Supplement*, 2 August 1974, p. 12) □

CHAPTER EIGHT

A Knickers Farce and Tribute to America

Dirty Linen and *New-Found-Land* (integrated plays)

After the production of *Travesties*, Stoppard adapted Jerome K. Jerome's *Three Men in a Boat* and collaborated with Clive Exton on the unpublished *The Boundary*, a half-hour TV play for the BBC described by David Pryce-Jones in *The Listener* (24 July 1975, p.117) as: 'Two lexicographers, trapped in their verbiage (as though belonging to their big brother of a play, *Jumpers*), find their files blown all over their gothicky work-room'. *The Boundary* won praise from Clive James:

■ The play's devices mostly seemed to reflect Stoppard's well-known obsessions: the don with the flighty wife (*Jumpers*), the bizarre stage picture which the action clarifies (*After Magritte*), the body on the floor (*The Real Inspector Hound*). Stoppard never minds using an idea a second time so long as the plot redefines it. And once again the plot was a honey, with the whole chain of events remaining unintelligible until a few minutes before the end, when a cricket ball flying through the window shook everything into shape. (*The Observer*, 27 July 1975, p.22) □

Stoppard saw *The Boundary* as a piece of fun and felt the same about the stage-play he was working on. This was *Dirty Linen*, which he called a knickers farce, and dedicated to the dynamic American director Ed Berman, the force behind Inter-Action, the powerful alternative theatre founded in 1968. In April 1976, *Dirty Linen* went on at the Ambiance Lunch-Hour Theatre Club, which operated under Berman's aegis for 11 years from 1972 at the Almost Free Theatre in Rupert Street near Piccadilly. The play transferred to the Arts Theatre in June 1976 and its long and successful run enabled the energetic Berman 'to set up a West End contract which gave everyone a share of the profits, including the box office lady'. It also allowed actors time off for other work in TV or film and provided opportunities for the understudies to perform. *Dirty Linen* thus made a social, even a political, contribution to theatre work, and the dedication to Berman is well deserved.

This farce-within-a-farce sends up the sexual mores of British politicians and their relations with a salacious press, anxious to discover peccadillos in order to sell newspapers. The central figure is Maddie, the typist at thirty words a minute of a select committee producing a report for the PM on the subject of press relations. Maddie has slept with the Home Secretary, the editor of *The Times*, journalists who report on MPs' sexual behaviour and every member of the committee. She has gone through the ranks 'like a lawn mower in knickers' (p. 84) and while the male characters around her are anxious to keep things quiet, she has no sense of wrongdoing. Wiser than they, she is responsible for the final draft memo, which says that the press should mind its own business. Stoppard told Oleg Kerensky he wrote the play in about three weeks and the *New-Found-Land* section during rehearsals: '*Travesties* took nine months and that's about par for the course' (Delaney, p. 85). To Ronald Hayman he observed:

■ *Dirty Linen* works nicely. But I don't think anybody would pretend that it was naturalistic. In fact I had a very sweet letter from the Clerk's Department of the House of Commons, inviting me for a drink and pointing out certain discrepancies between the play and the reality it purports to present. . . . I had no interest in the House of Commons, actually. I wouldn't have written the play at all but for the necessity to fulfil a promise. (Hayman, pp. 137, 141) □

Before the New York production, he tells Jon Bradshaw how the play evolved:

■ *Dirty Linen* grew like Topsy really [Topsy is the girl in Harriet Beecher Stowe's novel *Uncle Tom's Cabin* (1852) who, asked about her origins, replies that she just "grow'd"] . . . I couldn't think of a sketch relating to his [Berman's] particular needs, which were for a season of plays about America . . . I ended up using an idea I'd saved for some other occasion and that idea was to have a play about a committee of very high-powered people. I was thinking of the Archbishop of Canterbury and the prime minister, the equivalent of Einstein, some guy doing nuclear physics, a theologian, a philosopher, and they were going to have this committee meeting on some topic worthy of their brain power and there was going to be this staggering bird, who was there to sharpen the pencils and pass the water carafe around, and I was going to have her correcting them on points of theology and nuclear physics in a very bland sort of way.

... Finally, out of despair – you know, the usual deadline problem – I began writing that play in the form of a committee meeting to debate Ed Berman's application for British citizenship. Got sick of that, decided to hell with Berman's American problem, and just wrote *Dirty Linen*. And then, you see, because there is a God and he does look after writers, I realized that all I had to do was have an adjournment, put in fifteen minutes about America, and I'd solved Berman's problem as well. And the whole thing's a nonsense, of course, little more than an extended joke. (Delaney, p. 98) □

Later he told John Leonard, '. . . If it were a movie, it would have to be made by the Boulting Brothers . . .' (*New York Times*, 9 January 1977, Sec II, p. 1).

Knickers are conspicuous in the play, since various committee members produce them from pockets and they fill Maddie's desk drawer. The mechanical structure which characterises farce is again well in evidence. The committee is made up of stereotypes, all obsessed with Maddie's sexual attractions. 'The chairman·is off the shelf and Miss Gotobed is off another shelf. She's not a *real* character. What interests me is getting a cliché and then betraying it' (Delaney, p. 96). The committee-men fight to avoid exposure as the pace grows faster, and panic as props threaten to take over their lives. Maddie's skirt, slip and undergarments, not to speak of the physique they barely conceal, play a prominent role. The chairman cleans a blackboard with underpants produced from his 'brief'case and, as ever in farce, chaos looms and is finally avoided. The characters juggle desperately to keep the ball in the air, preserving their youth and verve. The old still bounce, no one is crushed and the ending is happy. The actors' brilliance and speed are part of the entertainment. *Dirty Linen*, despite its political content, remains farce, a time-honoured form and the most popular of dramatic genres. Any invitation to query the laughter, to engage in deep analysis, to discuss the importance of sexual disloyalty or the shame of private exposure would destroy the effect.

But the farce is not commonplace because it exhibits Stoppard's extraordinary gift for puns and love of jokes such as:

■ You do speedwriting I suppose?
Yes if I have enough time. (p. 93) □

It has fun with proper names, Latin and French tags, journalese and political rhetoric. The PM, whose mind is soaked in Tennyson's poetry, provides an instance in a memorandum: 'The morality of the honourable six hundred . . . has fixed its lance, determined to ride fearlessly into the jaws of controversy . . . ' (p. 100).

This is not a play for what Stoppard calls the 'lit-crit industry' to rephrase into 'a certain number of things worth saying but not worth listening to' (Delaney, p. 99). Style is more important than 'meaning'. Yet style for Stoppard is not, as he feels it was for Oscar Wilde, the means *and* the end: 'I'm not a writer who doesn't care what things mean . . . but despite myself I *am* a kind of writer who doesn't give a fair crack of the whip to that meaning' (Delaney, p.99). Critics can take *Dirty Linen* seriously. Hersh Zeifman argues that Stoppard's wordplay is not simply comic: '. . . what is impressive is the way Stoppard uses his puns both as a comic device and as an integral part of what his plays are trying to communicate' (*Modern British Dramatists*, Brown, p.107); Jenkins thinks: 'Stoppard . . . returns to his own past as a journalist, and begins to explore, however farcically, the rights of the individual' (p.131). If in *Dirty Linen* Stoppard has scarcely given the topic of human rights a fair crack of the whip, he has nevertheless paid a tribute to Ed Berman in the short interlude called *New-Found-Land*, cleverly interpolated into the middle of the play. When the committee room, which is situated just under Big Ben, empties temporarily, two Home Office officials enter (one fortunately rather deaf, the other, unfortunately not so). They are to consider what advice to give the Home Secretary concerning the application for British citizenship of a bearded American. It had strong appeal for the audience at the first performance, which knew that Berman's application had been successful. Stoppard first suggests acceptance hangs on whether the applicant has, or has not, a beard. Then the Home Secretary, in a hurry to get out of an embarrassing situation, signs without reading the papers: 'One more American can't make any difference' (p.135).

Stoppard also refers to Berman's City Farms I, a community arts project in Kentish Town that Berman ran among many other things: 'Did you say he farms in Kentish Town?' (p.123). In another tribute, the younger Home Office official embarks on a brilliant five-page travelogue of a train journey across the States from New York to New Orleans and California, using all the Hollywood clichés he can muster. He is wearing stars and stripes socks and a marshal's badge, which no doubt represent the invasion of England by American culture that Berman said he had come to Britain to escape from. The older official's preamble to this long speech sufficiently gives the tone:

■ Americans are a very modern people, of course. They are a very open people too. They wear their hearts on their sleeves. They don't stand on ceremony. They take people as they are. They make no distinction about a man's background, his parentage, his education. They say what they mean and there is a vivid muscularity about the way they say it. They admire everything about them without reserve or pretence of scholarship. They are always the first to put their hands in their pockets. They press you to visit them in their own home the moment they meet you, and are irrepressibly good-humoured, ambitious and brimming with confidence in any company. Apart from all that I've nothing against them. (p. 124) □

Such dialogue may be satire, not farce, but the satire is gentle and its objects various. The British are mocked as much as their breezy transatlantic brothers. Jokes cut both ways and they are especially at the expense of characters and audiences who take things straight. A tribute is paid to Berman's American generosity of spirit by way of the British official's suspicion. A sideswipe is made at British class-consciousness and at scholarly and other pretentious language. This recalls the courtesy but lack of servility that Maddie in the encircling play accords to all the ranks around her. Farce is egalitarian in this. If it has a moral value apart from its apparent celebration (from sources deep in the Greek past) of irrepressible sexuality, it is in the perception that sex, like death in tragedy, brings everyone to the same level. *'Toujours l'amour'*, says the formerly staid committeeman French, who now deserves his nomenclature. *'Finita la Commedia'*, says Maddie, ending the play. Maddie, too, has picked up the tags of learning – *Toujours la politesse; noblesse oblige,* etc. – with which the MPs began their committee meeting. Here, too, the farce achieves a democratic form. If one looks for serious meaning in a play that Stoppard casually calls 'an extended joke', it is probably here. Nor should one forget the friendly tribute to Berman and the social contribution it made to his company.

CHAPTER NINE

Ethics and Politics in Eastern Europe

Every Good Boy Deserves Favour and *Professional Foul*

Involvement with Ed Berman and his commitment to political action may well have contributed to the change in tone and emphasis of Stoppard's work during the mid-seventies, upon which many commentators have remarked. Stoppard's political concerns related strongly to Eastern Europe. He addressed a Trafalgar Square rally in August 1976 as an active member of the Committee Against Psychiatric Abuse and marched with others to the Soviet Embassy to deliver a petition. In 1977, he visited Moscow and Leningrad with an assistant director of the British section of Amnesty International and reported on it in *The Sunday Times* (27 February). In the same month, he also protested in *The New York Times* about the suppression of the human rights document, Charter 77, and the treatment of a signatory, the playwright Vaclav Havel, by the Czech government. He travelled to Czechoslovakia, the country of his birth, where he met Havel and Pavel Kohout, the inspiration of his *Cahoot's Macbeth* (1979). In July, his play *Every Good Boy Deserves Favour* was performed by the Royal Shakespeare Company and the London Symphony Orchestra at the Royal Festival Hall and enjoyed an extended run with a smaller orchestra at The Mermaid Theatre. In September, BBC Television transmitted *Professional Foul*, which received the *British TV Critics Best Play of 1977* Award.

Every Good Boy Deserves Favour

Every Good Boy Deserves Favour, known henceforth as *EGBDF*, combines, as the title intimates, an aesthetic with a political concern. A novel invitation by André Previn to write a play for a symphony orchestra engendered a whimsical but disturbing idea about Ivanov, a lunatic triangle player who imagines he is a member of an orchestra and occupies a cell in a psychiatric hospital alongside a political dissident. The triangle, which was the only instrument Stoppard had ever played, became a motif. The lunatic conducted the orchestra in his head and the London Symphony Orchestra on the platform alternately struck up to his imaginings or fell to silent miming at appropriate moments, when his sane cell mate, who is there for saying that sane men are placed in mental hospitals, was awake. Stoppard's meeting with Victor Fainberg and Vladimir Bukovsky, victims of Soviet misuse of psychiatry for the suppression of dissidents, was influential. He created a triple set consisting of a schoolroom, an office and a cell with two beds. The mad Ivanov's cell mate, Alexander Ivanov, has a son, Sasha, who does not want his father to die on hunger strike. Sasha is taught by an authoritarian Teacher, who disapproves of Sasha's redefinitions of Euclid, notably of triangles. The idea of direction, power and control thus runs across the different professions and institutions, be they school, hospital, prison, orchestra or state.

When asked about the provenance of the play, Stoppard speaks characteristically of the artistic challenge, rather than a serious political concern:

■ The idea, which was suggested by André Previn, appealed as much as anything to my incipient megalomania. I think I just love the idea of having a hundred musicians in a play. And I'm very in awe of conductors. Apart from Evel Knievel [the daredevil motorcyclist], I think the conductor of a great orchestra is the most awesome figure on earth.

You see, before being carried out feet first, I would like to have done a bit of absolutely everything. Really, without any evidence of any talent in those other directions, I find it very hard to turn down offers to write an underwater ballet for dolphins or a play for a motorcyclist on a wall of death. That's why I did this thing with André Previn. No one ever asked me to write a play with a symphony orchestra before. Probably no one ever will again. (Delaney, p. 98) □

Stoppard reminds his interviewer, Jon Bradshaw, of the elements of chance, ambition and fun that go into a decision to write a play. But, speaking to Milton Shulman, he also owns up to an ethical impetus:

■ There was no sudden conversion on the road to Damascus. I know human rights have been around for a long time and I have always been concerned with the daily horrors that I read in the newspapers . . . For some time I had been involved with Amnesty International . . . (Delaney, p. 109) □

Stoppard pinpoints the play's serious human concern by a concentrated pun: 'The subject matter seemed appropriate to the form. The dissident is a discordant note in a highly orchestrated society' (Gussow, p. 34). The suggestion recalls the use of allegory and fairy tales in prose satire. The fables in Jonathan Swift's *Gulliver's Travels* (1726) and George Orwell's *Animal Farm* (1945) sustain interest in themselves, but the allegorical parallel encourages readers to discover the underlying political implications. *Animal Farm* is superficially a children's story, but more profoundly it is about a fable being imposed upon a credulous community. In *EGBDF*, there is a fable inside the mad triangle-player's head that he wishes to impose on his cell mate Alexander and on the theatre orchestra that he (and the audience), but not Alexander, can hear. Megalomania embraces a fiction about the self and others that is not unknown to teachers, doctors and politicians, as well as musicians and conductors. Foucault, in *Madness and Civilisation*, demonstrates that dictators, apparatchiks and all repressive regimes are apt to propagate the menacing fable that subversives are insane.

Stoppard's target is not only politicians: 'Every member of the orchestra has a baton in his knapsack! Your turn will come' (p. 30). He pokes fun at the orchestra, at the three rigid and 'sane' professionals in charge of the patients – the Doctor, who plays a real instrument in a real orchestra, the Teacher, who tries to make Sasha toe the line and directs her own percussion band, and the Colonel, who orchestrates the prison/ hospital. The Doctor is in a hurry and does not pay attention when his patient, the lunatic Ivanov, is momentarily cured by his cell mate's laxative pills and announces: 'I've never had an orchestra'. Preoccupied with his own affairs, the Doctor rushes off to his concert and convinces the lunatic that the fantasy orchestra in his head is real after all. The Teacher is more sinister:

■ *Sasha*: **A triangle is the shortest distance between three points.**
Teacher: **Rubbish.**
Sasha: **A circle is the longest distance to the same point.**
Teacher: **Sasha!**
Sasha: **A plane area bordered by high walls is a prison not a hospital.**
Teacher: **Be quiet!** (pp. 25–6) □

The joke is on the Teacher, but it is a grim joke. The child tells her things she does not want to hear and she reduces him to tears. The tears of the child, as in the next play, *Professional Foul*, indicate the moral centre. Sasha moves between the different locations, through the orchestra, to his father who is as rigid in the interests of truth as the apparatchiks are in the interests of lies and power. 'Papa don't be crazy', he says at the play's closure. 'Everything can be all right.' But should Alexander Ivanov acknowledge his 'madness' of slandering the state or starve himself to death and deprive his son of a father? State blackmail is using his sense of parental responsibility to force him to capitulate. He has an appalling choice between personal and general responsibility. Those who create such a situation are condemned.

Stoppard conjures up a 'happy' ending. The KGB Colonel solves his problem of how to free a known dissident – and climb down without seeming to – by pretending each Ivanov is the other. The dissident Alexander Ivanov agrees he does not have an orchestra. The insane Ivanov agrees a Soviet doctor would not put sane people in a lunatic asylum. The answers are in the first case personally and in the second politically correct. The prisoners, sane and insane, are released. The triangle player will presumably continue to conduct his imaginary orchestra. But the sane will not be forced to join it – that at least is valuable.

David Cairns, in a review in *The Sunday Times*, argued that

■ Stoppard has allowed himself to be carried away by his own comic invention. The triangle-player runs such zany riot in the opening scene that the play is caught in his clutches and the theme half-smothered in its counterpoint . . . Perhaps, if Previn's accomplished anonymous score had provided something more positive than background music and interludes for reflection, the drama's tragic ironies might have struck home . . . (27 June 1982, p. 39) □

Another danger was that Previn's music, including his pastiche of Prokofiev and Shostakovich, and Stoppard's fun at the expense of the orchestra, would drown out the impact of the plot and dialogue. This was not the case for Thomas Whitaker, who eloquently describes the effect of the New York production:

■ The orchestra . . . seems a virtuoso actor: it delights the audience with its mimed passages, its various responses to its lunatic conductor, and its parody of the doctor's movements; it plays a threatening nightmare when Alexander sleeps and a bit of Tchaikovsky's *1812 Overture* when he confronts Ivanov over Tolstoy's *War and Peace*; it suggests through pastiche of Prokofiev and Shostakovich the controlling Soviet ethos and it becomes the percussion band in which Sasha bangs away without regard for the written notes. Conversely the actors often seem individual instruments: they enter into dialogues with the orchestra and antiphonal dialogues with each other, and Alexander's longest speech is scored and lit as a solo. Though Previn's somewhat cinematic and perhaps "overscored" music does tend to blur chronology and suspend the action, those effects are appropriate in the limbo of an asylum or a prison. And though the slender dramatic line may hold its own rather precariously against a full symphony orchestra on stage, that effect too is thematic. As massive visible and audible environment, the orchestra renders the inner and outer forces that have already dominated four characters and threaten to overwhelm the other two. At the Metropolitan Opera the orchestra nearly filled a bank of red-carpeted elevations that led up to a red-draped back wall. Within that ominously formal and often darkened space were the three small and separately lit playing areas – the prisoner's cell (in front of the podium), the Doctor's office (on a platform behind the string basses), and the schoolroom (on a platform behind the violins) – and through it Sasha finally wandered in search of his father. (Whitaker, *Tom Stoppard*, p. 141) □

Within the play's power and theatricality, the taut playscript communicates the experience of the dissidents Stoppard has met:

■ *Alexander*: If you don't eat for a long time you start to smell of acetone, which is the stuff girls use for taking the paint off their finger-nails. When the body runs out of protein and carbohydrate it starts to metabolise its own fat, and acetone is the waste product. To put this another way, a girl removing her nail-varnish smells of starvation. (p. 25) □

Stoppard's penchant for comic reversals is here less funny. It is striking to say that a healthy woman smells of starvation, but more shocking to think that a man or woman smelling of nail varnish remover is starving. In *EGBDF*, Stoppard calls attention to problems it is unpleasant to think about.

Yet the play retains a certain gaiety and Robert Cushman, in *The Observer*, made the quiet point that fun, too, has its ethical uses:

■ If a playwright wishes to fire us against injustice or the waste of life he must first convince us, in the quality of his own work, that life is worth living anyway. Mr Stoppard's gaiety is a moral quality in itself. (18 June 1978, p. 26) □

Bernard Levin put it more histrionically:

■ . . . as we emerged it was the fire and glitter of the play that possessed us, while its eternal truth, which is that the gates of hell shall not prevail, was by then inextricably embedded in our hearts. (*Sunday Times*, 3 July 1977, p. 37) □

The ending of the performance was powerful, more sombre for those who saw the KGB Colonel as deliberately manipulative rather than a bumbling fool. Sasha sings 'Everything will be all right!', but Katherine Kelly remarks: 'The sombre closing music of the symphony orchestra overrides Sasha's insistence on a bright future and drowns his hopeful-ness in a dark swell of deep sound' (Harty, p. 233). She also argues that the play marks a change in Stoppard's writing:

■ For the most part, Alexander and Sasha's dialogue bears little resemblance to the earlier speech of Stoppard's philosophers and aes-thetes such as George Riley's quasi-poetic reveries and Rosencrantz and Guildenstern's Beckettian music-hall banter. The new compressed speech helps Stoppard to create a new character type: the ordinary person forced by circumstances to express and defend a moral pos-ition. In striving to express this position, Stoppard creates a dialogue with a poetic depth, stretching his comedy vertically in the direction of tragedy. (Harty, p. 233) □

Professional Foul

Professional Foul seems to support Kelly's view that a new character type and a different form of naturalistic dialogue is emerging – though the naturalism owes much to the television medium. The play was first shown on BBC TV in September 1977 and seemed to confirm the change of direction seen in *EGBDF*. Kenneth Tynan's view was that 'history has lately been forcing Stoppard into the arena of commitment'. Robert Bergqvist wrote an article entitled 'This Time Stoppard Plays It (Almost) Straight'. Stoppard warned Berqvist not to assume he had changed direc-tion permanently:

■ . . . all my sense of purpose tells me now, I might write a play in which an English duchess comes through the French windows with a basket of begonias and a tennis racket and announces that the butler is dead in the library. I'm just not sitting here thinking, "From now on, I'm such and such a kind of writer". (Delaney, p. 138) □

Stoppard continues to insist on the right to surprise his audience. *Professional Foul*, however, invites classification with *EGBDF*, since, although it was more naturalistic in form, it, too, was about political repression and liberal attitudes: 'The BBC had been asking me to write a TV play . . . Amnesty International had decided to make 1977 Prisoner of Conscience Year and I thought a play on television might help their cause' (Delaney, p. 109). The play resembles a Sartre 'situation' play in which the central figures must make difficult choices to achieve their desired ends, but the effect is more comedic. It centres on a clever and imagina-tive Oxbridge Professor of Ethics (played by Peter Barkworth), who sees things at odd angles, rather like Stoppard. 'I should be the faculty almoner', he says. 'I like to collect little curiosities for the language chaps. It's like handing round a bag of liquorice allsorts. They're terribly grateful' (p.45).

Peter Barkworth prepared the part of Professor Anderson by watching Professor A.J. Ayer on TV:

■ I noticed, for instance, that his words had great difficulty in keeping up with his racing intellect, so he would rush the last words of one sentence because the next one had formed in his mind. I liked, too, his habit of delaying laughter at one of his own jokes; he would crack a joke, then say another sentence, then laugh at his joke during the sentence after that. I liked his mercurial changes of mood, violent changes really, revealing themselves so quickly in his face as the thoughts flashed by . . . (*About Acting*, p. 18) □

Stoppard and Barkworth catch the tone of academic discourse, whereby Anderson dispenses gems of ideas to others like a giver of alms. He is going to an academic conference in Prague as a guest of the Czech government to whom he therefore has a contractual responsibility. His real reason, however, for attending is to watch England play Czechoslavakia in a World Cup qualifying football match that becomes, like the orchestra in *EGBDF*, an allegory for both his professional game of philosophy and the more dangerous game of politics he finds himself drawn into.

The games connect amusingly through ambiguous words – left wing and centre in particular – and much play is made of the differences between discourses and languages. Interpreters are shown in close-up having problems with the ambiguities of simple English words like 'well'. The facile assumption that we only communicate by verbal language is mocked by exchanges of gestural 'theatre' language when Anderson waves his match ticket at his non-English-speaking taxi driver. Anderson also finds himself in a more serious situation where a command of the Czech language would be a considerable advantage.

Games with language lead to the real name of the game which, as in different ways in *Jumpers* and *EGBDF*, is ethical responsibility. A former student called Hollar asks the Professor to take a thesis back to England where the view it expresses – that a sense of good and evil is inherent in the individual, indeed in the child – stands a chance of publication. The Professor refuses, arguing that in accepting his fee to come to the congress he has entered into a contract with the Czech government. It is an argument whose apparent objectivity conceals his subjective anxiety for his own well-being and reveals to the viewer a disturbing form of unconscious hypocrisy. Stoppard, however, lends the professor a power of self-awareness and demonstrates an increasing capacity for creating rounded characters. Anderson recognises his bias, takes the thesis and regains the viewer's sympathy.

In this play, Stoppard argues the case for a fundamental human ethic. Three English philosophers, Anderson, Chetwyn and McKendrick discuss whether moral principles are relative or universal:

■ *McKendrick*: The mistake that people make is, they think a moral principle is infinitely extendable, that it holds good for any situation, . . . 'Morality' down there; running parallel to 'Immorality' up here – (*he scores a parallel line*) and never the twain shall meet. They think that is what a principle means.
Anderson: And isn't it?
McKendrick: No. The two lines are in the same plane . . . and if you twist the plane in a certain way, into what we call the catastrophe curve, you get a model of the behaviour you find in the real world. There's a point – the catastrophe point – where your progress along one line of behaviour jumps you into the opposite line; the principle reverses itself at the point where a rational man would abandon it.
Chetwyn: Then it's not a principle.
McKendrick: There aren't any principles in your sense. There are only a lot of principled people trying to behave as if there were.
Anderson: That's the same thing surely?
McKendrick: You're a worse case than Chetwyn and his primitive Greeks. At least he has the excuse of believing in goodness and beauty. You know they're fictions but you're so hung up on them you want to treat them as though they're God-given absolutes.
Anderson: I don't see how else they would have any practical value.
McKendrick: So you end up using a moral principle as your excuse for acting against a moral interest. It's a sort of funk. (p. 78) □

This hits a nerve and Anderson reacts angrily: 'You make your points altogether too easily, McKendrick. What need have you of moral courage when your principles reverse themselves so easily?' (p. 78). McKendrick can shelter behind his catastrophe theory. That too is a kind of funk. But Anderson has sheltered behind his own reasoning when refusing to take his student's thesis. He relents: 'I'm sorry. You're right up to a point. There would be no moral dilemmas if moral principles worked in straight lines and never crossed each other. One meets test situations which have troubled much cleverer men than us' (p. 79).

Anderson has met just such a test situation. He decides to take Hollar's thesis back to England and work for his now imprisoned former student's release. He hides the thesis in McKendrick's briefcase, which is not as likely as his own to be searched. His responsibility to Hollar, he decides, outweighs his responsibility to McKendrick. Personal responsibilities sometimes collide. He has reached the catastrophe point. But McKendrick doesn't enjoy the practical test of his theory:

■ It's not quite playing the game, is it?
Anderson: No I suppose not. But they were unlikely to search you.
McKendrick: That's not the bloody point.
Anderson: I thought it was. But you could be right. Ethics is a very complicated business. That's why they have these congresses. (p. 93) □

And the plane takes off with Hollar's thesis back in Anderson's briefcase. The sympathy is with Anderson's professional foul. He has taken a pragmatic decision and risked an acquaintance in the interests of a 'higher' ethic. Whether this is morally equivalent to the English footballer tripping a Czech opponent to prevent a goal is dubious, since the Czech team scores anyway. In Anderson's case he gets away with it. Chetwyn, who also has concealed luggage, but has not played unethical tricks, unfortunately does not. Ethics is indeed complex, since the outcome of an action is uncertain and the relation of ends to means is neither that the means always produce the ends nor that ends always justify the means. In Anderson's case, they do. The ethical centre, this play implies, resides in the feeling behind the reason that prompts the action. There is a difference of quality between feelings. Principles may sometimes be broken in the interest of the putatively higher principle when they collide. Pragmatism must sometimes take precedence. But when Hollar's son breaks into tears at the thought of losing his father, it gives credence to Hollar's argument for a personal ethic: 'I observe my son, for example', he says (p. 55).

In an article entitled 'Stoppard's Children', Richard Corballis argues that Stoppard shows children can be coerced into 'singing along' with the system, as in the case of Sasha fearing for his father's life in *EGBDF* (see Harty, pp. 264–5). This prevents Stoppard's view of the child's sense of natural justice from seeming too ingenuous. But Stoppard maintained his opinion (in an interview with David Gollop and David Roper, 1981). Of the Iron Curtain, a child would say: 'But the wall is there to keep people in. If it was good, people wouldn't want to leave'.

Of the scene in the play where Anderson meets his student's wife and child and a concrete case of right and wrong, Robert Cushman said: 'The hero's encounter with his imprisoned student's wife and son goes deeper than anything he has written before' (*Observer*, 2 October 1977, p. 28). Stoppard tells Melvyn Bragg:

■ . . . when I was at school – it's in the play – when you play football and the ball goes into touch, you know who touched it last, and you don't try to pretend that he did if you did. It just never occurred to you to do it. And yet, you know, we are all sitting there watching everybody being applauded for trying to steal some dishonourable advantage. And you know perfectly well that when both players claim the throw-in for themselves they both know whose it actually is. Now, what is going on? (Delaney, p. 120) □

Some Stoppard debates may be problematical, but in others the writer comes down off the fence: 'I can say that for the last few years I haven't been writing about questions whose answers I believe to be ambivalent . . . I want to live in a country where dispute can take place' (Delaney, pp. 164–5).

Anthony Jenkins observes of Stoppard's return to his Czech roots that:

■ The three plays which belong to that period will not support a theory of The Sudden Politicization of Tom Stoppard. The "politics" of undeniable human truths and inalienable human rights begins with *Jumpers* and continues to define the roles of Joyce and the Lenins in *Travesties*. What is new about Stoppard from that point on is the simplicity with which he formulates those ideas dramatically: the undeviating obsessive line which links *Dirty Linen* and *New-Found-Land*; the tight patterns that surround the madman and the prisoner in *Every Good Boy*, whereby the farce eats like acid into the authorities' bland and pompous reasonableness; the carefully worked out cause and effect structure that moves Anderson from 'correct' to incorrect' behaviour in *Professional Foul*. What is also new, and why Stoppard appears to become more political, is that each of the plays makes a direct unambiguous statement. For the time he abandons his intellectual "leap-frog", or rather his leap-frogging arrives at a distinctive terminus. Here Tom Stoppard does *know* things which before he had only suggested. (Jenkins, p. 142) □

The commentators agree. *Professional Foul* is disturbing, powerfully organised, formidably intelligent, highly characterised and, behind the light touch, even in the discussion of behaviour on a football pitch, eminently serious.

CHAPTER TEN

African Naturalism

Night and Day

Night and Day went on at the Phoenix Theatre on the 8 November 1978. It was directed by Peter Wood, with Diana Rigg and John Thaw in the main roles, and received generally favourable notices. Melvyn Bragg thought 'it will come to be regarded as Stoppard's most important play to date' and perceived ' . . . a change in Stoppard's work, not from less to more serious, or from more to less complicated, but a change in his personal commitment, and, especially in its dramatic expression toward naturalism' (Delaney, p. 116). The play is about Fleet Street journalists reporting a rebellion in an unnamed African state, interwoven with the story of the wife of an English mine owner who, to protect his interests, attempts to reconcile the rebels with the African President.

It begins strikingly at sundown and moves rapidly into darkness. Helicopter noise announces that this is an action play. Trees shake in the downblast; searchlights cross the stage; a jeep turns its headlights on the audience; a machine-gun rattles and a man falls in the helicopter searchlight. Quieter effects, reminiscent of Chekhov, follow. The helicopter recedes; a taxi stops; a dog barks; the taxi departs; a cassette radio begins to play (p. 20).

As it turns out, the opening is not 'real'. The man apparently killed in the spotlight, a war photographer called Guthrie, is shown sleeping in the garden as the light changes from night to late afternoon. Guthrie has been dreaming of what *might* happen and the chattering machine-gun is the sound of the telex machine. The dream sequence, however, is performed naturalistically. The characters are convincingly human, the exchanges are realistic and sharp, the setting, part room with a verandah, partly a garden, is real enough and the eve of civil war situation in an ex-British colony could be from a contemporary newsreel. This is not, as in *After Magritte* or *Jumpers*, a bizarre situation awaiting comic explanation or, as in *Travesties*, a scene filtered through a narrator's memory. The opening dream predicts a future event. Realism not comedy is the dominant tone.

The situation is complex. A rebel colonel has commandeered the mines, threatening the whole economy. Will secession be agreed if the mines are handed back? Is the dictator prepared to compromise? Both men probably want to rule the whole country. Their negotiations serve to gain time for clearing supply lines and making military preparations. The photographer, Guthrie, and two journalists, Dick Wagner and Jacob Milne, arrive at the house of the mine owner, Alastair Carson and his wife, Ruth. They are looking for a story and are attracted like bees to honey by Carson's telex machine.

Ruth is disturbed by Wagner's arrival because they have had a one-night-stand in London shortly before. (Ruth's son goes to school in England.) She also has experience of being hounded by the popular press. A discussion ensues about press freedom and Milne's idealism attracts Ruth, but Guthrie and Milne go off to contact the rebel and Milne is killed crossing the battle line. Meanwhile, Wagner sees a chance to 'scoop' Milne when he learns that the dictator is to arrive at Carson's house.

Complex information is fed to the audience with great skill. The scene is set by comparing the position of London in relation to Cheltenham and North Wales to the distances between the dictator in the capital Kamba City (KC) (London), Jeddu the town near Alistair and Ruth Carson's house (Cheltenham), and the hills (North Wales) where the rebel 'African Liberation Front' or ALF is holed up. The lines of communication form a similar dogleg.

The knowledge of press conditions is extensive. Wagner and Jake Milne argue over closed shops and union practice (see Richard Corballis, *Stoppard: The Mystery and the Clockwork*, pp. 118–21). Wagner has a tendency to use Marxist clichés which causes the bright, young Milne to say he has had his brains taken out and an electric typewriter golf ball put in their place. The older reporter argues for workers' solidarity. Jake tells Wagner they don't come any more solid than him. But Wagner is no fool:

■ A foreign correspondent is someone who lives in foreign parts and corresponds, usually in the form of essays containing no new facts. I'm a fireman. I go to fires . . . so don't imagine for a moment you've stumbled across a fellow member of the Traveller's Club . . . (p. 38) □

Wagner, the fireman, 'files facts not prose'. 'I admire Wagner rather a lot as a character', says Stoppard:

■ . . . I admire good professionals. I'm a bit of a journalistic groupie anyway. I think journalism is what Milne says it is, the last line of defence in this country. And surrounding this approbation is the knowledge that a great deal of journalism is despised and rightly so . . . nobody can have a cut-and-dried good/bad attitude toward Wagner or journalism because there are things to be said on different sides . . . (*Gambit*, No. 37, 1981, p.11) ☐

Reviews tended to focus on Stoppard's discussion of the British press. Michael Billington felt that

■ He never grapples with the question as to whether profitability should determine the right to publish opinion or the common-sense fact that the bulk of the national press supports one particular party. But it's a sign of the play's worth that one wants to argue with it. (*The Guardian*, 9 November 1978) ☐

In July the following year, he retracted the comment after Stoppard's rewrite:

■ Stoppard has rewritten the second act debate so that it becomes a reported conversation between Ruth and her eight-year-old prep school son. This both gives the argument a comic perspective (Ruth makes wounding points while spreading her son's Marmite) and also suggests there are two sides to the issue, that Britain has papers pushing every possible line from Hitler to St Francis of Assisi but that real power is still in the hands of vested economic interests. (*The Guardian*, 5 July 1979, p.8) ☐

The representation of political manoeuvring is also convincing. The LSE-educated President Mageeba has a grasp of political realities and considerable brutality behind the articulate façade. Stoppard may confess that he has created an African who speaks like himself, but the character is theatrically powerful, and dangerous.

Critics were also impressed by the characterisation of Ruth Carson. Steve Grant believed that 'this is by far the strongest and most potent part that he has yet written for a woman' (see *Plays and Players*, January 1979, pp.18–19). 'I was tired of people saying there are no good parts for women in my plays so I'll do one . . .', Stoppard told Shusha Guppy (Delaney, p.186). He provided Diana Rigg, playing Ruth Carson, with an intriguing problem – her husband is in the room when the death is reported of the reporter she is strongly attracted to. How should she react? Peter Barkworth describes what she did:

■ She put her glass down and clinked another one with it. A little later she walked, apparently calmly, across the stage and suddenly banged a pillar with her fist, and hugged it for a while. Her face gave nothing away.

I can imagine . . . that those brilliantly chosen actions were an immense help, night after night, to the recreation of the feelings induced by the news of the death of the boy. It's a bit like praying really . . . Thoughts inspire actions. Actions, rightly chosen, inspire thoughts . . . (Peter Barkworth, *About Acting*, p. 52) ☐

Stoppard had provided powerful material about a woman's position in a man's world that fused with the debate about the press. In an interview with Robert Bergqvist he declared:

■ The best thing that can happen to a writer is to discover that two plays he's been thinking about can actually be the same play. That way, with some luck, you can wind up with more than the sum of two parts. Journalism was an interest of mine. I wanted to write a . . . love story really, and finally the arcs intersected. (Delaney, p. 137) ☐

Melvyn Bragg asked what made him go for this complex of issues. Stoppard replied:

■ *Night and Day* is also a play about this woman and this young reporter. It's about something which is not journalism at all . . . I discovered pretty shortly after starting rehearsal that this play wanted to be more about that young woman and that young man than I had realized . . . (Delaney, p. 123) ☐

Stoppard knits the stories together by making Ruth Carson the victim of Fleet Street scandal sheets and inventing the stretched coincidence of her one-night-stand with Dick Wagner in London. Their second meeting in Africa, however (which Stoppard rewrote considerably when Peter Wood in rehearsal made him aware of 'a gaping hole in the text'), is powerful and abrasive. Ruth is the inactive centre of an action play and her presence adds a dimension to the world of politicians, businessmen and reporters, from which she feels excluded. To convey her thoughts, Stoppard makes original use of the non-naturalistic aside, which paradoxically adds to the realism of the play. The famous 'naturalists' avoided artificial asides and sought to establish character through subtext, silence and symbol. Chekhov gave his lonely characters long monologues. Stoppard divides his character into a private '*Ruth*' who conveys her inner life in asides, while *Ruth* without apostrophes comments caustically on the external and political world which is controlling her. He goes further still and enacts on stage Ruth's daydream of a love-relation with Jacob Milne. He only lets the audience know 'retroactively' (Stoppard's word) that the scene is wish-fulfilment. The Jake of this scene exists only in Ruth's imagination while the 'real' Jake is elsewhere, killed in crossfire in no-man's-land, as in Guthrie's prophetic dream of the opening sequence. The anguish of Ruth's unrealised wish enhances the poignant realism of a drama that develops beyond the initial action play, and the incorporated discussion play, to represent a collision between interior and exterior worlds. This explains why in rehearsal and performance she gained power and credibility. Critics would no longer say that Stoppard was unable to create female characters.

Critics, however, were divided over *Night and Day*. Bernard Levin and Peter Jenkins expressed disappointment and Peter Hall noted that it was about too many things:

■ ... everything that is in Tom's head at the moment, freedom of the press, the abuse of trade unionism, the position of women, the third world. Somehow he has tried to make it one play. It's four at least. (*Peter Hall's Diaries*, p. 475) □

The complex situation, however, enables the writer to focus on the isolation of a woman who, unlike Professor Anderson in *Professional Foul*, is a spectator who does *not* become involved in the political action.

Stoppard takes care to distance Ruth's sarcastic outsider commentary and balances her contempt for the gutter press against the quiet photographer Guthrie's widely quoted lines:

■ .I've been around a lot of places. People do awful things to each other. But it's worse in places where everybody is kept in the dark. It really is. Information is light. Information, in itself, about anything, is light. That's all you can say, really. (p. 92) □

Anthony Jenkins quotes this passage and adds that

■ ... to the cosy majority of his West End or Broadway audience, an idea like that does not burn on the brain ... Stoppard embarks on a debate whose pros and cons affect him deeply but which his audience would be apt to regard somewhat coolly. Stoppard does not seem to have allowed for that. For him, freedom of information is so vital an issue that he assumes debate in itself will be dramatic enough to provoke an equally passionate interest. English audiences have always loathed being lectured to in the theatre. (Jenkins, p. 143) □

Stoppard should not, perhaps, be blamed for an audience that is lukewarm about this issue, but Jenkins's criticism is ultimately an aesthetic one. He feels Stoppard has not communicated the *reality* of the two journalists, Wagner and Guthrie:

■ He can project his own humanity onto his professors and female neurotics but, familiar with the jargon and lifestyle of the press, he takes the journalists for granted, makes no such leap, and so they lack a dimension we too can enter. [But he adds] This is not the case with Jacob Milne . . . *Night and Day* is both entertaining and thought-provoking, a rare enough combination in the commercial theatre, but it fails to bond those qualities into a satisfying whole. Ruth's enigmatic performances pull us one way and the play's ideas, which do not vitally involve her, are not presented dynamically enough to pull us back. Ruth's two voices move us closer to her than to any other character, Milne included, and the face that she will never share with strangers makes us want to move still closer. Like all the major characters she is frequently undermined by the comedy, but that subversive laughter rarely detaches our sympathies, as it does from the others; since it nearly always rises out of her own self-mockery, we laugh *with* her. And Stoppard seems not to have realized that debate about a free press is not dramatic in itself. Animated as he is by that issue, he has not found a way of bringing the majority of his audience whole-heartedly along with him. (Jenkins, pp. 149, 152–3) □

Thomas Whitaker quotes other English and American responses. If Jenkins found the journalists unconvincing,

■ Harold Hobson called it "a comparatively straightforward play" that presents a social question "with the dialectical skill of a Shaw combined with the neat and moving melodramatic cleverness of a Rattigan". But he found Ruth Carson's presence "most mysterious", though granting that she was "played fascinatingly by the regal and Delilah-like Diana Rigg". When the play arrived in New York in November 1979, directed again by Wood but with Maggie Smith as Ruth, others objected more vigorously to its apparent incoherence. Douglas Watt thought Smith "divine" in this "Shavian drawing-room comedy" but was "not at all sure what the character she plays is doing there". Howard Kissel, who found the debate tedious, praised her rendering of "a totally extraneous part". Walter Kerr wondered whether Stoppard "is a true dramatist at all". The Shavian debate "really takes place in a void", he said. "Miss Smith's romantic life doesn't influence the argument in the least. Nor does the argument measurably affect the politics of Kimbawe" [the African state]. Even Jack Kroll, who understood that Stoppard was experimenting with conventional forms, thought the play "didn't hold together". (Whitaker, pp. 147–8) □

Whitaker, however, approves the mingling of genres and the effect of isolation:

■ At the keyboard of the telex, Wagner becomes a piano-player to whose chords Ruth sings Rodgers and Hart's wry lyric, "The Lady is a Tramp". But before she can utter that last word, Wagner tears the paper out of the machine and joins her. "Is that it?" she asks. "That's it." And a black-out completes Stoppard's ironic elucidation of our worlds of doubleness. (p. 152) □

The degree of Stoppard's irony is debatable. Guthrie's observation about the value of information and light seems straightforward. A picture, they say, is worth a thousand words (in the case of Wagner, Guthrie says, 'two thousand'). Guthrie's words identify the moral centre of a play about courage and waste and the value of knowledge. What is further to be done at the end is not answered and this justifies Whitaker's focus on irony. Ruth and Wagner are left alone, each continuing a life, which the man values and the woman does not. The conflation of the different genres leaves disturbing questions.

CHAPTER ELEVEN

Language and Czech Censorship

Dogg's Hamlet and *Cahoot's Macbeth* (integrated plays)

There has not been a great deal of analysis of Stoppard's bizarre reworkings of Shakespeare's *Hamlet* and *Macbeth*. Commentators repeat
Stoppard's own introductory observation that, though they were written
on separate occasions for different spaces, the second play depends upon
the first and the first is scarcely a play at all without the second. *Dogg's
Hamlet* is made up of two pieces: a reworking of *Dogg's Our Pet*, written
for Ed Berman in 1971 and *The Dogg's Troupe 15 minute Hamlet*, written for
performance on a double decker bus with the front seats taken out but
hilariously performed in front of the National Theatre in 1979. 'I'm waiting for the right moment to do a five-minute *War and Peace*', Stoppard
told Mel Gussow (p. 37). The *Macbeth* play was born out of Stoppard's
meeting in Czechoslovakia with Pavel Kohout and Pavel Landovsky
who, because they were banned from the stage, performed a 75-minute
Macbeth in a private room: 'Pavel Kohout told me about a living-room
Macbeth. Why don't I write a play about someone trying to do *Macbeth*
and getting interrupted?' (Gussow, p. 37).

 Dogg's Hamlet is about 'lettered' schoolboys called Able, Baker, Charlie
and Fox putting on *Hamlet* for Speech Day in a language called Dogg
(which is also the name of the headmaster). They are interrupted by a
lorry driver called Easy, who speaks only English and delivers blocks
with which the boys build a wall. The attempts to communicate provide
much rough humour. In *Cahoot's Macbeth*, an Inspector intrudes on a performance of *Macbeth* and warns the actors of the subversive nature of
Shakespeare. Easy enters speaking fluent Dogg to deliver his blocks then,
on 'Bleed, bleed, poor country', the Inspector returns and his henchmen
build a wall across the proscenium arch. A play about language becomes
a political allegory.

 The first combined performance of all three pieces was at the Arts
Centre, University of Warwick, on 21 May 1979. This was followed by a
successful London run from 30 July at the Collegiate Theatre, with Ed

Berman directing. Performances in Washington and New York in September and October of the same year followed.

Stoppard tells us that the first play derived from Wittgenstein's speculations in *Philosophical Investigations* (1953) about language comprehension. In certain circumstances, people may seem to understand each other when the words in the language they are using mean entirely different things for different groups. Thus the word 'plank' may mean for the speaker who is building a stage, 'I am ready to be thrown a plank'. For the listener assisting in the building, 'plank' has no significance apart from its recognisable place in a series of routine commands to throw different building materials. In context, it may signify 'ready' and misunderstandings will occur only if a plank is not the next item to be needed.

Wittgenstein's suggestion encouraged Stoppard to write a comedy around words that carry a negative charge in one 'language' and a positive or neutral charge in the other (which employs the same vocabulary). 'Git', for example, means 'sir' in Dogg. 'Dunce' means 'twelve'; 'moronic creep' means 'maroon carpet'. The game is light-hearted and, as a result of the misunderstandings, characters get hit over the ear or pushed through the wall they are building, on which rude words in Dogg appear. *Dogg's Hamlet* ends with a brilliant digest of Shakespeare's play, with the long speeches cut out and a few famous quotations left in. It lasts about fifteen minutes, not counting a hilarious encore lasting three. A masterpiece is massacred, always a source of disrespectful humour, here mixed with admiration for the playwright's skill.

The first play has attracted serious commentary from Keir Elam, who was one of the first to apply semiotics to theatre studies. He is interested in the effect of Stoppard's attempt to 'out-Wittgenstein Wittgenstein' by teaching the audience the code which at first mystifies Easy:

■ The protagonist Easy finds the code-cracking easy indeed, mere child's play . . . and at the end of the comedy has acquired perfect mastery of Dogg. Whether the audience attains a similar level of competence is another matter; the sense of semiotic inferiority is probably one of the main masochistic pleasures offered by the play [i.e., the audience enjoys being drawn into the chaotic incomprehension]. But in any event, in reversing Wittgenstein . . . Stoppard seems to suggest that dramatic discourse is itself a "primitive" language-game of a kind, being necessarily tied in its production of meaning to the simultaneous presence of ostended [a semiotic term for the act of holding up and showing] objects, bodies and gestures; but at the same time, even a so-called primitive game may not be all that it seems. It could be *this* too. The theatre, indeed, with its semiotic mix of objects, images and words is the privileged seat of pleasurably painful ambiguity. Or is not this, at least, what the tortoise would appear to have taught us? (Bloom, pp. 172–3) □

Elam's observation raises general questions about theatre, especially tragedy. What pleasure does an audience derive from watching the deaths of Hamlet and Macbeth? (T. R. Henn's *The Harvest of Tragedy* (1956) provides a summary of explanations, one of which is *Schadenfreude* or enjoyment of suffering.) Perhaps, suggests Elam, this relates to the ambiguous pleasure of the audience when the professor in *Jumpers* steps on his tortoise.

Elam also comments on non-linguistic forms of theatrical communication and Thomas Whitaker stresses this aspect of the original *Dogg's Our Pet*:

■ . . . Stoppard's ceremony leads us to participate in a nonsense language that makes its own sufficient sense. The most important theatrical communication is not verbal at all. It occurs through the miming of our ritual game-playing (building with blocks, tossing a ball, counting out flags, trading compliments and insults, making formulaic inquiries and announcements, delivering vacuous speeches), which actors can fill with easily graspable meaning regardless of the precise words they utter. In that respect *Dogg's Our Pet* is admirably designed as participatory theatre for all ages. And its playful logic shows Stoppard again to be, even when most obviously "verbal", a surprisingly non-verbal playwright. (Whitaker, p. 84) □

Stoppard reworked the original play and added his hilarious condensed *Hamlet* to make the more substantial *Dogg's Hamlet*. Whitaker's comment still stands – the play was meant for a special participatory purpose and needs to be seen and enjoyed. The audience may gain little from beginning to understand Dogg language (which Stoppard says was one aim of his experiment). At the end of the play it seems of no more importance than working out an anagram in a crossword puzzle, or as Whitaker remarks, 'a standard improvisation exercise in the theatre'. There remains, however, the question of the value of improvisatory fun.

Cahoot's Macbeth

Dogg's Hamlet forms a basis for the Macbeth play that establishes a closer allegorical parallel with the world of real events and enables the comedy to be seen as more than an intellectual game. This is probably why Stoppard insists the two plays should be presented together. *Cahoot's Macbeth* takes place in a private room and parallels the actual situation in Prague of the dissidents Pavel Kohout and Landovsky, who were acting 'in spite of circumstances'. It is interrupted by a knocking at the gate and

the entry, not of MacDuff, but of a jokey but menacing Inspector search-
ing for a reason to close the performance down. The situation parallels
the Czech reality and the actor Cahoot, who is playing Banquo, howls
like a dog:

■ *Inspector*: Sit! Here, boy, what's his name?
'*Macbeth*': Cahoot.
Inspector: The social parasite and slanderer of the state?
Cahoot: The writer.
Inspector: That's him. You're a great favourite down at the nick you
know. We're thinking of making you writer in residence for a
couple of years; four if you're a member of a recognised school,
which I can make stick on a chimpanzee with a box of alphabet
bricks. (*smiles*) Would you care to make a statement?
Cahoot: "Thou hast it now: King, Cawdor, Glamis, all
As the weird sisters promised . . . "
Inspector: Kindly keep my wife's family out of this.
Cahoot: ". . . and I fear
Thou playedst most foully for't . . . "
Inspector: Foul . . . fair . . . which is which? That's two witches. One
more and we can do the show right here.
Cahoot: ". . . Yet it was said
It should not stand in thy posterity . . . " (p. 193) □

The *Macbeth* quotations resonate within a modern tyranny and prophesy
its end. The Inspector's jocular use of cliché attracts dramatic sympathy
despite the sinister reference. Whether the fun Stoppard has in depicting
him works against the political satire is disputable. A writer who gives a
character lines such as 'when they gave you an inch you overplayed
your hand and rocked the boat so they pulled the rug from under you . . .'
(p. 193) has got to be joking. The exaggerated caricature attracts the
usual critical charge that Stoppard has relapsed into anarchic humour,
expunging the seriousness of the human situation that originally
engaged his sympathy. Colin Ludlow in *Plays and Players* observed:

■ . . . Were *Cahoot's Macbeth* written by anyone with less immaculate
credentials, the play might seem offensive and the motives behind it
dubious. As it is one can only conclude that the combination of
seriousness and absurdity is miscalculated and the result different
from what was intended. (August 1979, p. 28) □

Benedict Nightingale much prefers the TV play *Professional Foul*, which
ignores rather than invokes the *Macbeth* parallel: 'Both [plays] are about
usurpation and the abuse of power, but it is the one which ignores,

rather than specifically invokes, that parallel which comes the nearer to justifying it' (*New Statesman*, 20 July 1979, p. 105). Farcical fun with a masterpiece rides uneasily with satire. But the satire asserts itself when the actors begin to talk in a language the Inspector cannot understand. Easy, the lorry driver of *Dogg's Hamlet*, enters as Banquo's ghost speaking fluent Dogg. The actors perform *Macbeth* in Dogg to the discomposure of the Inspector, who loses command of the situation. He interrupts the final conflict between the tyrant Macbeth and MacDuff to order a wall to be built. The knockabout building and rebuilding of the wall of *Dogg's Hamlet* becomes, in retrospect, preferable to the Inspector's acolytes' construction of a grey wall across the proscenium arch. We do not see the tyrant slain.

Easy's final words after the sometimes rhythmically identifiable, but often incomprehensible, exchanges in Dogg are:

■ Double, double toil and trouble. No Shakespeare.
 (*silence*)
 Well, it's been a funny sort of a week. But I should be back by Tuesday. (p. 211) □

'Funny' implied 'strange', rather than 'amusing'. Whether the troupe would be back after their arrest was a moot point. But we now know that a real wall came down in 1989 and actors gained their freedom. The situation was real enough and although its representation was caricatural, the play is ironic about its own jokiness and suggests that an autocratic regime can be subverted by a language that is beyond its comprehension. Dogg is a metaphor for subversion, a 'clinical condition' that, as the play says, you don't learn but catch. Nor should the brilliant visual metaphor that ends the play be forgotten. For Felicia Londré, it makes a clear statement: ' . . . artists under a totalitarian regime are physically walled in, but their thoughts and creative imaginations will always find some form of expression – a whole new language if necessary' (Harty, p. 356).

CHAPTER TWELVE

Writing About Love

The Real Thing

If the Shakespeare adaptations for Ed Berman were about language and politics, the next original play, *The Real Thing* (1982), is about love with a minor political sub-plot. It was performed in November 1982, directed by Peter Wood, at the Strand Theatre in London. Roger Rees and Felicity Kendal played the main parts. Fourteen months later, on 5 January 1984, it opened in New York and was judged *Best New Play of the Season* by the New York Drama Critics Circle and given the *Tony Award for Best Play*. Jeremy Irons played the Roger Rees role of a dramatist involved in complex love relations who also writes a play about love called *'House of Cards'*.

The Real Thing is difficult to describe because it operates on different levels of reality. The characters are actors or writers and scenes from their private lives are intercut with the plays they write or perform in. Henry is the author of the drama called *'House of Cards'*, in which his wife Charlotte takes the part of the apparently adulterous wife of an architect. Max, the actor playing the architect, is married to Annie who is having an affair with Henry and subsequently marries him. Annie embraces the cause of a young soldier called Brodie, who protests against atomic missiles by vandalising the Cenotaph and being sentenced to a term in prison. During this time he writes a crude play about his experience that Annie wishes Henry to make fit for broadcasting, thereby publicising his case and cause. With some reluctance and considerable difficulty, Henry reworks Brodie's play, in which Annie performs along with Billie, an actor who has fallen in love with Annie, playing opposite her in John Ford's play about incestuous love, *'Tis Pity She's a Whore* (1633). They have an affair, which Henry manages to tolerate, and the play ends with Annie not answering Billie's phone call and covering Brodie's ungrateful face with the dips that accompany the wine to which he is liberally helping himself. Brodie has asserted that he was sprung from prison, not by Henry's efforts on his behalf (because Henry did it for Annie), but because 'the missiles I was marching against are using up the money they need for a prison to put me in. Beautiful. Can I have another?' (p. 81). The play ends with both Henry and Annie realising that neither Brodie nor Billie should endanger the feelings they have for each other. ('Fundamentally everything is OK', says Stoppard.) In the middle of all this, Henry and Charlotte's daughter Debbie goes off backpacking with her boyfriend. She provides a youthful viewpoint on the central love theme.

'Is this the nearest you've come to writing about love?', Mel Gussow asked.

■ *T.S.*: **Yes. As far as I'm concerned, this is all I'll do. For better or worse, that's it – the love play! . . . you can't do it again. I think love is the only area that might be private to a writer.**

M.G.: **You've written about sex.** *Jumpers, Dirty Linen* **have erotic moments.**

T.S.: **I suppose so, but none of it's private. It's all theatre sex, theatre lust, witty, articulate sex. Love is a very interesting subject to write about. I've been aware of the process that's lasted 25 years, of shedding inhibition about self-revelation. I wouldn't have dreamed of writing about it ten years ago, but as you get older, you think, who cares? (Gussow, p. 62)** □

Sheridan Morley asserted: 'Stoppard has come up with the warmest and most touching play he has ever written' (*Shooting Stars*, 1983, p. 339). In *The New York Times*, Frank Rich greeted the production as 'the most bracing play that anyone has written about love and marriage in years'.

The play was indeed about love – but also about the problem for a playwright (and his characters) of finding convincing language to express 'real' love, rather than 'theatre sex'. The play's title is that of a Henry James short story in which an artist finds it impossible to make a 'real' gentleman and a lady convincingly real in his book illustrations. Similarly, Stoppard and his playwright character 'Henry' seek a real language to express love. Guildenstern, in the earlier play, had a parallel problem of distinguishing a real death from a theatrical one.

Stoppard employs the complex device of the play-within-a-play to contrast the private speech of his fictional characters with the various witty, emotional or poetic discourses they speak in Henry's *'House of Cards'* or in Strindberg's *Miss Julie* or in Ford's *'Tis Pity She's a Whore*. T. S. Eliot suggested that poetry is the 'natural' expression of people who seek to express emotion, but the language of emotion varies with the situation from quiet utterance to rhetoric and theatricality, and *The Real Thing* plays with variations on banal, naturalistic and theatrical language to express what the characters pretend or believe is love.

In one sense, of course, all theatrical language is artificial. Even the 'sincere' is artfully constructed and rewritten. The difference between brilliantly written dramatic dialogue and 'natural' human speech lies in the time and talent it takes to put theatre exchanges together. Sustained displays of spontaneous wit in normal conversation are very rare and when they occur they are often carefully prepared. Oscar Wilde could do it in both his drama and his conversation. His improvisations had strong elements of artifice and Stoppard's central character is a playwright with a similar gift. Wit, however, tends to collapse under the stress of emotion. When a love relation breaks down, another language must be found to control the situation. Stoppard compares Henry and Max, Annie's two husbands. Max, the actor, fluent in betrayal within Henry's play, becomes in 'real' life incoherent with grief and rage. Henry, the playwright and second husband, manages, in company, to maintain control. The language he achieves can then claim to be 'real'. So, too, however, can the evident pain of Max, though his very incoherence may be a comment on the histrionic quality of the feeling that swamps his language.

■ *Max*: You're filthy.
You filthy cow. You rotten filthy –
(*He starts to cry, barely audible, immobile. Annie waits. He recovers his voice.*)
It's not true is it?
Annie: Yes.
Max: Oh God.
(*He stands up.*)
Why did you?
Annie: I'm awfully sorry, Max –
Max: (*Interrupting, suddenly pulled together*) All right. It happened. All right. It didn't mean anything.
Annie: I'm awfully sorry, Max, but I love him.
Max: Oh, no.
Annie: Yes.
Max: Oh, no. You don't.
Annie: Yes I do. And he loves me. That's that, isn't it? I'm sorry it's awful. But it's better really. All that lying.
Max: (*Breaking up again*) Oh, Christ, Annie, stop it. I love you. Please don't –
Annie: Come on please – it doesn't have to be like this.
Max: How long for? And him – oh, God.
(*He kicks the radio savagely. The radio has gone into music again – the Righteous Brothers singing 'You've Lost That Lovin' Feeling' – and Max's kick has the effect of turning up the volume rather loud . . .*) (pp. 36–7) □

The dialogue on the page is banal. Max's kick turns the scene to comedy and the characters do not rise to poetry. Yet this soap-opera dialogue seems 'natural'. Annie's quieter tone sets off Max's lack of adequate words, and within a dramatic frame in which more sophisticated language has its own inadequacies, the scene has great power. 'Please don't' may be more authentic than sarcasm, or bitter words, or poetry. It is echoed by Henry when Annie, in turn, betrays *him*. On that occasion it carries even more power, since Henry says it when alone. The nature of the expression varies with the situation and love has plural forms.

In *The Real Thing*, the witty Stoppard demonstrates the limitations as well as the values of witty language. In an interview with Joan Buck, he remarks that Henry 'leaves a woman who is pretty much his equal at the stuff which doesn't matter. The second wife, Annie, doesn't have the smart remarks. She's actually wiser than he is. He's cleverer, but she's wiser' (Delaney, p.170). Like Congreve and other post-Restoration dramatists, Stoppard is concerned with the wisdom of 'true' feeling that underlies different forms of wit and artifice. Truth, however, is not the same in art as in life and Stoppard, a playwright writing about a playwright, must not be identifed with his character:

■ The first idea I had was that I'd like to write a play in which the first scene turned out to have been written by a character in the second scene. That was what I started with. There is a strong – not autobiographical element – but strong editorial element because the man spouts opinions generally which I subscribe to. So in that sense there's a lot of me in it. (Delaney, p.259) □

The distinction here between opinions that are 'editorial' and autobiographical elements that are more private is worth noting. Henry is not Stoppard, though the relation is complex:

■ Because *The Real Thing* had an English playwright *editorializing* [my italics] about writing and love and marriage and all that, it was perfectly obvious that when he was waving his prejudices around, he was pretty much speaking for me. But then so are the people who contradict him. That's what playmaking is. You have to take everybody's side. (Delaney, p.229) □

Writing involves distancing the self from the work. It also helps to distance the audience and *The Real Thing* challenges the audience's sense of reality from the moment it begins to realise that the play has opened, against all dramatic convention, with a play-within-a-play. In it an architect appears to have detected his wife in an act of betrayal. The audience only realises in the second scene, when Henry's wife Charlotte comments sarcastically on the character she has played and accuses Henry of giving Max the best witty lines, that she and Max were acting in Henry's fictional play.

Charlotte is anxious that the audience should not interpret the play biographically:

- *Charlotte*: All those people out front thinking, that's why she got the job.
    You're right Max.
    Max: I never said anything!
    Charlotte: And also thinking that I'm her . . . coming in with my little suitcase, and my duty-free bag – It's me! – ooh, it's her! – so that's what they're like at home – he's scintillating and she's scintillated. (*Henry starts to speak*) Look out, he's going to scintillate . . .
    . . . you try playing the feed one night instead of acting Henry after a buck's fizz and two rewrites. (p. 20) □

Charlotte is wittier than the character she plays, while Max is far less witty than his. Henry remains witty, but his language varies according to his personal situation. Stoppard describes his plan thus:

- The idea is that you have a man on stage going through a situation. It turns out he's written it. Then you have the actor in the scene going through the same situation, except he reacts differently. Then you have the guy who wrote it going through the exact situation and he reacts differently too. It's quite a schematic idea. (Gussow, p. 40) □

Hersh Zeifman picks up Stoppard's comment, in his article 'Comedy of Ambush' in which he talks of Stoppard's 'replays':

- It is obvious that both replays are set up so that, structurally, each explicitly mirrors the opening scene; it is equally obvious that the reaction of the "real" husband to his wife's betrayal is, in both cases, utterly opposite to the wit under pressure displayed by the theatrical husband in the *House of Cards*. The structural similarities would thus appear to be deeply ironic, underscoring the disparity in emotional truth between theatre and life; we finally seem to have discovered "the real thing" but have we? Are those structural similarities there paradoxically to *clarify* the distinction between the artificial and the real, or rather to *cloud* it? Stoppard has one more ambush up his sleeve, for the claims of theatre cannot be so easily dismissed. Thus, in the first replay, Max discovers his wife's infidelity through an incriminatingly dropped handkerchief. At the very heart of this "real" scene then, we are implicitly reminded of theatre – of a highly theatrical, and therefore artificial, Moor who likewise bemoaned (and in blank verse!) the loss of his wife's handkerchief. Is Max's love, Max's pain, greater than Othello's? Is this discovery scene necessarily more real than

Shakespeare's theatrical discovery scene? [Zeifman is using the term in a literal sense. Shakespeare's stage has no curtain and therefore, in the technical, theatrical sense, it is not a discovery scene.] Similarly, while the pain felt by Henry is naked, intense and terribly moving, is it necessarily more "real" than the suffering of his theatrical alter ego in *House of Cards*? In both "real life" and Henry's play, the betrayed husband ransacks his wife's personal belongings; as Annie comments, in a direct echo of the opening scene, "You should have put everything back. Everything would be the way it was". In both "real life" and Henry's play, the accused wife claims no longer to know her husband. And the "real" scene ends with Henry alone on-stage, opening the present his wife has brought him from her adulterous trip to Glasgow. It is a tartan scarf. Unlike his theatrical counterpart, Henry does not laugh. But an audience, however much it genuinely feels for him, might be tempted to: life has a disconcerting habit of imitating theatre. Stoppard has ambushed us once again . . .

   The Real Thing keeps circling endlessly back on itself . . . Dizzy from this series of comic ambushes of our perceptions and preconceptions, we thus find ourselves at the end invariably questioning, among a host of other "realities", the precise nature of love – as Stoppard, of course, intended. Love speaks in many different tongues, with many different accents. Which of them, finally, is "the real thing"? (Bloom, pp. 149–50) □

Ambushes take various forms. Charlotte is ambushed because she fears the audience will assume a relation between Henry's play, in which she commits adultery, and her actual marital life as Henry's wife. We later find that she has indeed betrayed her husband and that Henry is ambushed because he does *not* know. This is different from Henry's play, in which the architect husband *does* know, or at least thinks he does (in which case he will be ambushed later, along with Henry's audience, in a play whose ending we do not know). Stoppard has ironic fun at the expense of many people – at the expense of authors who disguise personal experience in different ways; at the expense of his characters who either do not know or do not want others to know the 'real' situation; at the expense of Charlotte's prying audience 'out front' which Charlotte thinks will make the oversimple (but in this case justified) assumption of a direct relation between art and life, and some private fun at his own expense: 'It was me talking about myself before writing *The Real Thing*. The play contains self-reference jokes' (Gussow, p. 62).

   Henry shares with Stoppard a number of characteristics. He is a witty intellectual playwright who seems to be in the habit of teasing the audience. He finds it difficult to write about love; he is a professional writer who must make a living and is accused of having little time for good causes. He has a taste for popular music (and, like Henry, was interviewed, albeit later, on *Desert Island Discs*). He is against crude left-wing attitudes. The misuse of language, especially mixed metaphor, positively pains him. Henry, like Stoppard, is a rewriter of other people's plays and the opening scene of his play is Stoppardian in style.

To inquire further into private sources – the origins in Henry's author of Henry's lack of jealousy, for instance – would be prurient. Beneath the language lie problems of artistic intention, conscious and unconscious. But Stoppard does not tell us why or how his alter ego creates characters. Does Henry deliberately use his wife and himself as models for *House of Cards*? Charlotte implies he is biased against the wife. If she is right, unconscious or deliberate bias has damaged Henry's play (but not Stoppard's). But we do not know how far this is true, since Stoppard has not supplied Henry's ending – which may well privilege the woman, not the man.

Stoppard distances Henry from himself by seeing him through other characters' eyes ('You have to take everybody's side. That's what playwriting is'). But when Stoppard shows Henry doing what he does himself – distancing his main character – (for *House of Cards* does not reflect Henry's love for Annie or his ignorance of his wife's deception) – it brings the real and fictional playwrights closer again. Similarly, when the articulate Charlotte accuses her husband of having a 'joke reflex' instead of a sense of humour, Stoppard may be having a quiet joke at his own expense. The 'self-reference' joke emphasises a connection with the author, but a joke at the character's expense keeps him at an objective distance.

When Stoppard has differentiated his characters from the parts they write and perform, he introduces the other plays-within-the-play. Annie rehearses and acts in Strindberg's *Miss Julie* and Ford's *'Tis Pity She's a Whore*. The roles have a direct effect upon her life, but another dramatic function of the scenes is to invite the audience to compare and contrast the passion and sexual intensity of the famous roles with the shoulder shrugging, guiltless responses of Henry's wife and daughter, and (more subtly) with Annie's own refusal of guilt at her adultery. Henry, on the other hand, believes in passion, though his language is as different from Strindberg's and Ford's as theirs is different from each other.

Henry is a 'romantic' who feels pain when Annie betrays him:

■ . . . every object that meets the eye, a pencil, a tangerine, a travel poster. As if the physical world had been wired up to pass a current back to the part of your brain where imagination glows like a filament in a lobe no bigger than a torch bulb. Pain. (*pause*)
Debbie: Has Annie got someone else then? (p. 64) □

Debbie has glimpsed the subtext. Her forthright question indirectly suggests that Henry's simile both expresses and thereby sublimates the
feeling behind it. His language is powerful and original, unlike that of
Max, and it defines his 'real' pain when Annie reveals she has deceived
him. Henry's capacity for self-definition and self-distancing enables him
to endure infidelity. It attracts the audience's sympathy because, like his
author, he is an artist and can see the self with detachment.

Henry's pain is expressed in language which is unlike that of
Strindberg's *Miss Julie* and does not derive from fear of breaking class
conventions. Nor is it the passionate poetry of Ford's incestuous brother
and sister. Henry is a modern, suffering intellectual who analyses his
pain like a Schnitzler character (whom Stoppard had been translating).
But he does not act in accordance with Schnitzler's character's view that
'the highest love is beyond forgiveness' (see chapter thirteen). Henry
wants to stay with Annie. The desire to do so appears not to be a question of forgiveness, but to derive from a basic need.

A moral centre of the play seems to lie in the contrast between the
quality of Max's pain when Annie betrays him with Henry and Henry's
response when she betrays him with fellow actor Billie. Max and he both
feel pain, but Henry controls his and saves his relationship. Annie still
wants him and he refuses (unlike Max) to bore Annie with his pain and
use pain as blackmail. His sense of the other *as other* remains and his
definition of love begins with a definition of knowledge in the biblical
Greek sense:

■ Carnal knowledge. It's what lovers trust each other with. Knowledge of one another, not of the flesh but through the flesh,
knowledge of self, the real him, the real her, *in extremis*, the mask
slipped from the face. Every other version of oneself is on offer to
the public . . . but in pairs we insist we give ourselves to each
other . . . (p. 63) □

His daughter, Debbie's reply – 'exclusive rights isn't love it's colonisation'
– carries force, but Henry calls the phrase 'an ersatz masterpiece'.
Stoppard's dialogue, as ever, consists of statement and counter-
statement. Spectators will make their own decision as to who is right.
The power of the words suggests that the playwright is on Henry's side.
But, as ever, Stoppard tries to be fair. Debbie emerges as a more rounded
character than the children, who are the moral touchstones of the political plays. But, of course, she is older and has certainly lost her innocence.

Henry is still innocent. He tells Annie: 'I can't find a part of myself
where you're not important' (Annie has told him he will not be worth
loving if he doesn't find such a place). He is chosen and cannot choose
for himself – an admitted romantic. Hence the scene ends with the pop

song 'I'm a Believer' by The Monkees. Taken ironically along with Henry's incapacity to respond to classical music and his preference for pop music over Callas and grand opera, one might agree with Max that 'You've got something missing'. Perhaps this is why Henry finds it impossible to write a love scene. But Henry is not fully Stoppard and by virtue of Stoppard's objectifying in him a difficulty he has encountered in his profession, the play communicates a complexity which lies beyond identification with a single character: 'Everything should be romantic, love, work, music, literature, virginity, loss of virginity' (p.67), says Henry. 'You've still got one to lose', Charlotte replies.

Anthony Jenkins expressed some doubts about whether Henry's relation with Annie was as sound as he wanted to think it: 'If this is the real thing between herself and Henry there appear to be rocky times ahead' (Jenkins, p.171). But it was the political dimension to this complex drama that displeased some critics. Annie has taken up the cause of Brodie when he burns the wreath on the Cenotaph in Whitehall, apparently as a protest against nuclear missiles. He then beats up two policemen and is put in jail. Annie encourages Brodie to write his play and asks Henry to make Brodie's conventional dialogue presentable, but Henry gets no thanks for it. Brodie knows Henry wrote it for Annie, not for him. He doesn't 'owe him'; besides 'You wrote it clever', he says. Shortage of public money, not the pressure groups or the publicity of a TV play, has encouraged the authorities to release political protesters.

Brodie fights his corner, but Stoppard weakens his case by having Annie tell us his motive was only to impress her. However, Brodie has his supporters and Stoppard's representation of him has invited critical attack. C.K. Stead puts it thus:

■ Stoppard turns some of his best verbal fire against the kind of cant and half-truth to which the Left is prone. The mistake he makes, or the play makes . . . is confusing the cant and the cause. His playwright hero defends brilliantly and wittily his conviction that to be a writer you need, not a cause, but the skills of a writer. His adversary is permitted to put, but with no comparable eloquence, the counter-statement that to have the skills of a writer and nothing to say is not exactly a position of strength. What comfort will there be for those who attack (as Stoppard's play does) the failings of the language in which the anti-nuclear argument is put, if that argument proves nevertheless to be correct? (*London Review of Books*, 18–31 October 1984, p.25) □

Brodie's mixed motives, the argument goes, do not invalidate the political argument, which can be couched in more convincing terms than *The Real Thing* allows. Of course, in this play, Stoppard is less concerned with politics than private relations. This upset Michael Stewart of *Tribune* who calls Stoppard the 'Great Comforter' of the English middle class:

■ Here is a man with the impeccable credentials of spending the first two years of his life in Czechoslavakia to tell you how much more horrible the KGB would be. And he will do more. He can go on to consecrate every petty and craven feature of his adopted class as not merely the best of humanity but the very definition of it. All else is reduced to barbarism. (*Tribune*, 3 December 1982, p. 9) □

Others pursue the point more subtly. Thomas Whitaker remarks 'a certain glibness in the dismissive conception of the demonstrator Brodie', which he speculates may have arisen from Stoppard's too easy acceptance of W. H. Auden's aphorism: 'Public postures have the configuration of private derangement'. Whitaker, however, does not dwell on this and observes that 'Stoppard's comic shafts now reach our hearts as well as our heads' (Whitaker, pp. 167–8).

CHAPTER THIRTEEN

Adaptations

Undiscovered Country; On the Razzle; Rough Crossing; Dalliance

During his career, Stoppard has adapted many plays and novels for stage and film. They include *Tango* by Slavomir Mrozek in 1966 and Federico García Lorca's famous *House of Bernardo Alba* in 1973, Jerome K. Jerome's *Three Men in a Boat* for television in 1975, and in the same year, for the cinema, Thomas Wiseman's *The Romantic Englishwoman*, directed by Joseph Losey, with Michael Caine and Glenda Jackson. He wrote screenplays based on Vladimir Nabokov's *Despair* (1977) and Graham Greene's *The Human Factor* (1979). Recently he adapted Chekhov's *The Seagull* (1997).

Over the years, before and after *The Real Thing* (1982), Stoppard adapted four naturalistic comedies from central Europe, including two by Arthur Schnitzler, which are mainly about love and marital relations. These plays are worth independent consideration, since the adaptations are fairly extensive and vary considerably in their treatment of the central theme.

Undiscovered Country

A dramatisation of Schnitzler's *Das Weite Land* (*Undiscovered Country*) opened at the National Theatre in June 1979 and in August 1981 the National Theatre premiered *On the Razzle*, his adaptation of Johann Nestroy's *Einen Jux will er sich machen* (*He will go on the spree*). *On the Razzle* is a brilliant, if relatively conventional, farce, but the Schnitzler play is a major dramatic work and contains reflections on the nature of love, which are echoed in *The Real Thing*. For example, Schnitzler's Dr von Aigner observes: 'We try to bring order into our lives, but that very order has something unnatural about it . . . The natural condition is chaos. Yes, Hofreiter, the soul . . . is an undiscovered country . . . ' (p. 144). The lines recall Freud's analysis of love and sexuality in Schnitzler's Vienna, and the play is concerned with the importance of civilised control when betrayal in love threatens emotional breakdown. Stoppard, like Schnitzler, interrogates the value of those moments of bliss 'drunk on altitude' of which Schnitzler's Friedrich speaks (p. 149). In *Undiscovered Country*, summits and mountain climbing are metaphors for love and were incorporated visually into the mountain setting of the National Theatre's attractive production.

Stoppard discussed with Gussow the process of translation:

■ With *Undiscovered Country* I started by doing an obsessively faithful first draft – accurate but actable. Considerably shorter. It is a bit titivated. For someone like me, who enjoys writing dialogue but has a terrible time writing plays, adaptation is joy time. It is a craftsman's job, not 'my soul speaks through Schnitzler'. You go around with a bag of tools doing jobs between personal plays . . . (p. 36) □

Undiscovered Country (1979) may be 'Schnitzler not Stoppard', but it is the finest and most ambitious of his adaptations. 'Working on this play', said Stoppard, 'I often felt as if I were driving up the M1 in a Triumph Stag and finding myself overtaken by a 1922 Bentley' (*Peter Hall's Diaries*, p. 446).

■ I saw a copy of a literal translation . . . on Peter Wood's table. I was just being nosy. They had asked someone to adapt it but he pulled out. My interest was partly because Peter Wood would direct it and John Wood would act in it. Once I read the play I agreed with Peter. It was remarkable, a play completely unknown in England, and worthy to stand with Ibsen and English contemporaries. (Delaney, p. 132) □

At the National Theatre, William Dudley gave the play four striking and complex sets. Peter Wood directed a cast of 29, including Dorothy Tutin, John Wood, Greg Hicks and Michael Bryant.

Undiscovered Country is a naturalistic play that incorporates Ibsenesque poetic devices. The hotel high in the Alps conveys the proximity of danger and death, recalling *John Gabriel Borkman* and *When We Dead Awaken*. Schnitzler has learned from Ibsen's resonant use of offstage space. Doubles and singles tennis matches in the offstage distance suggest love games between couples who maintain a civilised façade to hide jealousy, injured pride, guilt and even relief from guilt when the partner joins in. The social background is the wealthy Austrian middle class that owns factories, or belongs to a military officer caste and resorts with successful poets and musicians. What matters most to them is the maintenance of 'honour' and control. The men observe an aristocratic duelling code – 'I am at your disposal' – and, like the women, are roughly divided into those who are capable of passion and those who, older and more sceptical, are now incapable of it, or always were.

The dramatic power of *Undiscovered Country* derives from a collision between different ages and temperaments, with the married couple at the centre sharing the characteristics of both groups. This couple's psychology is the central problem. The wife, Genia, has rejected a suitor who kills himself. This alienates her philandering husband, Friedrich Hofmeister, because her action does not absolve him from the guilt he feels about his own philandering and because he feels his wife (who continues to love him) is unconsciously blackmailing him. He is possessive, but does not wish to be possessed. He needs to be dominant and not at a moral disadvantage. When his wife finally takes a lover, Hofmeister kills him in a duel, not out of jealousy, so he says, but because he does not wish to be made a fool of. Yet Hofmeister is a kind of romantic. During a climbing holiday, 'drunk with altitude', he falls in love with a younger woman who vows eternal love. But his love does not last and the break-up of his marriage and his affair ends the play.

Adultery, with its varying effects upon the parties, is explored in the parallel situations in *The Real Thing*, but in Schnitzler the main focus is on an effete bourgeoisie, not on actors and writers. Stoppard reaffirms to Shusha Guppy that *Undiscovered Country* remains Schnitzler's:

■ I thought of Schnitzler as a modern classic, not to be monkeyed about with. But you're not doing an author a favour if the adaptation is not vibrant. So in the end I started "helping", not because Schnitzler was defective but because he was writing in 1905 in Vienna. When you write a play you use cultural references by the thousand, and they are all interconnected like a nervous system . . . (Delaney, p. 190) □

The play has been 'titivated' with 'extra flicks' and admittedly shortened. Richard Corballis argues that this has changed the original more than Stoppard implies:

■ So the extra flicks which Stoppard admits to having added often have the effect of simplifying the characters until they correspond to one or other of the two types he likes to juxtapose. That this simplification was undertaken quite deliberately is indicated by an important change in the speech, late in Act IV, in which Mauer comes as close as any of the characters to summing up the theme of the play. Provoked by Genia's assertion that life is no more than a series of foolish games, he protests, in Stoppard's version ". . . I assure you Genia . . . this hole in the corner posturing, this bogus civility between people made wretched by jealousy, cowardice, lust – I find all that sad and horrible . . . ". For Stoppard the civility is bogus . . . Schnitzler, on the other hand, has Mauer talk less absolutely of an "alternation of modesty and impudence, of cowardly jealousy and feigned indifference, of burning passion and empty lust". The moral judgement implied by Stoppard's word "bogus" is lacking here; for Schnitzler the modesty, impudence, passion and lust are equally real, and the jealousy and indifference equally despicable. He cannot reduce the complexities of the human psyche to the simple scheme that Stoppard prefers. (Corballis, p. 178) □

Corballis goes on to argue that: 'The very atmosphere is simplified too. The death motif that haunts *Das Weite Land* is severely curtailed in *Undiscovered Country*'; and he makes an extensive comparison between Schnitzler's original and Stoppard's adaptation, fitting Stoppard's play into the pattern of his book *The Mystery and the Clockwork*.

In performance, however, atmosphere and characterisation did not seem unduly simplified and Stoppard asserted that his alterations were an attempt to render the original theatricality:

■ My inventions for *Undiscovered Country* were guilty secrets, almost admissions of failure, bits of non-Schnitzler trying not to look un-Schnitzler, put in because I couldn't make the thing bounce properly. (Programme, National Theatre production of *On the Razzle*) □

And Michael Billington, who seems partly to agree with Corballis about a moral simplification, asserts nonetheless that the play is 'vintage Wiener Schnitzler':

■ What is fascinating is that the action is conducted against a background of tennis-parties, trips to the Dolomites, charade-like *affaires*, and summerhouse banter against Art Deco panels. Everything suggests a world of golden leisure and civilized deceit. But what Schnitzler shows us is the corrosive effect of habitual lying on this *Smiles of a Summer Night* atmosphere [in Ingmar Bergman's 1955 film of that title] and the destructive impact of the hero's contaminated sense of honour. (*The Guardian*, 21 June 1979) □

On The Razzle

The adaptation of *On the Razzle* was different:

■ I abandoned quite early the onus of conveying Nestroy intact into English. I'm not really a believer in the hypothesis of true translation. The particularity of a writer's voice is a mysterious collusion of sound and sense. The certain knowledge that a translation will miss it by an inch makes it less dreadful to miss it by a yard. (Programme note) □

If, in *Undiscovered Country*, he missed it by an inch, he decides in *On the Razzle* to miss it by a yard. This light-hearted, brilliant farce, also Austrian in origin, was written by Johann Nestroy in 1842 on the basis of an English one-act play by John Oxenford – *A Day Well Spent* (1835). Thornton Wilder's *The Merchant of Yonkers* (1938) and *The Matchmaker* (1954) are further reworkings – as is the musical *Hello, Dolly!* (1964). At the suggestion of Peter Wood, Stoppard adapted the play freely:

■ All the main characters and most of the plot come from Nestroy but almost none of the dialogue attempts to offer a translation of what Nestroy wrote . . . [it] makes no use of dialect, ignores period flavour in dialogue, and has no songs. It is still set in Vienna (though about fifty years later than *Einen Jux* [a 'spree']) but not essentially so. The two essentials which this play takes from the original are, firstly, the almost mythic tale of two country mice escaping to town for a day of illicit freedom, adventure, mishap, and narrow escapes from discovery; and, secondly, the prime concern to make this tale as comic an entertainment as possible. (Introduction, Faber & Faber edition, 1981, p. 7) □

It was performed in September 1981, first at the Edinburgh Festival, then at the National Theatre. Peter Wood directed Felicity Kendal, Dinsdale Landon and Joan Hickson in a cast of 24.

It is not a psychological exploration of human responses to betrayal like *Undiscovered Country* or *The Real Thing*. The usual farce plot of the older generation obstructing the young – a niece's love for a seemingly feckless suitor is thwarted by a guardian, but fulfilled when the young man improbably inherits money – runs alongside the story of two underlings in the guardian/businessman's shop who break the rules, go for a day out to the big city, and find themselves involved with their master's fiancée. With the usual good fortune, they avoid discovery and return to the provinces a little higher in social degree, immensely to their satisfaction. Property interest and social difference are mocked, but not questioned. The system is shaken up then replaced. The threat of chaos, the knockabout comedy, the catchwords, repetitions, mistakings, coincidental meetings and avoided disasters characteristic of farce are all there. The play even contains a direct comic address to the audience:

■ *Zangler*: Well, that seems all right. Just the ticket. First class. Why do I have a sense of impending disaster? (*He reflects*) Sonders is after my niece and has discovered the secret address where I am sending her to the safe keeping of my sister-in-law Miss Blumenblatt, who has never laid eyes on him, or, for that matter, on her either since she was a baby – while I have to leave my business in the charge of my assistant and an apprentice, and follow my new servant, whom

I haven't had time to introduce to anyone, to town to join the parade and take my fiancée to a fashionable restaurant in a uniform I can't sit down in.

One false move and we could have a farce on our hands. (p.309) □

Stoppard is having a day off from serious drama. This did not please Michael Billington, who observed that the 'verbal pyrotechnics' interfered with the momentum of the farce (*The Guardian*, 10 September 1981). Benedict Nightingale was even less pleased:

■ Dinsdale Landon replaces what's mean, tyrannical and potentially punitive in Zangler's character with a sort of goofy complacency, making it impossible to believe it would matter if he rumbled his disobedient underlings. Again, the tension of the main plot is dissipated; and without tension, danger, the threat of disaster, farce simply can't function. Third, it's hard to respond to raw comic event when your ears are turning somersaults lest they miss some pun, some spoonerism, some erotic innuendo, or some conceit or trick in what is, even by Stoppard's standards, a verbally hyperactive script. I myself found this doubly distracting, since I regard Stoppard's wit as a precious resource, but one, like gold or oil, that must also be finite. How could he squander so many good lines on what is – let's say it – an enterprise at best frivolous, at worst confused and silly? (*New Statesman*, 2 October 1981, p.27) □

The idea that wit, engendered by one play, is using up resources which could be saved for a different play is highly debatable. Verbal fun may be lost if the situation that produces it is ignored, and why should Stoppard not have his day off? If this farce had not fallen in Stoppard's way the hilarious lines would not have emerged from it. In any case they are not necessarily wasted and their discovery may serve as grist for some future mill. Nightingale suggests that the wit distracts from the farce situation and vice versa, but Robert Cushman has no problems either with the wit or the value of farce:

■ Apart from *Jumpers* and *The Importance of Being Earnest* there may be no script in English funnier than *On the Razzle*. From political farce and philosophical farce Mr. Stoppard has turned to writing farcical farce: both a raging example of the genre and a tribute to it . . . What makes *On the Razzle* unique is that every line in it is a joke or a part of one. (*The Observer*, 27 September 1981) □

Richard Corballis, on the other hand, acknowledges objections to the play, then tries to argue for 'something more substantial beneath the clockwork façade'. This he finds in references to time. The underling has to 'acquire a past before it's too late'. He quotes:

■ "Oh, Mr Weinberl, I have come into my kingdom and I see that it is the locked room from which you celebrate your escape! And if I have to wait until I am as old as you, that's longer than I've been alive!"

Christopher's response is to propose that they go on the razzle in Vienna. Weinberl hesitates momentarily but then indicates his support for the plan by declaring, "We'll stop the clocks". This turns out to be a malapropism for "cook the books" but for the initiates, Weinberl's slip of the tongue is a clear signal that we are about to leave the "clock-work" existence of the grocery shop for the exciting mystery of the real world. And indeed the ensuing razzle does enrich the lives of Christopher and Weinberl very markedly. (Corballis, pp. 182–3) □

Corballis's observations recall the time-clock girl in *If You're Glad, I'll be Frank* (see chapter three of this Guide).

The formal pattern of farce also raises important issues. Left-wing critics may assert (see, for example, Jean-Paul Sartre's comments on J. M. Barrie's *The Admirable Crichton* (1902) in *Sartre on Theatre* (1976)) that the farce structure shakes up the bourgeois social order only to reimpose it in Act III. But the anarchic linguistic fun of *On the Razzle* and the underlying social mockery and anarchic appeal of Act II are arguably as important as the happy ending.

It is, no doubt, unwise to be solemn about a play that has fun at the expense of solemnity, as Stoppard's anecdote about the 'flaming pudding' illustrates:

■ There's a certain moment in the play where they're in a restaurant, it was a curtain, it was a moment when an act finished and one wanted something, you know, which wasn't quite there.

I decided to have a waiter come on with what I called a flaming pudding, like a Christmas pudding, with lots of flaming spirit on it . . . So we rehearsed and rehearsed and of course you rehearse without props, the pudding or anything, you just do it, and finally we were there at the technical rehearsal: "OK where is the flaming pudding?" It turned out that because of the fire regulations at the National Theatre we couldn't have a flaming pudding. So, then there was a pause for consultation, and everyone turned to me as if it was my fault. Finally I said, "well, OK we'd better make it a cake with electric candles," so the fire people wouldn't mind. They said, "That's fine, we'll do that. Go and get me a cake with electric candles." I said, "Wait a minute. Whose birthday is it?" Nobody in this play was having a birthday. So I then made it the birthday of one of the women in the hat shop. So I said, "OK, it's *her* birthday."

When you do that – this isn't playwriting class, but I'll tell you anyway – you can't just suddenly say, "Oops, it's my birthday, here comes my cake," because the audience will not believe you. You have to get the birthday up front in Act One, and then have someone mention the birthday and finally by the time it gets to the cake the birthday must have been in the play really and properly several times and then the cake will work. Now then, this play was translated from Nestroy and without question somewhere there is an academic doing something about Nestroy or maybe even me and they say "ah". And then they write a paper or maybe set a question for some of you: "In *Einen Jux will er sich machen* (in the original) Mrs. Thing does not have a birthday. But in *On The Razzle* the plot has accommodated a whole new thread in which her birthday is really rather important. Why do you think that . . . ?" If this ever comes up you just write down, "because the National Theatre fire officers said, 'Get that fucking pudding out of here!'" (Delaney, pp. 208–9) □

Rough Crossing

Rough Crossing, first performed in October 1984, was the next adaptation that Stoppard undertook. It was first translated by P. G. Wodehouse in 1926 as *Play at the Castle*, from a play by the Hungarian dramatist Ferenc Molnár. Stoppard told Robert Gore-Langton: 'There is a great deal of invention, as I've explained, not more than a dozen lines of *Rough Crossing* will compare with the original dialogue' (*Plays and Players*, October 1984, p. 17). He thought less highly of it than the previous play:

■ *On the Razzle* was a wonderful production. It was tremendous fun and played to packed houses for however many shows it was at the National Theatre. And then it kind of disappeared. To my puzzlement, people kept reviving *Rough Crossing*, which isn't as good a play. I think *Razzle* is an expensive play to mount. That's certainly one reason, but *Rough Crossing* is quite expensive to mount, too . . . *Rough Crossing* Peter and I got rather wrong. It's worked much better in American productions I've read about. (Gussow, p. 105) □

Stoppard transposed the setting from a castle to a liner at sea and got a great deal of mileage or knottage out of the changed conditions, including puns on nautical terminology and the effect of a rough crossing on the actors' movements, especially those of the alcoholic steward Dvornichev, who reels in calm weather but finds corrective compensation in a storm.

Like *On the Razzle*, *Rough Crossing* is a high-speed farce with all the usual paraphernalia of repeated phrases, situations and actions, including Dvornichev's repeated consumption of the central character's cognac. The offstage ship's captain is an amateur playwright who suspiciously resembles the theatre-mad policeman in *Arsenic and Old Lace*. In return for his play being read by passenger and author Sandor Turai, he obligingly changes course to stop the ship rolling and allow a rehearsal to take place. How to keep the show on the road is Turai's and his co-writer's problem. They must write a musical during the four-day voyage in time for a New York opening and the project is threatened when their lovelorn and ingenuous actor/composer overhears a comically intimate love scene between his fiancée actress and her former lover from the sundeck below (there is a clever, horizontally split stage). The authors persuade the naive composer that the love scene is only a rehearsal of lines in the rapidly assembled musical.

The story enables Stoppard to have fun at the expense of commercial theatre, the successful theatre hack and the untalented but ambitious amateur. The actors have had 'a wonderful eighteen months in *Pauline Rides Pillion* and a *slightly* disappointing three weeks in *Romeo and Juliet*'. He also pokes fun at himself and at playwriting in general. Of his two commercial virtuosos, one is verbose and the other economical with words. Turai embarks on long discourses: 'You are an artist. For you there are no more women, only Woman, the female spirit etc. etc. . . . ' His partner comments: 'That gives you an idea of the kind of plays he would be writing if he didn't have me to stop him' (p.237). Stoppard knows how rhetoric and egotism can dull the critical sense. In *The Real Thing*, he illustrated the art of writing by an analogy with a cricket bat that, made and used with skill, can send a cricket ball two hundred yards in four seconds. Without the skill of the maker or performer, it sends the ball four yards and leaves the wielder clutching his hands. Similarly with writing – in *Rough Crossing* phrases go 'bonk!'. The amorous actor who can't write, but thinks he can, says: 'I love you as the moth worships the candle flame' and 'I love you as the Eiffel Tower loves the fleecy little cloud that dances around it in the summer breeze' (p.216). Turai incorporates these standard banal ingredients of commercial success into the play he is writing – the 'Cruise of the Dodo'. Meanwhile, Stoppard parodies his own problems of what to leave in and what to blue-pencil:

■ *Stoppard*: My particular twitch is to make the lines funny. (*He turns to Peter Wood*) It's not a particularly punny play is it? I can't remember.

Wood: It's extremely well-behaved. "Pre-madonna" has been cut.

Stoppard: I hope to get that back before we open.

Wood: Get it back and then you'll say, "What are they groaning at?" The moment they groan it has to come out.

Stoppard: **My family groan. My sons are like litmus paper.** (Delaney, p. 174) □

As ever, Stoppard's conversation revels in fresh metaphor. His play mocks the banal and also reshapes accidental errors of speech. 'Dodo' is a typographical mistake for 'Dido', the ship's name. Turai's play then becomes the 'Cruise of the Emu', since Dodo does not fit with Aeneas. Another typist's error, Robinsod for Robinson, is also gleefully incorporated into Turai's play which, it is implied, is likely to have more commercial success than one with a classical title. Stoppard continues to explore in different keys the problems of how to write (write about love). In *Rough Crossing*, the treatment does not encourage the audience to believe it is watching the real thing.

Dalliance

There are few critical comments on Stoppard's next, rather slight but haunting adaptation of Arthur Schnitzler's *Liebelei*. Directed by Peter Wood, *Dalliance* opened at the Lyttelton Theatre on 27 May 1986 and was predictably about love games in 1890s Vienna. It figured two pairs of young lovers and a number of minor parts, mostly musicians who furnished musical satire of the love relations between Fritz, a Hussar in the reserve, and the rather lonely daughter of a musican. The pair contrast with another couple, a light-hearted medical student and a theatre seamstress whose philanderings are perfectly understood by them as no more than a game. The dramatic tensions arise out of the dangers of Fritz's infatuation for an older married woman (who remains offstage) and the lonely young woman's love for Fritz that tempts her to risk scandal.

Dalliance begins with Fritz practising marksmanship and demonstrating that he is a poor shot. It ends when the target he has missed burns brightly in stage darkness. Fritz, in accordance with the military code of honour, is killed in a duel by the husband of the woman with whom he is infatuated. The play, like other Schnitzler plays and Stoppard's *The Real Thing*, explores the differences that exist between love, desire, infatuation and philandering. Should one be respectable and safe, it also asks, or should one follow one's impulses and 'live' – when living may easily mean dying? From a light-hearted comedy, the play turns sombre when the lonely girl expresses powerful disgust of the trivialising medical student, Theodore, who has encouraged Fritz to have 'fun', as her friend Mizi has encouraged her to do the same.

Compared with *The Undiscovered Country* or *The Real Thing*, the play is simple, though like them it is about the dangers of playing sexual and romantic games. Its importance lies in its examination of a romantic temperament, engaging dramatic sympathy for the 'romantics', but raising doubts about the nature of romanticism. As usual Stoppard, like Schnitzler, hedges his bets.

CHAPTER FOURTEEN

Later Radio and TV

The Dog It Was That Died and *Squaring the Circle*

During the period when Stoppard was adapting the four central European plays, he produced a radio drama, *The Dog It Was That Died* and a television play, *Squaring the Circle*. The first owed its existence to persistent letters and postcards from script editor Richard Imison and John Tydeman, Head of BBC Radio Drama, who directed Stoppard's six radio plays. It was broadcast in December 1982, ten years after his previous radio play, *Artist Descending*. Stoppard said, in his introduction to *The Plays for Radio*, that it 'grew from nothing other than the accumulating discomfort of failing to deliver'.

The Dog It Was That Died

The Dog It Was That Died is about a double agent called Purvis who has lost his sense of primary allegiance and wants to commit suicide. In the opening act he jumps off Chelsea Bridge, lands on a dog on a barge, and kills the dog instead of himself. Sent as a result to what another secret agent calls a funny farm, he finally wheels himself over a cliff near Cromer.

The radio medium lends itself to bizarre fantasy, which suits the atmosphere of spy stories, especially this one, in which Stoppard parodies 'Q6' and 'Q9', the equivalents of MI5 and MI6. All the characters, who regard themselves as sane, seem strange to the audience. The patients on the farm assume psychotic roles. One dresses as a matron; another is 'the Commodore'. But this 'real' insanity is not very different from the 'sanity' of the 'balanced' characters who run the spy network. They all have peculiar obsessions, manias or hobbies. Blair, apparently the sanest, is eccentric. He owns a 'folly' and collects clocks for which he has intense affection. Otherwise, his responses are unemotional and rather 'British'. But this, too, borders on the pathological. He does not, for example, seem worried that his wife, who has a good reason for stitching donkeys' wounds in the drawing room, may be having an affair with The Chief. The apparently sane Purvis lives with a Turkish ballet (or belly) dancer; the Chief smokes opium; a vicar is obsessed with the fabrication of cheese. The farm's Director loves roses, collects guano from bats in the church belfry, and is hard to distinguish from his megalomaniac patients, all of whom embrace authoritarian roles.

The parody centres on Purvis's questioning of his primary allegiance and consequent loss of identity. His second letter to Blair describes how he finds it again:

■ You might like to know that whether or not I left the fold all those years ago when my intellect aspired to rule my actions, I found at the end that my remaining affinity was with the English character, a curious bloom which at Clifftops [the 'funny farm'] merely appears in its overblown form. Looking around at the people I've rubbed up against, I see that with the significant exception of my friend in Highgate they all inhabit a sort of Clifftops catchment area . . . (pp. 189–90) □

Purvis, like Stoppard, feels at home with English eccentricity – the kind of thing Orwell commented on in 'England Your England' (see *Inside the Whale and Other Essays* (1962)) – and it seems to breed the bizarre strain in Stoppard's work. But although *The Dog It Was That Died* spoofs eccentric behaviour, it hints at questions about identity which have concerned dramatists since Shakespeare. Lunatics, lovers, poets and playwrights are near allied. The condition in which a writer subdues his personal views in order to give full dramatic and even moral force to opposite viewpoints is not far from schizophrenia, the invasion of the self by other voices which Pirandello speaks of in *Six Characters in Search of an Author*, or Keats in his famous letter about 'negative capability' – the creative dissolution of personal identity. Coleridge was right, too, when he spoke of children in play never allowing the role to eclipse the person they are. The trick is to retain a sense of self or one goes over the edge. And writing a play, like playing a game of doctors and nurses, is to visit but not to become a patient at the Clifftops. *The Dog It Was That Died* seems, in part, to be about its own processes.

Anthony Jenkins takes a different approach and sees the play as a parody of Stoppard's need, as a Czech, to overcome the threat of not belonging:

■ Stoppard has always had a fondness for eccentrics, and much has been written about his English guise, "plus anglais que les anglais"; his "costly casual dandyism" [Tynan in *Show People*, pp. 46–7], his love of cricket, his Home-Counties life-style. Colleagues have even suggested its connection with his unwillingness to take sides; "He's basically a displaced person. Therefore he doesn't want to stick his neck out. He feels grateful to Britain, because he sees himself as a guest here, [like Professor Anderson in Prague in *Professional Foul?*] and that makes it difficult for him to criticize Britain." Partly he is laughing at that lurid picture of himself when he laughs at these mad dogs of Englishmen (the play's title comes from Goldsmith's "Elegy on the Death of a Mad Dog"). The whole play turns on this fellow-feeling for the English; no malice waits to pounce from behind the farce. Instead, individualism is revealed as England's saving grace, more powerful than any "system". Consequently his eccentrics are all well-meaning; the "firm" has been completely defanged; the Blairs' marriage ambles along despite Pamela's liaison with the Chief; a general regard for the right of other people to live their own lives prevails. (Jenkins, p.175) □

If Stoppard's 'Englishness' is a defence mechanism, he has certainly objectified it by parody. For the listener, however, despite (or because of) the parodic treatment of madness and suicide, this spy story remains troubling.

The Dog It Was That Died could be considered a dry run for *Hapgood* (1988), the stage drama about espionage. Before that, however, Stoppard made a foray into documentary TV with a play about the Polish *Solidarity* movement of 1980–1.

Squaring the Circle

Squaring the Circle was transmitted on Channel 4 in May 1984 and is very different in tone and genre from *The Dog It Was That Died*. 'Whether it is a play at all or a drama documentary, is a question, though perhaps not a vital one', says Stoppard in his introduction. It has 122 scenes and uses 44 settings plus 50 named characters and many extras – witnesses, aides, secretaries, policemen, etc. The cast included John Woodvine, Roy Kinnear, Bernard Hill, Tom Wilkinson and Alec McCowan. Mike Hodges directed.

Stoppard's description in his preface of the economic and cultural pressures on this high-cost production is fascinating. He recounts a struggle for artistic freedom against the American firm Metromedia that parallels the Polish struggle against the communist regime. Metromedia thought that financing the TV film gave it absolute control of the script. Mike Hodges and Stoppard fought the company and eventually won back important features that the company wished to eliminate. These mainly involved the figure of the Narrator, usually a functional device to link complex historical material and save time by narrating the offstage story, like the Chorus in *Henry V*. Narrators, even Shakespeare's, become suspect when they express opinions; Stoppard wished to remind the TV audience of the dangers of expounding history and created an unreliable Narrator, as Conrad and Henry James had done in fiction many decades before. This procedure led to a dispute with a company that wanted to supply its audience with an acceptable and simplified product. Metromedia was dubious about whether raising an audience's doubts would improve business. Author and director, however, managed to rescue most of the original 'final' draft.

One way of representing historical process is by dramatising scenes involving opposing power groups and bringing them together in dialogue and conflict at crucial points of decision when they spell out the political and economic pressures they act under, or combat and attempt to control. Moral preference for one side or the other, for the 'free world' over communism, for example, may be communicated by loaded forms of presentation. The TV public may prefer to be confirmed in its prejudices, and many producers assume that this is the case. But *Squaring the Circle* avoids propaganda though it employs caricature and satire.

The play opens with two meetings between Leonid Brezhnev and the Polish CP leader Edward Gierek. The camera cuts between caricatures of the leaders in dark suits to a replay of them wearing Hawaian shirts and slacks. The effect, which stage drama cannot easily copy, challenged the validity of the caricatural process in the name of realism.

The same scene is repeated in further meetings between Brezhnev and subsequent Polish leaders: 'In an atmosphere of cordiality and complete mutual understanding the two leaders had a frank exchange of views' (p. 191). Diplomacy conceals historical exchanges that will not be in the public domain for many decades if, indeed, they ever emerge from the archives. 'Who knows?', says the Narrator to the camera, and when indeed he presents loaded scenes (dressing the Politburo as gangsters, for example, or having children make comments on the democratic socialist leader, 'poor Mr Kuron'), he is corrected by a Witness who calls attention to the Narrator's bias (but makes judgements of his own). Thus, as in *Travesties*, where Stoppard presents his historical characters through the prism of the unreliable memory of Henry Carr, the Narrator in *Squaring the Circle* emphasises the essential complexity of historical writing and the dangers of speculation and caricatural simplification. The spectator is not patronised but invited to consider modes of presentation. Brecht, who liked problematic endings, would not have disapproved.

In a play that presents conflict between powerful institutions, the representatives of those institutions must debate the issues. The Soviet Union exerts pressure from outside, afraid of the break-up of the Warsaw Pact countries it then dominated. Within Poland, the power groups are the Party, the Army, the Government, the Church and *Solidarity*. In the course of the play, General Jaruzelski acquires power and comes to represent the first three of these. Then he engages in a crucial private debate with Archbishop Glemp and Lech Walesa, the respective representatives of the fourth and fifth groups. How the meeting went and who sided with whom is not known, so Stoppard dramatises the players' potential differences and shared interests in three successive, alternative, scenes. In each the three characters play a card game and Jaruzelski at first takes the tricks. A fallacious metaphor? A three-handed card game in which two players gang up on the other is perhaps a simplified image. But it may be closer to the truth than the conventional comparison with two opposing politicians playing chess. (Why is it always chess? asks the Witness.) For the Narrator, 'Everything is true except the words and the pictures. It wasn't a card game' (p.258). The visual metaphor, he reminds us, only stands for one possible mode of representation.

By comparison, the general settings seem more 'real', partly because they lack visual appeal (but not interest) and the language that accompanies them is appropriately 'realistic', abrasive and utilitarian. Characters speak their minds directly, frankly, brutally (and occasionally ironically to the enemy, when playing political word games). Stoppard's usual fun with English words would be scarcely appropriate in a play about a Poland struggling to achieve freedom. He therefore employs 'transparent' dialogue, which calls attention, not to itself, but to historical situations in which characters interrogate how events can be controlled.

Film image and editing rather than dazzling discourse is the mode of communication. The spectator is moved rapidly and vividly in 122 cuts from seashore to car, to café, to office, to street, to prison, to boardroom, to hospital, to courtroom, to steelworks, to parade ground, to playground, to police cell, to seashore. But the aesthetics of film discourse are of minor importance compared with the play's central thesis that independent unions and Soviet socialism cannot be squared, any more than a circle.

The winner of the contest (before 1989) was the 'head waiter', Jaruzelski, who predicted that a military solution was the inevitable outcome – 'We'll get there – you have my guarantee' (p.213). How far the play is fair to Jaruzelski is uncertain; but this distinguished piece of documentary film – a fictive 'faction' – stands with (and against) the post-1968 political drama of Trevor Griffiths, David Hare, Howard Brenton and Howard Barker.

'What comment does it finally make?', one may ask. Joan Dean observes: 'In some ways *Squaring the Circle* contains Stoppard's most "Brechtian" dramaturgy. (Ironically, its politics are decidedly anti-Brechtian or at least anti-communist)' (Harty, p.249). Anthony Jenkins also remarks on Stoppard's caricatural 'Brechtian' practice and defines Stoppard's views, following Stoppard's own description, as conservative with a small 'c':

■ Enlarging these gangster types to farcical proportions, Stoppard ensures that we see his monsters as cardboard shams. Like an image from an old movie, First Secretary Kania, smothered in his barber's shaving lather, inveighs against "people who think that the Party boss can run the operation like a Chicago gangster" (64) and lists a string of disasters ("Al Capone wouldn't have lasted out the week") as if he were in some sort of farce. But the social circumstances make it a bitter one.

The "quirky bits" provide Stoppard with a way of saying what he thinks about the regime, because simply to blast them as gangsters, cheats, shams and liars would have sounded as banal as love did to Henry [in *The Real Thing*]. But the quirkiness also provides him with a way of threading together a vast amount of factual material, as it did in *Jumpers* and *Travesties*. One of the wonders of this script is the economy with which he moves from scene to scene, using his comedy and the vocabulary of film with a sense of design that has grown more subtle and supple since the days of *Neutral Ground*. To convey the unyielding circle around the reformist's zeal, a large conference table interspersed with flags gives a quick sketch of a Warsaw Pact meeting which we come in on as the East German minister concludes his fulminations against the Polish government's weak reaction to "an attack on social- ism, an attack on everyone here" (66). A pause adjusts the rhythm of the scene and out of that, Brezhnev, seated across from the Polish dele- gation, explains "in a fairly friendly manner" that Poland once had its own free trade union – "He is in a lunatic asylum now, poor fellow" – and that if the Polish Party "cannot defend itself . . . it must be defended". The picture instantly dissolves to a group of high-ranking officers in greatcoats who casually watch their armies' off-screen manoeuvres. Marshall Kulikov turns to Jaruzelski and adds the punchline to this cartoon: "Well, I don't know what this is doing to the Poles but it's scaring the hell out of the Americans" (67) . . . The scene changes to the First Secretary's office where a flunky arranges files on the empty desk; the General walks in, takes possession and, pleased with what he sees, flicks at his uniform: "You don't think the effect is . . . a bit South American?"

Theatrical illusionist, serious gamester, fence sitter, master tacti- cian, cold formalist: the old labels could all be applied to the Stoppard of *Squaring the Circle* without accounting for their changing combin- ation from scene to scene and without getting him quite right. That they describe the *way* he writes, rather than *what* he writes, points up the unarguable fact that it is the style of each play that hits us first. But to stop there is to ignore the man who makes the stylish strokes with each well-made cricket bat [a reference to *The Real Thing*]. Behind his dash, finesse and complexity, Stoppard's values are small-'c' conservative and surprisingly simple. Endlessly curious about seeming and being, the way people misunderstand each other, the words that entrap or betray them, and humbled by these confusions, Stoppard distrusts slogans yet loves to pick at clichés. He is essentially benevolent, though wary of sentiment, and his truths are self-evident and inviolate: individuals have a right to be happy and free, and to mistreat people or to persuade them that happiness and freedom are other than they *know* them to be is wrong. (Jenkins, pp. 180–1) □

Jenkins describes the way, in *Squaring the Circle*, that caricature defines false ways of seeing, and thus contributes to the realism of the play. He also states that Stoppard takes a human, not a political, stand, a form of 'liberal humanism', which can be castigated as 'sitting on the fence'. Joan Dean asserts, without criticising Stoppard, that, unlike Brecht's drama, '*Squaring the Circle* does not intend to galvanize the audience to action' (Harty, p. 249). One answer to this would be that an attempt to render the complex truth of things communicates to its audience a form of political awareness that encourages beneficent change when conditions are ripe. For Stoppard, journalism was far more effective in prompting immediate change, as he says in his 'ambushes' interview (Trussler, p. 67). In certain circumstances, of course, the need for political action may be more important than producing a political drama. But a writer can scarcely be blamed for attempting to write impartially, especially when the political structure allows a free debate.

CHAPTER FIFTEEN

Triple Twinning

Hapgood

Stoppard's next big project, *Hapgood*, opened at the Aldwych Theatre on 8 March 1988. Felicity Kendal, Nigel Hawthorne and Roger Rees took the main parts and Peter Wood again directed. Act I has five scenes and five sets, repeated in Act II with two more added. Stoppard described to Shusha Guppy what happened to the text in rehearsal:

■ I am suffering from the usual delusion that the play was ready before we went into production. It happens every time. I give my publisher the finished text of the play . . . but by the time the galleys arrive they're hopelessly out of date because of all the changes I've made during rehearsals. (Delaney, p. 178) □

A theatre script is never final, and Stoppard is not a writer who would have it so. In *Hapgood*, the female secretary Madge became the male 'Maggs', so that he could understudy another part. *Hapgood* became two acts rather than three to suit audience preferences for a single interval. Changes in lighting were thought necessary in a play where light became a metaphor for human personality. Stoppard also realised that the audience required certain plot information in the second, not the third, scene: 'it's like pulling out entrails', he told his interviewer.

Ostensibly, *Hapgood* is a spy story in which the central figure, Elizabeth Hapgood, her superior, Blair, and an American agent, Wates, are setting a trap to find which of their secret agents has betrayed them to the KGB. The prime suspect is the Russian scientist, Kerner, who has been 'turned' some years before by Hapgood, but the actual traitor is a less attractive figure called Ridley. 'Whodunnit?', however, matters less than 'how?', and beyond the 'how' lie complex questions about the natural world and human personality:

■ The subject matter of the play exists before the story and it is always something abstract. I get interested in a notion of some kind and see that it has dramatic possibilities. Gradually I see how a pure idea can be married with a dramatic event . . . For *Hapgood* the thing I wanted to write about seemed to suit the form of an espionage thriller. (Delaney, p.179) □

The original idea arose out of Stoppard's interest in mathematics:

■ I didn't research quantum mechanics but I was fascinated by the mystery which lies in the foundation of the observable world, of which the most familiar example is the wave/particle duality of light. I thought it was a good metaphor for human personality. The language of espionage lends itself to this duality – think of the double agent . . . (Delaney, p.180) □

Stoppard's interest in natural science and human identity combined with a new spy story and the standard farce strategem of confusing pairs of identical twins. Like *Shakespeare's Comedy of Errors, Hapgood* has two pairs. Stoppard even adds a third, since the main character pretends to be her own non-existent, but very different, twin sister.

Twins challenge the idea of single identity. In Shakespeare's *Comedy Of Errors* twins are mistaken for one another, sow confusion, and begin to doubt their own sanity, but the audience is aware of the existence of twins and laughs at the characters' ignorance. The audience of *Hapgood* remains ignorant and must guess that there are two pairs of twin spies in order to solve the problem of a spy being in two different places at the same time. In farce the audience has superior knowledge, but in the spy story secrets are buried and the audience seeks to be relieved of its uncertainty. The twins in *Hapgood* solve a puzzle.

The challenge for Stoppard's audience, however, does not mainly reside in finding the 'mole'. It lies in trying to work out Stoppard's analogy between the ambiguity of the natural world and the duality of human character:

■ *Gussow*: If there's a central idea in the play, it is the proposition that in each of our characters is the working majority of a dual personality, part of which is always there in a submerged state.

Stoppard: That was the hypothesis which generated the play itself, that the dual nature of light works for people as well as things, and the one you meet in public is simply the working majority of that person. It's a conceit. It may have some truth to it. (Gussow, p.78) □

To enable the audience to focus on such complex problems and at the same time to follow the convoluted plans and subtle minds of those who will trap the mole, Stoppard breaks the conventions of the spy genre and identifies the traitor in the first act. Unfortunately, many playgoers and reviewers still found the complexity of the process too great for their concentration:

■ *Hapgood* was a kind of struggle from the word go and I was still dealing with it at the Lincoln Center, trying to explain, simplify. We started off by referring to it as a melodrama. The way you label something is very helpful: it gets you out of the corner. Once I began to think of *Hapgood* as a melodrama, I felt much more comfortable with it, because it is melodramatic. It's not satiric about the spy business. It operates on a heightened, slightly implausible level of life. It's probably the only play I've written, as far as I can remember offhand, in which somebody shoots somebody onstage. [It also happens in *Jumpers*] (Gussow, p. 106) □

Melodramatic it may be, but the play goes a long way beyond the simple moral oppositions of a melodrama and its mode of suspense is very different. Stoppard's initial natural suspect, the likeable Russian, Joseph Kerner, has been planted as a 'sleeper' in England and, as aforesaid, 'turned' into a 'joe' by his lover, Hapgood, the female head of the British operation to whom he has given a child, also called Joe. But Kerner is not the guilty party. Ridley inadvertently lets slip what only a Russian agent could have known – that twin Russian agents are at work. Kerner obliquely confirms Ridley's guilt and his own innocence by commenting on genre conventions in spy stories that pin the guilt on the most likeable and therefore least suspected:

■ When I have learned the language I will write my own book. The traitor will be the one you don't like very much, it will be a scandal. Also I will reveal him at the beginning. I don't understand this mania for surprises. If the author knows, it's rude not to tell. In science this is understood: what is interesting is to know what is happening. When I write an experiment I do not wish to be *surprised*. It is not a joke. That is why a science paper is a beautiful thing . . . (p. 47) □

Stoppard, through Kerner, is talking about the method of his own play. He has surprised his audiences in the past but is now, like Kerner, less interested in jokes and surprises than in the duplicity of the natural world that is revealed by quantum mechanics and Einstein's theory of relativity. He voices disapproval of the standard means of keeping an audience in suspense by suppressing a simple secret.

When the mole is identified early, the technical problem resides in finding another form of suspense – the kind that invites a spectator or reader to see or read a play a second time for its human and intellectual interest and for its dramatic skill. Visual choreography and rapid scene changes add powerfully to the dramatic appeal, and the vivid monologues of Kerner concerning the ambiguity of nature and the electron discuss fascinating ideas, while they remain metaphorically and naturalistically relevant to the human drama:

■ *Kerner*: . . . One day Konstantin Belov jumped out of his bathtub and shouted "Eureka!". In Russian it means, "Twins!". Maybe he shouted, "By jimini!".
Hapgood: You're mischievous.
Joseph: Maybe he was asleep in his bath. The particle world is the dream world of the intelligence officer. An electron can be here or there at the same moment. You can choose; it can go from here to there without going in between; it can pass through two doors at the same time, or from one door to another by a path which is there for all to see until someone looks and then the act of looking has made it take a different path. Its movements cannot be anticipated because it has no reasons. It defeats surveillance because when you know what it's doing you can't be certain where it is, and when you know where it is you can't be certain what it's doing: Heisenberg's uncertainty principle; and this is not because you're not looking carefully enough, it is because there is *no such thing* as an electron with a definite position and a definite momentum; you fix one, you lose the other, and it's all done without tricks, it's the real world, it is awake.
Hapgood: Joseph, please explain to me about the twins.
Kerner: I just did but you missed it.
(*pause*)
Hapgood: So you did. It's crazy.
Kerner: (*unmoved*) Oh, yes . . . but compared to the electron it is banal. . . . (p. 48) □

Dialogue which dovetails the electron with twin double agents is worth hearing twice.

Subtext in the play also becomes very important. Stoppard observes to Guppy: 'The ideal is to make the groundwork so deep and solid that the actors are continually discovering new possibilities under the surface' (p. 179). This dimension is to be found in the games of dominance between spies and national spy networks. An apparently simple exchange, for instance, where the American agent asks Blair to come to the washroom and Blair sends him a message to stop washing his hands, has a strong flavour of Pinter's subtextual games in which two characters strive for dominance or attempt to set up an undisclosed alliance at the expense of a third. This occurs in Pinter's *The Caretaker* (1960) and, of course, Stoppard himself in *Squaring the Circle* had dramatised concealed motives and possible alliances between Glemp, Walesa and Jaruzelski.

Even without subtext, the basic story is complex enough to remain intriguing. The second or even third performances help to clarify the plot. The unconventional ending also retains a power to surprise. The 'traitor' is shot by a woman – or is this no longer against convention? But for Stoppard, as we have said, the story is a means to a different end; the investigation of fascinating, important and complex subject matter: the nature of Nature and human identity. The relation between classical or Newtonian mechanics that seems to provide a satisfactory explanation of the world we know, and the micro-world of atomic physics in which the single electron in a hydrogen atom resembles a fluttering moth in an empty cathedral – which can also be in two places at the same time – is a metaphysical problem. The powerful notion and the poetic description lend a dimension to the play well beyond melodrama.

As ever, Stoppard's imagination leaps between normally separate fields. Indeed his description of the way a play evolves – two trains running on the same line simultaneously – resembles the behaviour of the world as conceived by the German physicist Max Planck (1858–1947), the originator of quantum theory. Stoppard adds the nature of the writer's creativity to the question of dual identity and the metaphor of the 'double' characters who are duplicitous and double crossing. Two Russians pretend to be the same person and enact a 'drop' in the bewildering choreographed opening, based on a well-known mathematical conundrum concerning the seven bridges of Königsberg and the impossible task of crossing all of them while crossing each only once. This is impossible unless one person is in two different places simultaneously or unless there are identical twins. If we are very quick, we may identify Ridley as half of an identical twin pair. Our identification probably occurs only late in the play. One twin, we find, has carried out a murder, while the other provided an alibi by sitting elsewhere in a car with the spymaster Hapgood. As aforesaid, Stoppard revealed the mole, Ridley, in Act I, but he concealed his twin. In this way Stoppard follows as well as subverts the convention.

Hapgood herself, in the trap to catch Ridley, pretends to be her own twin, alike in appearance, very different in behaviour and language. The 'working majority' gives way to a submerged self or, as Stoppard puts it in another interview:

■ The play is specifically about a woman – Hapgood – who is one person in the morning but who finds that, under certain pressures, there is a little anarchist upsetting the apple cart. The central idea is that

inside Hapgood One there is Hapgood Two sharing the same body; and that goes for most of us. (Delaney, p. 194) □

Other kinds of 'twinning' occur – names echo each other and have two meanings. Kerner's and Hapgood's child is called Joe and his father is a 'joe' in more than one sense. Characters oscillate between public and private behaviour. Hapgood operates on many levels – she plays mental chess and solves her son's school problems over the phone. (He has lost a key and must track it down – another metaphorical parallel.) At the same time she sorts her mail and foils the suspicions of the American agent, Wates, that she is herself a Russian agent. Her ability to play four games simultaneously makes her a kind of quadruple agent, like the Russian physicist who fathers her son and keeps a photograph of him despite the requirements of his profession. Hapgood and Kerner have a private world as well as a public function. The two inevitably get mixed up when secrets from private lives are used as pressures to 'turn' the agents one way or the other.

Set against Hapgood and Kerner are two characters who know where they stand. Blair, as in *The Dog It Was That Died*, and the American, Wates, have no identity problems, though they lie and play games. They seem very little different, morally, from the world of the KGB that doubles the British Intelligence Service. Blair, unconventionally, turns out to be a villain but not a spy, since he manipulates Hapgood's son in his games to trap Ridley, who is less of a villain because he acts out of sympathy for the child. Ultimately, perhaps, despite the similarity of eastern and western spy systems, the play comes down on the side of the west. And though the Russian Kerner wishes, like the double agent in *Neutral Ground*, to go back home, he lingers at the end as his son plays rugby. The western system, Kerner says, has in it the democratic seeds of its own reversal.

We have since seen, just as Stoppard in 1987 could not, that two years later the Soviet regime could be upended. The seeds of a reversal of the eastern system as well as the western might arguably be found in Marx's original human sympathies, which remained ingrained in the political system that Lenin and Stalin developed. What is striking in *Hapgood* is the continuing existence of personal feelings within opposing spy systems that seem equally inhuman.

The ending of the play, which suggests that Kerner may stay in the west for his son's sake was, for Anthony Jenkins, too easy, and this is the note on which he ends his book. He refers back to *The Dog It Was That Died* and the despair of the double agent Purvis:

■ Espionage is a blacker joke in *Hapgood*, but Stoppard does not allow Elizabeth [Hapgood] to confront that darkness [Purvis's suicidal despair] and thereby reassess her values or defend them knowingly. No chasm yawns for her. Disheartened by the fact that she must have been "buying nothing but lies and chickenfeed since Joe was in his pram" (87) she "opts out of it" and turns instead to her son and his school's conservative standards: a relatively painless escape. Like her, we glimpse the randomness behind those standards without fully experiencing what that implies. The political and moral dualities of Stoppard's theme slide away beneath the last scene's gentle, but inadequate pathos. In consequence, *Hapgood* rocks our minds and senses but, in all its wondrous symmetry, leaves life much as we thought it was. (Jenkins, pp. 191–2) □

Both Elizabeth and the audience might have learned more from a tragic confrontation. But *Hapgood* is a comedy, a play of ideas, and a thriller with elements of farce. The relative optimism of the ending may be justified by the comic frame within which the audience is invited to see things for the first time. Katherine Kelly would go further and argues that the play's value lies in its showing spectators that interpretation resides in their own heads:

■ *Hapgood* does not attempt to improve upon *The Real Thing* as a treatment of the art-life exchange, but to give it a new theatrical expression that accounts for the presence of the interpreting spectator . ... the power of metaphor finally belongs to the spectators, following clues, watching demonstrations, sifting evidence, making connections. *Hapgood* attempts to present in the theatre an image of the mysteries of human behaviour that cannot be solved and to recognize that in the act of observing these images, we are in part determining the meaning we will find in them. (Kelly, pp. 157–8) □

Heisenberg's uncertainty principle is thus applied to the theatre audience, who, if they see the play as a comedy, will remind themselves that it is they who partly project it.

CHAPTER SIXTEEN

Discovering the Past and Predicting the Future

Arcadia

Stoppard's next full-scale stage play, *Arcadia*, opened at the Lyttelton Theatre on 4 April 1993. Trevor Nunn directed Harriet Walter, Felicity Kendal and Bill Nighy in a cast of twelve. Paul Delaney describes the response:

■ First-night reviews of *Arcadia* . . . ranged from denunciations of "The play's central vacuum, its fatal lack of living contact between ideas and people" to celebrations of an "unusually moving" play in which "Stoppard's ideas and emotions seamlessly coincide". In any event, Stoppard's first full-length original play to be performed at the National since *Jumpers* played to sold-out houses and the National Theatre book-stalls broke all records for sales of a playscript. (Delaney, p. 265) □

If *Hapgood* was a mixed play that Stoppard called a melodrama, it is tempting to label *Arcadia* a tragicomedy. For this play, however, Stoppard didn't need a label:

■ *Gussow*: How would you categorise *Arcadia*?

Stoppard: Because I was happy with it anyway, I didn't need to label it. I didn't need to get myself off the hook.

Gussow: Some people think it's your best play [This is becoming a critical consensus].

Stoppard: I know they do. I think that's what they're talking about. The story works best.

Gussow: Did you feel you got it more together than in other plays?

Stoppard: I did, yes. *Professional Foul* was another one; it seemed like that. The other kind of play – *Travesties* being a good example – at that time of my life, the passing show, the showing-off, if you like, the pastiche and the jokes and the theatricality of it, was what the play was flourishing and boasting about. What one did was to attach it to a pretty stripped down little wagon, just so that these things had some wheels to run on. *Arcadia* and *Travesties* are like opposites of one another. (p. 107) ☐

Stoppard felt that *Arcadia* had moved beyond the fireworks and intellectual display of *Jumpers* and *Travesties*. It is about a young girl in the early 1800s who anticipates the discoveries of post-Newtonian science. After her death her tutor becomes a hermit who seeks to develop her insights. Their story and that of visitors, including Lord Byron, to the country house in which she dwelt, are investigated by twentieth-century researchers in scenes which alternate with those set in the early nineteenth century. While the play was 'cooking', Stoppard said: 'It's about literary detection . . . about people speculating about what happens . . . and in theory the fun is seeing how wrong they can be, because we've been there and they haven't' (Delaney, p. 259). The remark suggests that the play is mainly comedy at the expense of the researchers, but the complexity of the scientific ideas and the presence of witty characters of high intelligence prevents any full sense of audience superiority. Sombre notes are sounded at intervals and become louder at the end, so that the label of tragicomedy seems closer to the mark.

Stoppard says that his plays originate in ideas and *Arcadia* is about kinds of creativity – about creating gardens and landscapes, writing literary history, writing or failing to write poetry, making scientific and historical discoveries, or inventing false explanations. Mel Gussow suggests that the play originated from reading James Gleick's book, *Chaos* (1988). Stoppard demurred. The creative process is not an 'orderly natural development':

■ *Stoppard*: . . . It's like a river with more than one source. There's no 'where' about it. You just mentioned the *Chaos* mathematics book. At the same time, I was thinking about Romanticism and Classicism as opposites in style, taste, temperament, art . . . The romantic temperament has a classical person wildly signalling, and vice versa . . .

Gussow: No single acorn?

Stoppard: It's more than that. I have the feeling that you throw the acorn away at some point . . . an alternative way of making a picture of the process would be to say that it's something that starts you up . . . like a cranking handle. Then you throw the handle away, and drive off down the road somewhere and see where the road goes . . . I don't think *Arcadia* says very much about these two sides of the human personality . . . I don't think it's in the play. It's by no means in the foreground. And yet, it's firing all around the target, making a pattern around the target. (Gussow, p. 89) □

The analogy between the analytical classical and 'intuitive' romantic sides of the personality recalls Kerner's description in *Hapgood* of the wave/particle experiment with light. *Arcadia*, despite Stoppard's denial, suggests the duality of his own creative temperament and stages a comparison of different creative temperaments. The play, in short, is about the processes of its own creation within a much wider vision of the natural and historical processes that go on around it.

Stoppard observes that the 'subconscious usefulness' of general reading can subvert the primary conscious mind to the advantage of the creative state: 'I'd read one or two books about Byron over the years . . . with a faint sense of undisclosed purpose' (Gussow, p. 90). Ideas from Byron and landscape gardening combined with the original ideas. *Arcadia* became a study of the nature of historical and scientific research. Vivid characters inhabit a world in which the passage of time casts a long shadow over them, whilst a bright light is shed on their endeavour.

Formally, if not theoretically, it is very different from *Hapgood*. Instead of a series of complex scene changes, the whole action takes place in a single, unchanging, classically elegant room in a stately home. What changes is the unseen space outside. The park has, in the early eighteenth century, been a symmetrical Italian garden, recreated later by Capability Brown in a tranquil English style. When the play begins in 1809, it is being retransformed into a picturesque, Salvator Rosa-inspired, Gothick landscape with mock ruins and a phoney hermitage. The unseen outdoors is evoked by sound effects: steam engines are digging trenches to create artificial lakes, gunshots indicate that grouse, rabbits, hares, or even men are being shot – for what is in this pastoral, indeed Arcadian landscape is a tomb with an inscription, *Et in Arcadia ego*: 'even in Arcadia I, Death, am there' (or 'I, who am now dead, lived once in Arcadia').

Unlike *Hapgood*, *Arcadia* has no puzzling visual choreography until the end when twentieth-century characters don period costume for a fête and mix with their early nineteenth-century counterparts. The drama plays with time rather than space, alternating the action between 1809 and the present, and counterpointing vivid characters who speak in a decorously caustic eighteenth-century manner against descendants and researchers who speak with often abrasive, colloquial, modern voices. Characters from each period, however, are engaged in finding things out. 'It's wanting to know that makes us matter. Otherwise we're going out the same way we came in' (p. 75), says Hannah, a twentieth-century literary historian investigating the romantic period whose classical temperament corresponds to her sardonic subject, Septimus Hodge, the tutor of the brilliant young early nineteenth-century mathematician, Thomasina, whose insights into the processes of nature relate, in their turn, to the research of a modern Oxford post-graduate student called Valentine.

Thomasina sees the future in pictures. Her vision is as sombre as Byron's poem *Darkness*, which Hannah quotes:

■ I had a dream which was not all a dream.
The bright sun was extinguished, and the stars
Did wander darkling in the eternal space,
Rayless, and pathless, and the icy earth . . . (p. 79) □

Both anticipate the second law of thermodynamics – the law that states that the irreversibility of the transfer of heat leads to the extinction of energy and the death of the universe. The young Thomasina sees entropy in pictures. Yet her gaiety and vitality contrast with the sombre vision that is to send her tutor mad. Arcadia is a happy place, yet we are reminded of the speaker of *'Et in Arcadia ego'* in the poignant final reminder to Thomasina to be careful of the candle she is taking to bed. We know that fire will consume her as it will eventually consume the earth.

Nevertheless, gaiety suffuses a play that first shows the audience events of 1809 that the twentieth-century characters, especially a 'media don' called Bernard Nightingale, struggle to construe on slender evidence. Bernard jumps to wrong conclusions as his romantic enthusiasm collides with Hannah's classical caution. Other characters interpret according to their temperament and Stoppard makes play with their conflicting lines of thought:

■ *Bernard*: Where was I?
Valentine: Pigeons.
Chloe: Sex.
Hannah: Literature. (p. 55) □

Oscar Wilde also contributes to the play's gaiety in the person of Lady Croom, suspiciously similar to Lady Bracknell in her speech rhythms and stern views:

■ *Lady Croom*: Pray what is this rustic hovel that presumes to super-impose itself on my gazebo?
Noakes: That is the hermitage, madam.
Lady Croom: I am bewildered.

Brice: It is all irregular, Mr Noakes.

Noakes: It is, sir. Irregularity is one of the chiefest principles of the picturesque style.

Lady Croom: But Sidley Park was already a picture, and a most amiable picture, too. The slopes are green and gentle. The trees are companionably grouped at intervals that show them to advantage. The rill is a serpentine ribbon unwound from the lake peaceably contained by meadows on which the right amount of sheep are tastefully arranged – in short, it is nature as God intended, and I can say with the painter, *'Et in Arcadia ego!'* 'Here I am in Arcadia,' Thomasina.

Thomasina: Yes, mama, if you would have it so.

Lady Croom: Is she correcting my taste or my translation?

Thomasina: Neither are beyond correction, mama, but it was your geography caused the doubt.

Lady Croom: Something has occurred with the girl since I saw her last, and surely that was yesterday. How old are you this morning?

Thomasina: Thirteen years and ten months, mama. (p. 12) ☐

In Arcadia it is eternal spring. Work, ownership, walls, conflict and the passage of time are eliminated. Yet there is a tomb in the landscape which Lady Croom's mistranslation ignores. Sure enough, gunshots are heard. Pigeons are being shot, it later appears, by Lord Byron, and Valentine's game books record the slaughter of grouse, rooks, partridge, snipe, teal and the culling of the herd – a two-hundred-year calendar of slaughter, the Arcadian world of the early nineteenth-century aristocracy.

Within this environment, the dialogue is amusing but scarcely consolatory. Thomasina is involved in solving Fermat's last theorem. She asks:

■ When you stir your rice pudding, Septimus, the spoonful of jam spreads itself around making red trails like the picture of a meteor in my astronomical atlas. But if you stir backward the jam will not come together again. Indeed the pudding does not notice and continues to turn pink just as before. Do you think this is odd?

Septimus: No.

Thomasina: Well, I do. You cannot stir things apart.

Septimus: No more you can. Time must needs run backward, and since it will not, we must stir our way onward, mixing as we go, disorder out of disorder into disorder until pink is complete, unchanging and unchangeable, and we are done with it for ever. This is known as free will or self-determination. (*He picks up the tortoise and moves it a few inches as though it had strayed, on top of some loose papers, and admonishes it.*) Sit!

Thomasina: Septimus, do you think God is a Newtonian?

> *Septimus*: An Etonian? Almost certainly, I'm afraid . . . (pp. 4–5) □

The problem of the rice pudding runs through the play. You cannot stir time backward. In the next (modern) scene, Valentine attempts to discover a pattern for the varying number of grouse shot each season. He is distracted by what he calls 'noise', that is, irrelevant information. Other characters, too, are distracted – by the cacophonous sound of the steam pump beating out the seconds, or occasional gunshots, or the piano discordantly played in the next room. All of these interfere with their desire for harmonious solutions in a universe where ordered systems inevitably tend towards the random.

The implications of the second law of thermodynamics are sombre, but harmonious patterns exist – such as Thomasina's graphs of nature and chaos, which Septimus with only pencil and paper goes mad in his hermitage trying to solve. Valentine, however, creates them on his computer, thereby suggesting that some things can be recovered from time. Arcadia contains a tomb but, like the garden of Eden, it also contains a tree of knowledge. And when the silent character called Augustus or Gus, offers Hannah an apple, and then hands her the evidence she needs to identify her hermit, the joy of rediscovery counters the sombre concept of entropy. The play enacts a moment when things come together. Septimus and Thomasina, Hannah and Gus waltz – smoothly in the one case, more awkwardly in the other – but Hannah has learned to dance. This counts for something, though not perhaps as much as the catastrophe that is to come.

In literary tradition, Golden Ages exist in the past or in the future. Catastrophes – flood, death, doomsday – always separate us from Arcadia or Paradise or the Garden of Eden. But at the heart of this brilliant, witty and ultimately sad play, there is a vision of beauty in the present, even though Thomasina doubts her mama's geography when she declares: 'Here I am in Arcadia.' A golden moment, if not an age, occurs as a state of consciousness saved from time.

■ *Valentine*: The heat goes into the mix.
  Thomasina: Yes we must hurry if we're going to dance.
  Valentine: And everything is mixing the same way, all the time, irreversibly.
  Septimus: Oh, we have time I think.
  Valentine: Till there's no time left. That's what time means.
  Septimus: When we have found all the mysteries and lost all the meaning, we will be alone on an empty shore.
  Thomasina: Then we will dance. Is this a waltz?
  Septimus: It will serve. (p. 94) □

Past and present mingle on the stage and speak simultaneously in a moment of time that the play has created. The quiet Gus lives in both periods. He gives Hannah her apple and she joins the dance. Septimus and Thomasina waltz and embrace amid a vision of time ending.

It seems appropriate to quote an extract from James Gleick's aforementioned *Chaos*:

■ . . . the twentieth century's best expression of . . . flow needed the language of poetry. Wallace Stevens, for example, asserted a feeling about the world that stepped ahead of the knowledge available to physicists. He has an uncanny suspicion about flow, how it repeated itself while changing:

"The flecked river
Which kept flowing and never the same way twice, flowing
Through many places, as if it stood still in one."

Stevens' poetry often imparts a vision of tumult in atmosphere and water. It also conveys a faith about the invisible forms that order takes in nature, a belief:

"that, in the shadowless atmosphere,
The knowledge of things lay round but unperceived."

When Libchaber and some other experimenters in the 1970s began looking at the motion of fluids, they did so with something approaching this subversive poetic intent. They suspected a connection between motion and universal form. They accumulated data in the only way possible, writing down numbers or recording them in a digital computer. But then they looked for ways to organize the data in ways that would reveal shapes. They hoped to express shapes in terms of motion. They were convinced that dynamical shapes like flame and organic shapes like leaves borrowed their form from some not-yet-understood weaving of forces . . . their conception came close to what Stevens felt as an "insolid billowing of the solid":

"The vigour of glory, a glittering in the veins,
As things emerged and moved and were dissolved,

Either in distance, change or nothingness,
The visible transformations of summer night,

An argentine abstraction approaching form
And suddenly denying itself away." (Gleick, p. 196) ☐

To this may be added a quotation from the original National Theatre programme. It comes from Paul Davies's book, *The Cosmic Blueprint* (1987), in which the idea of entropy is challenged:

■ Hidden deep in the overall process of running down towards total disorganisation where all atomic activity is flattened out to zero, nature organizes pockets of resistance where time's arrow is swung around to point in the direction of continuing creation. □

If some first-night reviewers felt that such ideas had not been fused with the human interest, others felt that they emphatically had. In 1995, Michael Billington reviewed Stoppard's career up to *Arcadia*:

■ A new Stoppard is always an event. It also provokes an ongoing assessment of his output. Two years ago a *Guardian* headline asked: "Can *Arcadia* revive a faltering career?" Well, we all know the answer to that one. *Arcadia* is still running at the Haymarket even as a new work – *Indian Ink* – is about to open at the Aldwych. Meanwhile in New York, Stoppard will shortly become the first playwright to have two plays running concurrently at the Lincoln Centre: *Hapgood* in the Mitzi E. Newhouse Auditorium and *Arcadia* opening on March 2 in the Vivian Beaumont . . . [Stoppard's career] has an organic shape to it and an ability to respond to perceived deficiencies. Just as people were beginning to question his stylish, apolitical detachment, he wrote *Every Good Boy Deserves Favour* and *Professional Foul* which dealt with fundamental issues of human rights. Can't cope, for all his cleverness, with the quotidian emotions of love, pain and grief? He disproves it with *The Real Thing*. No good at writing convincing female characters? He responds with *Hapgood* and *Arcadia*. (*The Guardian*, 8 February 1995) □

Billington read Paul Delaney's anthology of interviews, *Tom Stoppard in Conversation*, and remarked on Stoppard's 'unusual awareness of his strengths and limitations', presumably implying that an awareness of what he has not yet accomplished lies behind his capacity to continue to develop. He argues that Stoppard has changed his approach:

■ What is new is his increased willingness to accept the chaos and unpredictability of personal relationships or universal laws, his belief in the heroic nature of curiosity. As the literary scholar says in *Arcadia*: "It's wanting to know that makes us matter." □

Billington then remarks on the pattern of 'collision' in the plays, only to hesitate to apply the word to Stoppard's recent drama, with 'its emphasis on harmony and continuity as much as disjunction and opposition'. He quotes Hannah again, and Valentine's exultation at the collapse of simple scientific determinism: 'It's the best possible time to be alive when almost everything you thought you knew is wrong'.

■ This is totally new Stoppard. Where the early work is filled with fear of chaos, darkness, the decline of moral absolutes and scientific certainties, the later work has an almost defiant optimism . . . by emphasising the cyclical continuity of history, the endless appetite for knowledge and the possibility of love, Stoppard strikes a distinctive note.

His early work, to misquote Disraeli on Gladstone, now seems inebriated with the exuberance of his own virtuosity; his later work with its acceptance of mortality and muddle, strikes me as more mellow and durable. Whether *Indian Ink* is equally indelible we shall soon know. (*The Guardian*, 8 February 1995) □

CHAPTER SEVENTEEN

From Radio to Stage

In The Native State and *Indian Ink*

In between the stage productions of *Hapgood* and *Arcadia*, Stoppard directed the film of *Rosencrantz and Guildenstern Are Dead*. This delayed by a year the promised delivery of a major radio play, *In the Native State*, which was broadcast on BBC Radio 3 on 21 April 1991. It predates *Arcadia*, with which it has things in common – both plays switch across time and in each play we see modern researchers trying to recover the past. After *Arcadia* (1993), the play was expanded into a stage play and renamed *Indian Ink* (1995).

In The Native State

In The Native State, directed by John Tydeman, went on air with a cast of 13 almost ten years after the previous radio play, *The Dog It Was That Died*. Felicity Kendal played the part of a poetess, Flora Crewe, who goes to India in 1930 and dies there of consumption. Peggy Ashcroft played the role of her sister, Mrs Swan, still alive in 1990, who entertains a literary biographer, and the son of the Indian painter, Das, who painted Flora before she came to enjoy a posthumous fame. The play gains its power from the alternation between pre- and post-independent India and from the discovery of events, enacted and narrated in letters by Flora, which took place in 1930. John Tydeman felt it was the best thing that Stoppard had written: 'It has flesh and blood. One is moved by it. So often in the past his cleverness has got in the way and he's hidden his feelings under the pyrotechnics . . . ' (Delaney, p.252). Stoppard tells Gillian Reynolds (*Daily Telegraph*, 20 April 1991) how he finished directing the film of *Rosencrantz and Guildenstern* in July, 'got going in September, and delivered the radio play in October':

■ It began as odd pages, dialogue and stuff. I kept trying to find what play they belonged to. I thought I was going to write a play simply about the portrait of a woman writing a poem and her poem is about being painted. Then I found the idea of her poetry so perversely enjoyable I went on writing her poetry for far longer than you'd believe. (Delaney, p. 249) □

The play typically combined two kinds of creative activity – this time poetry and painting rather than playwriting and acting (*The Real Thing*), science and the art of double crossing (*Hapgood*) or acting and scientific discovery in the film of *Rosencrantz and Guildenstern*. It led into *Arcadia*, a play, as we have seen, about poetry, science and creative research.

But *In The Native State* is not only about poetry and painting. When asked by Paul Allen about its origin, Stoppard said:

■ Certainly the main one was a rather generalised idea to write about the empire, and more particularly the ethics of empire. And I'm not saying that *In the Native State* is *that*. In a way I still want to do that. This play is some sort of introduction to the subject for me. (Delaney, p. 240) □

As usual there were several points of departure, but Stoppard stresses that 'the process of writing the play determines the way it goes much more than one starts off thinking it will' (Delaney, p. 240). The character of Flora took a powerful and somewhat unexpected grip on the play within the world of empire that encloses her and about which Stoppard feels that there is still a play to do. Felicity Kendal certainly felt the main focus was on poetry and the way language in radio can be used to create poetic cross-connections:

■ This play is to do with language rather than action and it lends itself particularly well to radio; it isn't the story that's the thing, it's the spider's web of ideas and circumstances, written very carefully with a lot of loops that loop into something else. (Delaney, p. 252) □

The play seems very Chekhovian. The characters hint at experience behind the stage action and they possess secrets. Flora's is that she is seriously ill and tells only the painter, Das. She feels he has revealed a private confidence when she discovers everyone from the English Resident to the Rajah is aware of it. But letters have been opened – her English contacts make her politically sensitive – and Flora's private life is revealed as part of a public web. Just as Chekhov's plays create space and time around the action, providing a rich Russian social background for his leisured gentry, Stoppard's sick poetess, Flora Crewe, having her portrait painted in Jummapur, is involved in a sense of the decline of the British Raj and the post-war independence of the sub-continent.

The play moves between Flora's death in India in 1930 and England in 1990 where her poems and letters have made her an important subject for literary research. An American academic, Eldon Pike, is editing a collection of letters and writing a biography. He interviews Flora's sister, Mrs Swan and Anish Das, the son of Nirad Das, who painted Flora 60 years earlier. His interviewees decide not to reveal all they know, in particular the existence of a second painting, a nude, which would raise personal questions of a kind they feel should remain private. The full answers to Pike's questions are, in any case, only known to the dead, and his biography of Flora will remain incomplete.

Around this story about art, creativity and the interpretation of the past, Stoppard weaves suggestions of personal lives in England as well as India. Mrs Swan has been the mistress of a communist candidate in British General Elections and has had – and lost – a child by him. She has married Francis Swan, an official of the Raj, now dead. Back in England and more conservative in her old age, she plies Anish Das with tea and cakes. Das has recognised his father's painting on the cover of Flora's *Collected Poems*. They talk in 1990 of the Raj, of Indian Independence, of the Mutiny, of Moslems and Hindus, of Gandhi and the nationalists, of the English community. So, in alternating scenes, do Flora, Das and a young English officer David Durance, from their pre-Independence viewpoint in 1930. The literary life of London in the 20s is recalled briefly and intriguingly. H. G. Wells, Mrs Blavatsky and the Theosophical Society, Diaghilev, and J. C. Squire (poet, journalist and editor of the Georgian poets and *London Mercury*) battle with the Sitwells. Flora tells us she broke off an engagement while at an exhibition of Modigliani's paintings at Heal's in Tottenham Court Road. Visits to Rome and Venice are left a mystery. In India the life of the English Club is briefly evoked, together with the looming of independence and the history of the Raj, including the effect of the opening of the Suez canal and the subsequent export of Anglo-Indian wives. The play ends with Flora reading on a train from Emily Eden's impressions of India in 1839:

■ . . . and we one hundred and five Europeans being surrounded by at least three thousand mountaineers, who, wrapped up in their hill blankets, looked on at what we call our polite amusements, and bowed to the ground if a European came near them. I sometimes wonder they do not cut all our heads off and say nothing more about it. (*The train clatters loudly and fades with the light*) (p. 83) □

The vivid and varying discourse of the characters and further brief hints of their personal lives – Flora and Mrs Swan, for example, have lost their mother on the *Titanic* – give the characters the flesh and blood of which the director, John Tydeman, speaks. Contributing strongly to this sense of life is the atmosphere of India, the heat, the beauty of moonlight and sunrise, the sense of time past and the need to live in the present.

Literary and political references enhance this poetic play and the evocation of Indian literature and painting creates a further dimension. Stoppard said he had 'read a million words about India when I needed a tiny fraction of that reading' (Delaney, p. 239). But the reading enables his Indians to refer with apparent authority to schools of Indian painters and strengthens the vivid counterpointing of Indian with English culture.

Stoppard pays tribute in the play (p. 30) to Forster's *A Passage to India* (1924) that also subtly portrays the powerful tension between cultures. Paul Allen suggests in interview that the play has 'a kind of polarised feeling in which you very fairly give a shout to both sides'. Stoppard replies:

■ . . . that's mixed up with the personalities who have to carry nearly all of the dialectic in the 1930s scenes. I think that there *are* two oppositions at work in the play, but they're not cut and dried. Just to take the first and most obvious point, it's the Indian who loves things English . . . his references are English and he obviously is in a kind of thrall to English culture. And it's the Englishwoman who finally says: "It's all bosh you know. It's your country and we've got it; everything else is bosh". (Delaney, p. 243) □

Stoppard's point is that the cultures and languages overlap, and he demonstrates it in Das and Flora's language game:

■ *Flora*: While having tiffin on the verandah of my bungalow, I spilled kedgeree on my dungarees and had to go to the gymkhana in my pyjamas looking like a coolie.
Das: I was buying chutney in the bazaar when a thug who had escaped from the choky ran amuck and killed a box-wallah for his loot, creating a hullabaloo and landing himself in the mulligatawny. (p. 209) □

English has absorbed Indian culture, but English is also the language which united India, providing the *lingua franca* in which nationalists communicated. And there are other Anglo-Indian paradoxes: Anish Das is married to an Australian and considers England his home. His father, though in thrall to English culture, was an Indian nationalist. The Rajah of Jammapur, however, educated at Harrow, approves of the British Raj and the furniture in his palace is from Heal's. On the other hand, Mrs Swan, wife of an Anglo-Indian, thinks of NW India as 'home'. Her house in England is furnished with Indian furniture; yet in India it is full of reminiscences of England. The cultures overlap and yet maintain a separation. At the English club, the natives are kept rigidly away, even the educated Indians. Only the servants are allowed to enter.

Stoppard weaves this tension into the discussion of the nature of creativity, notably in a comparison between the nude and clothed portraits of Flora. The nude portrait impresses both Flora and Mrs Swan as an accomplished work of art, whereas the other is too pre-Raphaelite, too English, too imitative and yet glaring in an Indian style. The nude portrait mixes styles differently. It is both naturalistic and Indian – flat, ornate and symbolic, compared with the European three-dimensional style. But it has what the play defines as *'rasa'*, a mysterious quality that seems to have arisen from a strong sympathy between sitter and painter and which is lacking in the clothed painting. During the sitting for the latter, Flora has begun to write a letter instead of her poem. Her action spoils the rapport when the painter, Nirad Das, assumes she is dissatisfied.

■ *Das*: You looked at the painting and decided to spend the time writing letters. Why not?
Flora: I'm sorry
Das: You still have said nothing about the painting.
Flora: I know.
Das: I cannot continue today.
Flora: I understand. Will we try again tomorrow?
Das: Tomorrow is Sunday.
Flora: The next day.
Das: Perhaps I cannot continue at all.
Flora: Oh. And all because I said nothing. Are you at the mercy of every wind that blows? Or fails to blow? Are you an artist at all?
Das: Perhaps not! A mere sketcher . . . (pp. 234–5) □

Flora struggles to prevent Das taking down the easel. This sets up a new rapport, which results in Das painting the private nude. Flora has wanted Nirad Das to be more Indian, not to speak or paint to please *her*, but to please himself. This kind of selfishness, Stoppard interestingly suggests, is important for an artist. Art is not about politeness, and when Modigliani painted her, Flora points out, he painted her as an *object*: 'when I paint a table I don't have to show it to the table' (p. 210). He did not paint a portrait as a gift to the sitter.

This might suggest a view of art as fundamentally cold. The transaction between Nirad Das and Flora, however, derives from her unspoken poem about heat and sex. It results in the second private painting and – so we discover if we are attentive – in Das spending the night with Flora (Durance sees Das on the road as he comes to collect Flora at sunrise). Heat, art and desire are subtly connected with cold creativity. India combines with England and the separation between nations and cultures that Forster defined in *A Passage to India* is momentarily overcome.

The historical background, in this complex play, gives force, often by contrast, to the creative life within it. The attractive English officer, Durance, who also falls for Flora, has the attitudes of his class. He loves India, but feels superior to the Indians and lives at the Club with the English community. He proposes to Flora and is flatly turned down. This is partly because Flora is ill. But this pleasant man is also, the play suggests, destructive in nature, for he would kill the moths and shoot the sand grouse. Flora is surely right to refuse his proposal of marriage, as she refused her fiancé when he burned her portrait by Modigliani.

Art emerges as mysterious and important, and in the discussion of it the term *rasa* is crucial. Das tells Flora it is a feeling created by the moon, the scent of sandalwood, an empty house:

■ *Das*: *Rasa* is what you feel when you see a painting, or hear music; it is the feeling the poet must arouse in you.
Flora: And poetry? Does a poem have *rasa*?
Das: Oh yes! Without *rasa* it is not a poem, only words. That is the famous dictum of Vishvanata, a great teacher of poetry, six hundred years ago.
Flora: *Rasa* . . . yes. My poem has no *rasa*.
Das: Or perhaps it has two *rasas* which are in conflict.
Flora: Oh . . .
Das: There are nine *rasas*, each one a different colour. I should say mood. But each mood has its colour – white for laughter and fun, red for anger, grey for sorrow . . . each one has its own name, and its own god, too. (p. 221) □

Stoppard is less concerned with the white *rasa* of laughter than with the blue-black *rasa* of erotic love, which goes with all other *rasas* except cruelty, disgust and sloth. Its god is Vishnu and it is called Shringara. Moonlight has stimulated it and perhaps the empty house that Das speaks of is the life Flora is about to leave. Death may destroy, but the idea of death, as Forster again once remarked, is creative. *In the Native State* deserves more critical attention than it has yet received.

Indian Ink

After writing *In The Native State*, Stoppard worked on *Arcadia*, then adapted his radio play for the stage. Renamed *Indian Ink*, it was first performed at the Yvonne Arnaud Theatre in Guildford and had its London première at the Aldwych Theatre on 27 February 1995. Peter Wood directed and Felicity Kendal, Margaret Tyzack and Art Malik took leading roles in the increased cast of 18.

Stoppard admitted to Mel Gussow (p. 108) that his work had changed. His characters, as John Tydeman remarked, were fuller and more completely individualised. And in *In The Native State*, the two central roles were female. Gussow observes: 'You used to say, though I never completely believed it, that all your characters sounded like you'. Stoppard replies: 'I think everybody in *Night and Day* sounds like me'. Stoppard may, previously, have heavily relied on the actor's physical presence and voice to characterise his articulate language, but he adds: 'it's less true now. It's certainly not true of *Indian Ink*' (p. 108). Characters in the play are highly individualised, both within and across the racial divide. Apart from the silent servant, they are very articulate, but the Indian dialogue is strongly differentiated from the more sober speech of the Europeans. It tends to be ebullient and exclamatory, rejoicing in dead metaphor – 'top-hole', 'red-letter day' – personal without always being frank, making sweeping statements, 'jumping through hoops of delight', as Flora says, and very courteous. Stoppard admits to having picked up forms of Indian speech from books, but it has vitality and makes convincing individual rhythms in the head. The film *Shakespeare Wallah* (1965), which shows the Kendal family playing Shakespeare in India, was doubtless an important source. *Indian Ink* is dedicated to the memory of Laura Kendal, and Felicity was a child among the travelling players.

In The Native State and *Indian Ink* are not written for the same media and although the substance of the two plays remains similar, and many of the observations about the radio play apply also to *Indian Ink*, it is worth noting their differences. The stage play does not require as much narrative description of setting since the set is in view. Sound effects are less prominent. There is no need to specify, for instance, that footsteps walk across a sandy, not a metalled surround, or that a table has a brass top to emphasise the chink of teacups. Mrs Swan no longer needs a stick as a radio sound effect, since her movements can now be seen. She can be younger and her stage movements consequently easier. So Stoppard places the play in the mid-80s and gives Mrs Swan's year of birth as 1909.

Radio plays are very versatile and change scenes instantaneously by the use of sound effects and verbal reference. Sophicated stage techniques, however, make the relative clumsiness of theatre scene-shifting less of a problem. Thus the opening scene, which the radio play describes by letter in Scene Nine, is enacted on stage. Flora arrives in Jammapur, sitting alone at dusk in a moving train approaching the station. By the end of her first speech she is on the station platform. Seven lines of dialogue later:

■ *The handshake which begins on the station platform ends on the verandah of the 'Dak Bungalow', or guesthouse. The guesthouse requires a verandah and an interior which includes, or comprises, a bedroom . . .* (p. 1) □

The scenes of *In The Native State* alternate in place and time, whereas in *Arcadia* they alternate only in time. In the final scene of both plays, however, characters from different periods mingle. The stage is not demarcated between England and India. A preliminary note suggested that *'floor space, and even furniture, may be common'*. Lighting changes and careful direction shift the temporal and spatial focus. Clever use is made of letters written by Flora, picked from a pile in England by the American researcher, Pike, and read aloud by Flora, over 50 years dead. The sense of time passing, which lends a particular poignancy to *Arcadia*, is again strongly present. It owes itself in both plays to the ironic contrasting of two groups, one aware of the past, the other focused on its daily and immediate life. The Chekhovian sense of time and sudden stabs of sadness also emerge from Pike's footnotes to Flora's letters:

■ The man was probably the Junior Political Agent at the Residency, Captain David Arthur Durance, who took F.C. dancing and horse-riding. He was killed at Kohima in March 1944 when British and American troops halted the advance of the Japanese forces. (p. 62) □

A feeling that flesh is grass, present in *Artist Descending a Staircase* and, for that matter, in *Rosencrantz and Guildenstern Are Dead*, grows stronger. Flora's death occurs very soon after she leaves Jammapur for the hills. Her intention 'to take years and years about it' is not fulfilled.

Thomasina in *Arcadia* also died young and the writing of *Arcadia* may have prompted the development of Pike in *Indian Ink*. He is given an Indian assistant, Dilip, and his role is considerably expanded. He is more serious and less vital than *Arcadia*'s Bernard Nightingale, but, like that researcher from Sussex, he is excited by literary discovery. He does not jump so rapidly to conclusions on insufficient evidence, but possesses the same capacity for misinterpretation. He quotes Flora's letter:

■ *Pike*: "I had a funny dream last night about the Queen's Elm". Which Queen? What Elm? Why was she dreaming about a tree? So this is where I come in, wearing my editor's hat. To lighten the darkness.
Mrs Swan: It's a pub in the Fulham Road.
Pike: Thank you. This is why God made writers, so the rest of us can publish. (p. 4) □

Pike is kept in the dark about the nude portrait as, the play implies, he deserves to be. He is not allowed to exaggerate, for his own aggrandisement, the importance of a detail in a poet's private life that only the dead characters know. Dilip tells him:

■ You are constructing an edifice of speculation on a smudge of paint on paper, which no longer exists.
Pike: It must exist – look how far I've come to find it.
Dilip: Oh, very Indian. (p. 61) □

The American is thinking like an Indian, the Indian like a European. Stoppard mixes the characteristics and mocks national caricatures. Pike's enthusiasm distorts his logic but drives on the search. The portrait exists, but although the play tells the audience, no one tells Pike. History and the Partition have destroyed the Dak bungalow. Pike sifts assiduously through the wreckage of time, but some things must remain hidden and what is lost cannot be produced as verifiable research. It can only be imagined in a dramatic fiction that represents a general, not a particular, truth.

The history of empire, the smells and sounds of India, pi-dogs fighting, the sweat and heat and the beggars, create a strong sense of reality. At the play's centre is the twin theme of death and creativity embodied in Flora's poem, which lends *'rasa'* to the portrait being painted simultaneously. Again, Stoppard's central question is creativity and it is not surprising that his next play is about an authentic, not a fictional, poet.

CHAPTER EIGHTEEN

Scholarship and Poetry

The Invention of Love

Two years after *Indian Ink*, *The Invention of Love* (a play about A.E. Housman), directed this time by Richard Eyre, opened at the Cottesloe Theatre on 25 September 1997. A cast of 13, including John Wood as the old Housman, Michael Bryant as Charon and Paul Rhys as the young Housman, played 23 characters.

The life and poetry of A.E. Housman would not at first appear to be a promising dramatic subject, since neither his personal life nor his professional life were eventful. Flamboyant extroverts are more obviously theatrical material and Housman might seem to lack dramatic colour, compared with a number of his contemporaries, especially Oscar Wilde and the older Oxford dons such as Pater, Pattison, Ruskin and Jowett, all of whom appear in the play. Stoppard, however, saw dramatic potential in Housman's dual character. The finest classical scholar of his time, with a highly combative, acerbic scholar's wit, was, at the same time, a poet obsessed with the twin themes of love and loss.

Stoppard's interest in Housman emerges in the previous play. At the beginning of Act II of *Indian Ink*, the Resident asks Flora, the poetess, whether she has 'come across' Alfred Housman:

■ *Flora*: Yes, indeed I have!
Resident: A dry old stick isn't he?
Flora: Oh – come *across him* –
Resident: He hauled me through *'Ars Amatoria'* when I was up at Trinity.
Flora: The Art of Love?
Resident: When it comes to love, he said, you're either an Ovid man or a Virgil man – *omnia vincit amor* – that's Virgil – "Love sweeps all before it, and we give way to love" – *et nos cedamus amori*. Housman was an Ovid man – *et mihi cedet amor* – "Love gives way to me".
Flora: I'm a Virgil man.

Resident: Are you? Well it widens one's circle of acquaintance.
(p. 46) □

Unlike Flora in fiction and Oscar Wilde in fact, Housman's circle of
acquaintance was certainly restricted. Oscar, who is a Virgil man, makes
a late entrance in *The Invention of Love* and asks Housman who their common friends are: 'Did you know Henry Irving? Lily Langtree? No? The
Prince of Wales? You did *have* friends?' (p. 97). 'I did have colleagues',
Housman replies. Housman's friends are a fellow classicist, Pollard, and
an athlete and scientist, Moses Jackson, for whom he had an ideal, life-
long, unrequited love. Apart from these, the characters in *The Invention of
Love* include a colleague, Chamberlain; his sister, Kate, the only woman
in the play; a number of Oxford and Cambridge notables; three famous
journalists who are not acquaintances; and Charon who ferries the dead.

The play has no substantial plot. It consists of nearly 40 short scenes,
most of them duologues, connected associatively rather than causally.
The old Housman is dying in the Evelyn Nursing Home in Cambridge in
1936, but instead of an obvious and naturalistic setting, Stoppard creates
a scene in keeping with the imagination of a classical scholar. He places
him on the banks of the Styx, where he encounters old memories and
waits for Charon to ferry him over.

Without a dramatic situation to build on, the play slowly creates its
own past by enacting scenes of Oxford life watched by the old Housman.
Charon arrives, thinking Housman is two people, the scholar and poet.
He meets one and waits for the other. Meanwhile, Housman's young
student friends and his younger self arrive; the Oxford scholars converse,
creating offstage space by talking mainly of the doings of Oscar Wilde.
The young Housman speaks to his friend Jackson and to two of the dons.
Then AEH, the older Housman, meets his younger self and discourses
with him for 16 pages of script. Jackson and Pollard arrive and converse
with the young Housman. Then Charon is seen poling the Oxford don,
Pattison, across the Styx. AEH remarks: 'When he died it was the first
time Pattison finished anything he started' (p. 49).

These words begin a long three-page simulation of a classics class at
the end of Act I, in which Housman gravely and amusingly holds up to
scrutiny the flat or. faulty Latin translations of the students. The poetic
quality of Housman's mind, as well as his astringent wit, come clearly
through his own renderings of material which parallels his personal
situation *vis-à-vis* Jackson:

■ Here is Horace at the age of fifty, pretending not to mind, verse 29,
me nec femina nec puer, iam nec spes animi credula mutui – where's the
verb? anyone? *iuvat*, thank you, it delights me not, what doesn't?
neither woman nor boy, nor the *spes credula*, the credulous hope,

animi mutui – yes, well, mutual mind is roughly right, shared mind,
yes but he means love requited . . .
    – never mind, here is Horace not minding, taking no pleasure in
woman or boy, nor the trusting hope of love returned . . . (p. 51) □

The surface dialogue, as ever, is entertaining in itself. The tension lent by
dramatic subtext slowly builds, as Housman's hopeless love for Jackson
both intensifies his life and takes half of it away. It is reminiscent of
Henry James's advice to L. P. Smith: 'If you want to be a writer there is
one word you must inscribe upon your scutcheon – loneliness'. It also
bears a similarity to Stoppard's description in *Indian Ink* of the Indian
culture-seekers: 'like children with their faces jammed to the railings of
an unattainable park' (p. 6). Isolation and introversion are not un-
dramatic, only harder to deal with in a theatre that conventionally
favours characters who externalise feelings.

To energise the slow build-up of the story, Stoppard uses the technique he employed in *Travesties* – an old man looking back at his younger
self – but rather than, as in the earlier play, creating a virtuoso role in
which John Wood could play both the old and young selves of the same
character, he divides the Housman part between John Wood and a
young actor, Paul Rhys. The two can now debate instead of alternate. In
this way the old comedy pattern of the split self takes on a graver tone.

Stoppard makes imaginative use of location. The stage is necessarily
sombre, like the poetry, but the Styx doubles with the Isis at Oxford and
the stage lightens when the younger Housman with his two friends row
up and down the river. Act II begins with the young Housman and his
sister at sunset looking westwards to Housman country and beyond
Shropshire into Wales and the Black Country. The young men picnic on
the banks of 'Hades'. The darkness closes in when Charon ferries his
souls, but the night is starry and bonfires glow on Jubilee Night, June
1897 (exactly a hundred years before the play was put on). Then Charon
and Housman fade into the mist.

The contrast between Housman and his more extravagant contemporaries also has dramatic force. The journalists, Labouchère, Harris and
Stead have no personal connection with Housman, but their discussions
evoke the historical context of Housman's personal tragedy. Harris, a
notorious liar, who, according to Max Beerbohm, only told the truth
when his imagination failed him, lends more colour to the dialogue. The
journalists contrast with the aesthetes, Pater and Wilde. They create the
world around the play, talking of General Gordon, the Siege of Paris,
Oscar Wilde's visit to America, and the Criminal Law Amendment Act
relating to homosexual practices. They contrast with each other in their
moral and amoral attitudes, as do the scholars Pater and Ruskin, Jowett
and Pattison. The journalists bring in the present; the scholars speak of

the past: but 'Greek' practices form the subject matter of both, building up to the entrance of Oscar Wilde and his imaginary dialogue with Housman in Act II.

The play thus consists of a series of encounters, rather like the forest meetings and joustings between Shakespeare's wise men and fools in *As You Like It*. It uses both pastoral and ironic anti-pastoral, suffused by a melancholy that Shakespeare's play dispels, but that is dominant here in the sombre setting. The scholars discourse as they play croquet to get them on and off stage. Jackson, the runner, enters in running kit, exhausted like Adam in Shakespeare's play, but young, not old. Pater and Wilde wear extravagant costume; literary and historical references fill out the story; and Stoppardian themes, such as the dangers and value of biography, or the question of how to shed light on present and past, return to intrigue the spectator.

At the centre, as in *Indian Ink*, the play revolves around love and death. The climax to which the play builds is Jackson's discovery of Housman's 'Greek' tendencies:

■ *Housman*: . . .Virtue! What happened to it? It had a good run – centuries! – it was still virtue in Socrates to admire a beautiful youth, virtue to be beautiful and admired, it was still there, grubbier and a shadow of itself but still there, for my Roman poets who competed for women and boys as the fancy took them; virtue in Horace to shed tears of love over Ligurinus on the athletic field. Well, not any more, eh, Mo? Virtue is what women have to lose, the rest is vice. Pollard thinks I'm sweet on you, too, though he hardly knows he thinks it. Will you mind if I go to live somewhere but close by?
Jackson: Why?
Oh . . .
Housman: We'll still be friends, won't we?
Jackson: Oh!
Housman: Did you not really know, even for a minute?
Jackson: How could I know? You seem just like . . . you know, normal. You're not one of those aesthete types or anything – (*angrily*) how could I know?
Housman: You mean if I dressed like the Three Musketeers you'd have suspected? You're half my life . . . (pp. 79–80) □

The conversation ends with Jackson putting out his hand:

■ (*Darkness, except on Housman*)
Housman:
He would not stay for me; and who can wonder?
He would not stay for me to stand and gaze.

I shook his hand and tore my heart in sunder
(*Light on A E H*)
And went with half my life about my ways. (p.81) □

Poetry (and light), economically used, is highly dramatic when placed within convincingly natural dialogue and a human situation.

In this case, as has been said, Stoppard uses the lyrical poetry of an actual poet rather than inventing lines for a fictional one. This treads on the boundaries of biography that, Stoppard reminded us in *Indian Ink* and *Arcadia*, is a suspect way of shedding light on lives that wish to remain private. In this play, a character again expresses misgivings:

■ *Housman*: . . . my life was not short enough for me to not do the things I wanted to not do, but they were few and the jackals will find it hard scavenging . . . (pp.98–9) □

A dramatic biography is selective, evidently semi-fictional and need not scavenge. The pains and joys of personal lives set within a general situation have been a subject of drama since Greek tragedy and Shakespeare's Histories. There the lives were the mainly public ones of heroes and kings. Stoppard's protagonist is relatively private, even muted. But *The Invention of Love* lends fresh life to Housman and his poetry, vividly representing him in dialogue and situations of character-istic paradox. Through Housman, connections with the past, with Ovid, Virgil and especially Horace, are renewed. The apparent academic lumber is brought alive again in the present.

CHAPTER NINETEEN

Film Scripts

Shakespeare in Love

Stoppard has written and co-written a number of screen and TV plays. He wrote the early, short TV plays, *A Separate Peace*, *Teeth* and *Another Moon Called Earth* and was commissioned by Granada TV in 1965 to write a play for a series on myths and legends. The result, *Neutral Ground*, based on Sophocles' *Philoctetes*, used outdoor locations and was transmitted in 1968. In 1974, he adapted Jerome K. Jerome's *Three Men in a Boat* for BBC Television and scripted for the large screen *The Romantic Englishwoman*, directed by Joseph Losey. The following year, he co-wrote with Clive Exton *The Boundary*, a half-hour play, broadcast live by BBC TV. In 1977, *Professional Foul* received the British Television Critics Award for the best play. Yet, in 1977, we find him saying to Anthony Smith in a British Council audio-recording, 'I don't feel I've done any films. A chap did a short film of a radio play of mine, *The Dissolution of Dominic Boot* . . . '.

Some of the work may be described as 'professional writing' and it is not always easy or even possible to separate Stoppard's contribution from that of his co-writers and directors. This, for example, is what he says of *The Romantic Englishwoman*:

■ . . . it was a film which didn't interest me in the least. I was very interested in working with Joe Losey, and I rewrote most of the dialogue, and changed the plot, but it was far from my heart as a job.

I've written a film based on the life of Galileo, which nobody ever did (it was commissioned by Paramount but not done), which I think is probably quite a good script in a literary way. You know how it is, they say, "Would you do this film?" and I say, "you do realise I'm rather sort of verbose, a literary kind of writer," and they say "yes, that's why we want you . . . " and then you write the script and they say, "well, you know, it's rather wordy . . . ". I wrote a film version of *Rosencrantz and Guildenstern* which was never done . . . but this year I have adapted a Vladimir Nabokov novel called *Despair* (1978) . . . for the German director, Fassbinder, and this week the word is that this will be shot in April with Dirk Bogarde. And if that happens, as far as I'm concerned, that'll be my first film. (A. Smith, British Council recording, 1977) □

Stoppard was attracted by the aesthetic and intellectual possibilities of film but pessimistic, at this stage, of achieving control: 'There's a lot of technicians, and a lot of money, and little time, and a lot of muscle, and a lot of people over the title, and, you know, the position of the writer in films is notorious, i.e. supine' (A. Smith, British Council recording, 1977).

By the year 2000, however, Stoppard's screenplays included *The Human Factor* (1979), from the novel by Graham Greene; *Brazil* (1985), directed by Terry Gilliam; *Empire of the Sun* (1987), from the novel by J.G. Ballard and directed by Steven Spielberg; *Rosencrantz and Guildenstern Are Dead* (1991), directed by himself; and the tremendous box office success (co-scripted with Marc Norman), *Shakespeare in Love* (1998).

Brazil, directed by Terry Gilliam, shows important signs of Stoppard's hand. Felicia Londré, in an essay in the collection edited by John Harty, *Tom Stoppard: A Casebook*, argues that much of the film bears his clear imprint:

■ Stoppard has frequently spoofed the complexity of modern life as he does in *Brazil* with the many plugged phones and the ubiquitous ducts. Sam is an ineffectual hero trying to rise above those complexities in the tradition of George Moore in *Jumpers*, or the title characters of *Albert's Bridge* and *Lord Malquist and Mr Moon*. In the latter work, Mr Moon receives wounds in both hands; in *Brazil*, Sam's beloved Jill has a bandaged hand, Mr Kurtzman hurts his hand so he can't sign a check, and Sam's hand is the focus of the torturer's work . . . Stoppard's fixation on boots (a constant throughout his work) is echoed in *Brazil* when Sam's mother wears a leopardskin boot as a hat, and similarly, Jill wears a black boot on her head at the surreal funeral. (p. 357) □

Londré specifies further details. A fly drops into a typewriter, changes a name from Tuttle to Buttle and sets in chain a series of Stoppardian events threatening the innocent bearer of that name. And it is easy to see Stoppard in the film's spoofs of modern life, its ineffectual hero, its motifs, its fascination with chance events, its shifting perspectives, visual and aural incongruities, and interchange between the real and the imaginary: 'The very structure of *Brazil* . . . is an alternation between one man's mental reality and the external reality that is constantly driving him to seek refuge in his own mind', says Londré. This is well said, but it is impossible to attribute all this to Stoppard. Terry Gilliam and, for that matter, the other scriptwriter, Charles McKeown, have strong claims. And we might add that Sam Beckett has had an indirect hand in it. A film, more than the performance of a play, is the creation of its director, actors and technicians, and the writer is subordinate.

Stoppard achieved dominant control, however, when *Rosencrantz and Guildenstern* was eventually filmed in 1991. He abandoned the old, presumably wordy and literary 1968 filmscript and decided to direct it himself because he was the only person ruthless enough to cut his own material.

■ **It was really easy to cut . . . mainly I was trying to add things which I was now able to think of because I could now change the frame – which frankly is the only difference between theatre and film for me.**

In the theatre you've got this medium shot, fairly wide angle, for two and a half hours. And that's it folks. You can't do jokes which depend on close-ups or different angles. That's what I was really thinking of. And I had a good time actually. (Sid Smith, *The Theatre Magazine* no. 1, April 1991; Delaney, p. 236) □

Film does not possess the tension of live performance and the excitement of an action that can go wrong at any time. (One reason why the escapist Houdini's venture into cinema failed was because spectators knew that the exploit was already over.) But film compensates for the absence of physical presence by its visual and aural flexibility and Stoppard demonstrated an immediate mastery of the film medium – not surprisingly, in view of the numerous TV and filmscripts written since the 1960s.

Stoppard cut his dialogue ruthlessly. The film gained naturalistic action: a horseman hammering at a window and powerful indoor and outdoor settings – a mountain path and a forest, a castle with hall and stairways apt for spying. The camera homed in on the actors' stage business, the realism of their wagon (reminiscent of Bergman's *The Seventh Seal* (1957)), the enactment of fights. It enabled quick cross-cutting from cups to daggers, slashed sleeves, a quivering rope. Close-ups of props such as the hourglass were substituted for poetic and philosophical speculation. Spatial effects, often created by the sound of birds, wind, water, music, eerie effects of echoing voices and clinking coins, took the place of language.

Stoppard also added more of Shakespeare to the content of the play: the death of Ophelia, the graveyard scene and the duel. He developed, too, the relationship between the rational Guildenstern and the slower, but more intuitive and childlike Rosencrantz. The latter, as was said in the earlier chapter on the play (see chapter two), is often on the edge of a great scientific discovery. He sails little paper boats; an apple drops on his head and he ponders; he watches a paper aeroplane fly; he is intrigued by bathwater rising and falling; tests whether objects of different weights drop from a balcony at the same speed. But he never cries 'Eureka'. He is an ordinary man, not an Archimedes, Newton, Galileo or Leonardo.

Stoppard gained the major award at the Venice Film Festival for his first film. How far he should be credited for the awards and success of *Shakespeare in Love* (1998) is more problematic. John Madden directed and Stoppard was joint author of the screenplay with the experienced Marc Norman. The credits run to 12 pages and there are 51 named parts, including cameos by famous actors, such as Judi Dench as Queen Elizabeth. Antony Sher is the spoof Dr Moth, the inaugurator, according to the filmplay, of a 'false dawn' of psychoanalysis. In many ways the film is a light-hearted romp. A mug, a 'Present from Stratford', is among the props; a wherryman is instructed to 'follow that boat' in an early chase sequence; Fennyman, whose business closely resembles the gang-land Krays, becomes a 'born again theatre groupie' solely concerned with his own part. Another actor shows scant respect for his lines – 'typical', says Shakespeare, played by Joseph Fiennes.

Parallels with *Romeo and Juliet* and other Shakespeare plays are seen throughout. A western-style saloon bar brawl between the Lord Chamberlain's and The Admiral's Men on the Rose Theatre stage suggests the battle between Capulets and Montagues. Hints of Falstaff in the laundry basket in *The Merry Wives of Windsor* appear when Shakespeare, to avoid suspicion, dresses in women's clothing, looking to Lord Wessex, Shakespeare's competitor in love, like a laundry woman.

The action is rapid, energetic and hilarious, but there is a serious element behind it. The film spoofs the creation of *Romeo and Juliet*, which begins as: *'Romeo and Ethel the Pirate's Daughter'*, a title with popular crowd appeal. But it also raises questions, albeit light-heartedly, about the evolution of a play from original sources, a process that Stoppard in interview consistently insists is, if not haphazard, certainly less under control than solemn scholars would wish.

Will Shakespeare has writer's block; his producer, Henslowe, needs a script to pay his debts; Will needs a muse to write his play; the theatre is closed by the plague; there is competition from Burbage and Marlowe at The Curtain; the Puritans want the theatres closed for good; Will Kemp, the Clown, wants to play tragedy; Will Shakespeare needs fifty pounds to desert Henslowe and join the Lord Chamberlain's Men. As Henslowe says to the man he owes money:

■ Mr Fennyman, let me explain about the theatre business . . . The natural condition is one of unsurmountable obstacles on the road to imminent disaster. Believe me, to be closed by the plague is a bagatelle in the ups and downs of owning a theatre.
Fennyman: So what do we do?

> *Henslowe*: Nothing. Strangely enough, it all turns out well.
> *Fennyman*: How?
> *Henslowe*: I don't know. It's a mystery. (p. 23) □

The last line is repeated through the play. In it there is a gentle mockery of academics, interviewers and others who would solemnly rationalise the process.

Shakespeare's new play arises both from observation and personal experience. The author picks up lines in the street, making mental notes when the Puritan Makepeace cries: 'A plague on both your [Rose and Fortune play]-houses' and claims the line as his own. When the film begins he seeks escape from his writer's block, firstly with the deceitful Rosaline (in Shakespeare's play Romeo first falls in love with a Rosaline) then with his true muse, Viola. Their tempestuous lovemaking and subsequent separation begets in Shakespeare both Juliet and the resourceful Viola of *Twelfth Night*, a play that, according to standard chronology, comes at least six years after *Romeo and Juliet* in the canon. But what of that? Shakespeare himself is no respecter of chronology and *Twelfth Night* is an appropriate choice for the Bard's next play because it implies, as does this film, that laughter can defeat melancholy and art can be born from the heart of loss.

Shakespeare in Love, of course, plays jokes and games with *Romeo and Juliet*. These engagingly raise questions of identity, gender and playacting. Joseph Fiennes's Shakespeare speaks the lines of both Juliet and Romeo. Gwyneth Paltrow brilliantly plays Viola de Lesseps, playing Romeo, then Juliet. Each character has dual identity and takes on the opposite gender, as does the boy actor who plays the female part. The play within the play allows both comic and serious comment on the creative link between art and sexuality, as well as on the nature of commercial competition between theatre companies and on relations between director, actors and writer in the mystery and excitement of the theatre process. The film employs the old stage technique of the play-within-a-play to bring the audience within the play frame. *Hamlet* does this by creating an identification between the audience and stage spectators watching the Player King and Queen. Recalling the artificiality of the playframe has traditionally provoked laughter and the film's anachronisms – 'I had Christopher Marlowe in my boat once' – achieve this. But if there is a second frame within the play, the theatre audience forgets that the onstage actor/spectators are themselves artificial, and becomes involved more deeply in the action even as it laughs with them at the play within.

Sometimes, too, the play-within-a-play is not entirely comic. This rumbustious film has a tragedy at its centre and if some members of a cinema audience prefer to ignore it, they resemble Shakespeare's lovers and spectators in Act V of *A Midsummer Night's Dream*. Lysander and Hermia, Demetrius and Helena mock the 'tragical mirth' of Bottom and company's *Pyramus and Thisbe* – the play within a play which closely mimics the tragic deaths of *Romeo and Juliet* and the frightening experience the lovers have gone through in the wood outside Athens.

But *Shakespeare in Love* is far from tragedy; it is an exhilarating comment on the nature of theatre. Philip Kemp (in *Sight and Sound*, February 1999) praises the heterogeneous mixture and fine acting. He credits Stoppard with 'some literary gags that may bypass the groundlings' and in particular with the addition of the young and bloodthirsty John Webster, 'a mischievous small boy, given to tormenting mice':

■ The final triumphant première of Shakespeare's first true masterpiece conveys something of what Nabokov called *shamanstvo* – the "enchanter quality" of great theatre. It reinforces Henslowe's remarks – which may also be those of Geoffrey Rush the actor – smiling beatifically as the whole shambles comes magically together: "It's a mystery". (p. 53) □

CHAPTER TWENTY

Theatre Views: Director, Actor and Author

PROFESSOR JOHN Russell Brown (in his introduction to *Modern British Dramatists*, 1984) points to the importance of the director to a playwright:

■ The physical and organisational conditions of the first performance of a stage play have become ever more crucial elements in the successful launching of a new playwright. So much depends on what is called the "set-up" that more and more established dramatists insist that their work be staged only by the directors they have come to trust over a period of years. Each new play by Harold Pinter is directed by Peter Hall; Peter Wood directs Stoppard's; and Harold Pinter Simon Gray's ... even plays that are staged very simply are presented more satisfactorily by a director and special group of actors who are known to the dramatist and respond fully to his ideas; so many options are now open in technique, style and physical resources that a secure base for the production of a new play seems almost obligatory. (p. 7) □

John Russell Brown's views are corroborated by Stoppard, who freely acknowledges his debt to actors and to the director Peter Wood who creates theatrical moments the author has not thought of. In an interview with Melvyn Bragg (Delaney, pp. 123–4), Stoppard says: 'Peter Wood susses things out in my plays which somehow I've left to just look after themselves', and cites the way in which, in *Night and Day*, the director works with the actors (Diana Rigg and Peter Machin) 'with such persistence and detail' to determine the exact moment when Ruth falls in love with Jake – a moment Stoppard had only generally specified. 'And I sit there knowing I am the beneficiary of what happened in that scene.'

The relation between author and director is symbiotic in other ways. He and Peter Wood perceive different spectators. Wood visualises one who is

■ . . . a cross between Rupert Bear and Winnie the Pooh. He assumes bafflement in order to force me to explain on a level of banality. If I had an ideal spectator it would be someone more sharp-witted and attentive than the average theatre-goer whom Peter thinks of . . . (Delaney, p. 186) □

Wood has a less flattering, or more realistic, view of a listener's capacity to apprehend the subtleties of Stoppard's lines, but he acknowledges that in rehearsal the author's explanations are valuable: 'Over and over again I've had immense light suddenly vouchsafed on a line or a moment I'd totally underrated when I read it'.

   This symbiotic exchange between author and director has much to do with a different sense of rhythm:

■ *Stoppard*: My plays for me – in my head, before anyone gets hold of a text – make a certain quality of noise, which rises and falls at certain places, and slows and speeds up at certain spaces, and much of our rehearsal time consists of my trying to explain what this noise is like, and trying to make the actors make this noise; and then Peter and the actors, working from the other end, show me how the action can speed up in a different place, and not get loud there but very quiet, and it's my turn to be shown an alternative orchestration for these voices. (Cited by Hayman, Delaney, p. 147) □

A sense of rhythm or pace must relate to the whole play as well as to dialogue. Thus Wood can suggest structural changes in *Night and Day* by making the author aware 'of a gaping hole in the text'. He says:

■ This lady goes through the play as a ball-breaker, mowing down everyone before her. Until that man can make her say "Ouch", there's no play. But Tom's instinct was that Ruth wouldn't say ouch out loud, at least not yet, and not to Wagner. So he wrote that speech for Wagner, and her reply comes out as "If you're waiting for me to say 'Ouch', you're going to get cramp." So my offer was taken up but turned upside down in a way that refined it . . . It was a great thrill when you phoned me on the Sunday . . . and said in that comfortable way you can: "I've written a bloody good speech for Wagner." (p. 148) (Ronald Hayman, *The Sunday Times Magazine*, 2 March 1980; Delaney, pp. 148–9) □

Stoppard adds: 'the author is there to save the play from the director and the director has to be there to save it from the playwright. That's quite a good way of describing our relationship' (Anthony Smith interview, British Council audio-cassette, 1977).

   Peter Hall is another director who admires Stoppard. He remarks on the importance for a director of listening to the cadences of an author's voice: 'The greatest guide to playing a dramatist is to listen to his tone of voice in everyday life: Beckett, Pinter, Shaffer, Stoppard, Ayckbourn, Brenton – I could go on' (*Diaries*, p. 274). This is particularly interesting in view of Stoppard's observation that his (early) characters tend to talk like himself. An author's speech rhythms can help directors determine the pace of the dialogue, though, as we have seen, an author's and director's rhythms may not be the same.

As administrative director of the National Theatre, Peter Hall has commented on a different quality in Stoppard – a readiness to engage with the press. Max Hastings had interviewed Hall and written two highly critical articles in the *Evening Standard* that encouraged a *Guardian* leader about the 'Colossus of the South Bank', recommending that Hall's power as director of The National Theatre be reduced. Stoppard helped fight Hall's corner. Hall records that Stoppard wrote a 'wonderful article in the *Standard* today . . . taking Max Hastings to pieces' (*Diaries*, p. 260).

Actors have commented on Stoppard in rehearsal. David Hall, touring with Ed Berman's British American Repertory Company, responded to a questionnaire sent out by Felicia Londré as follows:

■ Tom Stoppard was great fun . . . He would jump up to alter a line or improvise a new gag, sometimes spending fifteen minutes or more improvising a bit of dialogue he would then discard. There was a helmet . . . Himmler . . . Hamlet gag in *Dogg's Hamlet* for a couple of rehearsals. Tom or Ed suggested it, Tom developed it, the actors rehearsed it, we all laughed a bit, and Tom cut it. (Harty, p. 348) □

Another respondent, Stephen D. Norman, wrote:

■ As Stoppard so typically put his sharing of brainstorming sessions with the company, he was "taking us into his lack of confidence" . . . To watch ideas born in a brilliant man . . . lends a participatory pride to one's feeling about the play. (Harty, p. 362) □

Peter Barkworth published two books for drama students – *About Acting* (1980) and *More About Acting* (1984) – based on long experience of directing, teaching at RADA and acting (including the role of Professor Anderson in *Professional Foul*). Discussing the choice of speeches for audition in his second book, he recommends three Stoppard plays – *Night and Day*, *The Real Thing* and *Travesties*. He says: 'The best speeches . . . are those which are self-sufficient, needing little preamble . . . a memory, a story' (p. 88). This says something about the structure of Stoppard's drama, tightly composed, but often built around quite long speeches, set within a carefully organised pattern, but often detachable for auditions.

It does not make Stoppard easy to perform. The actor Roger Rees feels that 'Stoppard is quite hard to do, and requires a great deal of physical energy. It's like digging a hole in the road every night'.

Fellow authors also make comments. Stoppard is seen as a conservative writer, but antagonism to him is rare in the professional theatre. David Hare, the most successful and, earlier, one of the most hard-edged of the post-1968 'Fringe' political dramatists, writes:

■ I never find him politically narrow in any way. His friendship and encouragement and generosity to writers are legendary. We have far more in common than in conflict. (Quoted by Gussow, 'The Real Tom Stoppard', *New York Magazine*, 1 January 1984, p. 22) □

But among theatre commentators on Stoppard's work, the author himself is uniquely important. In dozens of interviews, many already quoted, he provides illuminating replies to questions about form and content. Questions concerning the latter often relate to political commitment. More frequently, interviewers ask about the nature of the creative process during and prior to rehearsal and production. This is, of course, a major theme that has already been referred to. An early interview with John Russell Taylor (broadcast on BBC Radio 4, 23 November 1970) summarises how a play forms in his mind:

■ One is the victim and beneficiary of one's environment, history, sub-conscious, say, and – for me personally – 80% of my time is spent in looking for something to write *about*. To put it crudely, it's a bit like waiting to be struck by lightning . . . when it actually happens . . . it's as though at the far end of this gilded hall, the double doors have opened and a butler bearing a silver tray turns up and slowly approaches with the idea, or even the manuscript . . . which he just puts in front of me while the trumpets sound. At that moment one has this surge of relief that perhaps there is just one more play left in one . . . (Delaney, p. 25) □

The 'idea' announces itself pictorially and the semi-conscious search results in a gift on a silver tray which takes the form of a 'concrete situation' (Delaney, p. 28) with a substructure which can be dramatically and theatrically explored.

The act of writing must also take account of available resources. Stoppard says, speaking of the origin of *Travesties*:

■ When one pursues these memories of how plays came to be the plays they are, one finds that the convergence of threads includes threads which are, you know, pretty ordinary yarn; I mean there are very practical reasons; to put it another way, I wanted to write a play for John Wood, a tall thin actor who has the gift of speaking very quickly, but very clearly. I knew he didn't look like Lenin and I didn't know what Tsara was like, but when I found a photograph of Tsara I knew he couldn't be played by John either. And then I began thinking about Joyce . . . and then I thought, no, I want a big part for John Wood and this play was turning into a play about three people rather than a play about John Wood, and I needed a fourth person . . . and came across the figure of Henry Carr (in *Ulysses*) . . . so, who knows? . . . I might have settled for a very different play about a much more historically truthful Zurich. (Anthony Smith, British Council audio-cassette, 1977) □

More personal elements are involved, of course, though Stoppard plays down the importance of biography and is not sympathetic to a romantic/expressive view of the nature of art. The idea for a play comes from observation and reading as well as personal experience. He admits to 'a neurotic element' in the early *Albert's Bridge* (1967), but defines this as a worry, not about himself, but about the functioning of technological society. He is astonished that it seems to work – that the law of supply and demand operates as mysteriously 'as the peace of God' and some-times – reassuringly – 'goes spectacularly wrong' (Smith, British Council cassette, 1977).

It is characteristic of Stoppard that confusion provides reassurance, whilst perfect functioning becomes a worry. It indicates a writer with a penchant for farce – a genre that delights in confusion – whose methods owe much to (Stoppard's word again) 'temperament':

■ There's a certain kind of joke, which consists of constructing some-thing with infinite care and then just, sort of, putting your hand through the bottom layer so the whole thing collapses; this Samuel Beckett con-struction of that nature, where you build up piece by piece a proposition, and the last piece negates it. I enjoy that as a humorous device. □

A temperamental leaning, however, is strengthened by knowledge of the comic tradition and careful observation of Beckett's methods. The collapse of stout parties is traditionally comic and jokes often depend on the puncturing of expectation: 'You do speedwriting I suppose', the secretary in *Dirty Linen* is asked. She answers, we remember: 'Yes, if I'm given enough time'. The 'collapse' is also a visual and structural theatre device, as when, in *The Real Thing*, a house of cards, carefully built up, collapses as a door slams. And it operates in the analysis of character. In the same play (p. 22) the wife says:

■ You don't really think that if Henry caught me out with a lover, he'd sit around being witty about place mats. The hell he would. He'd come apart like pick-a-sticks. His sentence structure would go to pot, closely followed by his sphincter. □

A concern with chaos, personal and social, runs right through Stoppard's work as more than a comic device. He admires, he tells us, not an anarchic mind but an anarchic spirit (interview with Taylor, Delaney, p.27). The distinction is clear in his work from *Rosencrantz and Guildenstern* to the fascination with chaos theory in *Arcadia*, a play that interrogates confusion in the natural world as well as in language, human relations, the individual mind and social structures.

Chaos might be thought a description of the writer's mind in the early stages of composition, but this may only be a surface impression. In an interview with Ronald Hayman, Stoppard defines this condition as one of extreme compression:

■ In an ideal state all the meaningful and referential possibilities in a work of art exist in a highly compressed form in the mind of the artist, probably before he even begins and the existence of that nucleus dictates what the tentacles do at the extremities of his conscious gift. What's wrong with bad art is that the artist knows exactly what he's doing. (Hayman, *Tom Stoppard*, p.2) □

The process Stoppard describes is like the conscious elaboration of a half-understood dream. The mind works logically and technically upon a nagging core of meaning. The logic, image and form seem chaotic, but they have an inner coherence. Such may well be the process informing the multiple perspectives of a Shakespeare play that make students protest – possibly in self-defence – 'No one could have been that intelligent'. The play is 'precipitated' from material that has been worked over at length and not entirely consciously. It is no accident that Stoppard's plays in the 90s are concerned with poets and the nature of poetry. This, of all forms, is the most concentrated and compressed, and the closest to unconscious process.

CHAPTER TWENTY-ONE

Academic Criticism and Stoppard

SINCE HIS first success, academics have written about Stoppard in many foreign, as well as English, journals – in French, German, Italian, Dutch, Polish, Japanese, Serbo-Croat and other languages. A penchant for puns marks many of the English titles. The effect is not always happy. 'Tomfoolery' is one of the better examples. 'I am not only witty in myself', Stoppard might say with Falstaff, 'but the cause of wit in others . . . '.

The number of entries by the year 2000 in the MLA database (many of which are to be found in the Canadian journal, *Modern Drama*) was 57 between 1969 and 1980; 122 in the 1980s and 68 since 1990. The majority are concerned with individual plays – principally *Rosencrantz and Guildenstern Are Dead* (43), *Travesties* (31) and *Jumpers* (20). *Dogg's Hamlet* and *Cahoots Macbeth* attracted eight articles, *Professional Foul* and *The Real Thing* seven, *Hapgood* rated only four and *Artist Descending* and *Arcadia* only two. (The numbers do not include articles that make limited references to the plays.) Judging from the journals, the height of academic interest seems to have been in the 1980s. Full-length books, however, continue to appear at regular intervals and the number is now over a score.

A fair idea of the *areas* of academic interest may be gained from the following rough list of topics: Play (12 articles); Language (11); Comedy (9); Adaptation (8); Absurdism (8); Parody (7); Audience response (6); Dramatic structure (6); Politics (6); Values/beliefs (5); Theatricality (4); Deconstruction (2); Tragedy (2); Creativity (2); Symbolism (2); Character (2); Gender (1); Realism (1). Further topics include pastiche, satire, farce, play within play, monologue and dialogue, defamiliarisation, history, space and time, identity, *différence*, repetition and metadrama.

A number of articles make comparisons with twentieth-century dramatists. Wilde, Beckett, Albee, Shaw, Anouilh, Orton, Bond, Ibsen, Molnár, Schnitzler and Pinter are the most frequent. Shakespeare, of course, looms in the background. As regards articles of a more theoretical nature, 61 appeared in the MLA list in the 1980s as opposed to 36 in the 1990s and 19 before 1980. These mainly discuss dramatic form and cannot be divided chronologically into diverse schools of criticism – liberal humanist, formalist, Marxist, feminist, structuralist, post-structuralist, deconstructionist, cultural materialist, new historicist, etc. – as is possible with classical single texts written 100 or more years ago. There is much useful thematic analysis and plot interpretation, but this leads to considerable overlapping and repetition.

Theoretical and evaluative perspectives on Stoppard, scattered over the last three decades, cannot be organised into a pattern easily, but a number can be defined. Of these, the first must be the description of him as 'absurdist'. The early debt to Samuel Beckett and Harold Pinter has been amply acknowledged. In the late 50s, when Stoppard was, as a journalist, trying his hand at stage drama, the so-called absurdist theatre was in the ascendant. Martin Esslin's well-known book *The Theatre of the Absurd* (1961) promoted the term and, in a final chapter entitled 'Beyond the Absurd' (1980 edition), Esslin comments:

■ The plays of Tom Stoppard clearly show the impact of the Theatre of the Absurd, in spite of the obvious difference in other aspects of their approach, and the tradition – that of English high comedy – which they represent. *Rosencrantz and Guildenstern Are Dead* (1966) uses standard elements of *Waiting for Godot* (1953) while *Jumpers* (1972) concludes its brilliant and zany absurdist exploration of the problem of good and evil . . . with a direct paraphrase of lines from *Waiting for Godot*: "At the graveside the undertaker doffs his top hat and impregnates the prettiest mourner". To which the character of Archie and surely the author of the play also, adds: "Wham, bam, thank you Sam". The play's debt to Samuel Beckett could not have been more clearly emphasised. (pp. 433–4) □

Esslin goes on to say that some absurdist writers 'have naturally and smoothly reintegrated themselves into the main stream of the tradition' and others 'have clearly contributed to the negative and disruptive trends which tend towards the destruction of the tradition itself . . . '. His observation that Stoppard relates to the tradition of English high comedy indicates that he sees Stoppard as going beyond the theatre of the absurd, and Stoppard himself demurs at the 'absurdist' tag.

The concept of the absurd is central to the existentialist reaction against essentialist philosophy and it developed from explorations of the dramatic mode of tragedy by Kierkegaard and Nietzsche. A sense of the 'death of god' is strongly present in the novels of Dostoievsky and Kafka. The French existential writers Camus and Sartre made the concept (and experience) of the absurd a keystone of an atheistic philosophy, which denied meaning to the world except that created by man himself. '*In the beginning was the Word*' was replaced by '*In the beginning was the World*'. God became a hole in the sky and the world 'absurd'. God, if he exists, is deaf (*'surdus'* in Latin) and the anguish created by his absence or silence must be faced and filled with man's own meaning. Kierkegaard suggested that this situation compelled an existential leap of belief: *credo quia absurdum est* (I believe *because* it is absurd). The atheist existentialists denied all leaps into idealism as 'bad faith'.

The drama of Beckett is absurdist insofar as his characters (and audience) wait for explanations which are denied. Godot, probably a parody name for God (Charlot is the French name for Charlie Chaplin), either does not come or is not recognised when he appears. Pozzo (meaning 'cesspit' in Italian) in Act I, is in charge of Lucky, his slave, who enters tied to his master by a long rope. In Act II, Pozzo is blind and is pulled along by Lucky on a shorter rope. Insofar as a statement is made, the double stage image allegorises, among many other things, a historical shift from an authority (God) in charge of man, to a man in charge of an authority figure, or from essentialism, which assumes a transcendent meaning, to atheistic existentialism, which does not. At the same time Beckett parodies the attempt to find ultimate meanings.

Stoppard acknowledges the influence of Beckett, but denies that he finds existentialism an attractive philosophy. The world of some plays, such as *After Magritte*, begins absurdly with an apparent phantasmagoria, but the absurd picture has an explanation. The audience and the bewildered characters are illuminated. The stage images are only *apparently* absurd. The play shows people working in the semi-darkness, making hilarious mistakes at which an audience can laugh when light is shed.

Some Stoppard characters fail to emerge from varying degrees of darkness. Rosencrantz and Guildenstern progress into the light of knowledge only to retreat again. Other characters do emerge, such as Inspector Foot in *After Magritte*. He comprehends the grotesque situation, but Constable 'Holmes' does not (and he is the one asked for an explanation). In *Arcadia*, the researcher Hannah finds what she is looking for. One might argue, however, that Stoppard still belongs to the absurdist tradition because, in that play, the larger mystery of the death of the young and brilliant Thomasina encloses her brief illumination of the darkness and ends her final dance. But in this respect Stoppard relates to the broader tragicomic tradition that subsumes the 'theatre of the absurd'.

When Stoppard began writing, the American naturalists, Arthur Miller and Tennessee Williams, followed by the 'Kitchen Sink' school of Osborne and Wesker in England in the late 50s, had created a new vitality and superannuated an older school of successful West End writers represented by Terence Rattigan, just as Beckett had superannuated the poetic drama of Fry and T.S. Eliot in 1955. In 1956, the Soviet invasion of Hungary and the British invasion of Suez aroused a powerful political conscience. The arrival of Brecht's *Berliner Ensemble* in London in the same year had as strong an impact as the absurdism of Beckett and Ionesco or Osborne and Wesker's lower-class naturalism. In the plays of John Arden, a new political drama arose. Edward Bond fused absurdist patterns with a hard political edge and in the later 60s, with the lifting of censorship, political drama appeared to have won the day. Stoppard was assigned an inferior place as 'absurdist' and entertainer by a radical movement embracing the dramatic structures and modes of performance that Brecht advocated and evolved from Marxist theory.

Brecht's view of the theatre as a radical form sprang from his experience of the rise of Fascism during the Weimar Republic. Radical drama must ask hard questions, not mediate modes of entertainment that reconciled playgoers to the status quo. Nor should it project an existential angst in response to what it saw as a universal condition. Traditional forms both of comedy and tragedy were suspect because they presented life as unchangeable. The 'well-made play' was 'bourgeois'. It might disturb the audience with its multiple confusions and its upending of the social order, but ultimately the social order is restored and the audience reconciled. (As an example, Sartre cited *The Admirable Crichton*, in which a butler takes control then returns to his former inferior position. One might also cite Stoppard's adaptation, *On the Razzle*.) In a comparable way, Brecht repudiated tragedy and the Aristotelian effect of catharsis/ purgation of emotion (which led to political passivity and reconciliation with the political status quo). Anger, for example, was not to be purged. A century of capitalism, competition and world war demanded an active and radical political response.

Marxists saw absurdism as a regrettable product of early twentieth-century modernism. The Marxist Georg Lukács expressed it thus in *The Meaning of Contemporary Realism* (1963):

■ As the ideology of most modernist writers asserts the unalterability of outward reality (even if this is reduced to a mere state of consciousness) human activity is, *a priori*, rendered impotent and robbed of meaning. The apprehension of reality to which this leads is most consistently and convincingly realised in the work of Kafka . . . this vision of a world dominated by angst and of man at the mercy of incomprehensible terrors, makes Kafka's work the very type of modernist art . . . Kafka is not able, in spite of his extraordinary evocative power . . . to achieve that fusion of the particular and the general which is the essence of realistic art . . . what matters is the basic ideological determination of form and content. The particularity we find in Beckett and Joyce, in Musil and Benn . . . is essentially of the same kind. (pp. 36–45) □

It is easy to see how this can also be applied to Beckett's *Waiting for Godot*, which, Lukács feels, lacks a progressive form. Its pessimism results in characters who do not possess the three-dimensionality of the 'critical realism' of which Lukács approves in Thomas Mann and Solzhenitsyn. Lukács traces the development of a 'phantasmagoric' literature and drama from Dostoievsky to Camus, and repudiates the existential angst that undermines the belief in the future that a Marxist philosophy undoubtedly embodies. Any Marxist who felt that the theatre was an instrument for communicating truths about the material world was bound to be suspicious of works that found their source in such early twentieth-century movements as Symbolism, Expressionism, Dada and Surrealism. In these movements, dream and hallucination were projected as more real than the capitalist and class-ridden world of which the theatre was a part. Existential angst, Lukács argued, created a phantasmagoria that arose out of the imperialist and class crisis leading into World War I. It must be combated if a more just society was to be achieved, by a progressive drama that did not project an anguished state of mind as a universal condition.

In this context, then, attitudes to Stoppard's plays, either as entertainments or as 'absurdist', tended to be dismissive. This was reinforced by observations Stoppard made about Marxism, and especially Leninism, in an interview in *Theatre Quarterly* (Vol. V, No. 17, 1975):

■ The repression which for better or worse turned out to be Leninism in action after 1917 was very much worse than anything which had gone on in Tsarist Russia. I mean, in purely mundane, boring statistical terms which can sometimes contain the essence of a situation, it is simply true that in the ten years after 1917 fifty times more people were done to death than in the fifty years before 1917. □

In *Stages in the Revolution* (1980), Catherine Itzin asserts that Stoppard opted for human solidarity rather than 'class solidarity':

■ . . . he pursued his mission to expose the repressions of Soviet communism in 1977 with *Every Good Boy Deserves Favour* . . . In 1978 Stoppard's *Night and Day* dealt with internecine political strife – a guerilla war – in an easily identified African state and with analogous internecine strife within the world of journalism and its embattled unions. Again Stoppard was concerned with freedom and freedom of speech. (pp. 185–6) □

But she adds that this concern was 'from a liberal or right of centre perspective' and identifies Stoppard with the theatre journal *Plays and Players*, which congratulated him for standing out against current left-wing views associated with Brecht, Bond and the French director, Roger Planchon. With these few words, in a very detailed summarising book on political theatre, Stoppard is dismissed.

The 1980s saw the development of 'cultural materialist' criticism, deriving from the work of Marx and the elaboration of the new discipline of cultural studies by Raymond Williams and Richard Hoggart in the 1950s and 1960s, and subsequently by other academics such as Terry Eagleton at Oxford and Jonathan Dollimore and Alan Sinfield at Sussex University. The figures of Brecht and Foucault loom large behind their concern with the ideological implications of dramatic structures, the power relations within a culture, and the contribution made by writers to the economic and political systems of which they are a part. They see moral codes as created by the cultural system and are suspicious of 'myths' that invoke transhistorical and transcendent values. Systems and institutions project such myths as 'natural' in order to reinforce their power.

Cultural materialists claim that certain writers, notably Shakespeare, have been embraced by national institutions as enunciators of universal truths. To challenge Shakespeare's text and the hierarchical system that (conservative critics say) his plays embody is to challenge a national icon and subvert society. Brecht did just this when he rewrote *Coriolanus* to give the lower ranks a stronger dramatic and ideological case.

Stoppard's handling of Shakespeare is interesting in this regard. He recasts Shakespeare and might therefore be seen, like Brecht, as a radical, subversive playwright. In his first major success, the power groupings are decentred and Rosencrantz and Guildenstern become central figures. In *Dogg's Hamlet* and *Cahoot's Macbeth*, too, the powers of the authoritarian censorship are satirised. Surely, then, Stoppard is a radical writer? Sinfield disagrees. In an article in *The Shakespeare Myth* (1988), he says:

■ It seems that the Shakespeare myth is challenged in two ways, formally, . . . in that the natural flow of the Shakespeare text is disrupted . . . and thematically in that the 'tragic hero' is displaced from the centre of his own play . . .

Formally *Rosencrantz and Guildenstern* may seem to offer the radical undermining of ideology that we associate with a Brechtian alienation effect. In that effect no discourse is allowed to become established as simply dominant, as the natural and self-evident way to think about the action. The audience is denied the secure relationship with the text that characterises the process through which ideology normally normalises itself. . . . Stoppard's play seems to present a double alienation effect, for it disrupts the experienced audience's relationship with the text of *Hamlet* and disrupts also its own surface by playing incessantly with audience expectations of text and narrative.

However, *Rosencrantz and Guildenstern are Dead* is actually a very conservative play. As the discourses of the play are reduced to one set of notions (illusion, allusion, contrivance, acting joke, logical play) a new meta-discourse emerges behind them, controlling them and reassuring the audience . . . (p. 131) □

Sinfield attacks the absurdist genre to which he assigns the play:

■ . . . When the audience locates *Rosencrantz and Guildenstern are Dead* within this genre, it knows where it stands. While the characters are increasingly baffled and anxious, the audience becomes more confident in its knowledge. This is because its members understand about the absurd, and also about *Hamlet*. Turns of event which baffle Rosencrantz and Guildenstern – such as the contents of the two letters to England . . . offer for the audience a pleasant little surprise, for they pick up the cues from *Hamlet*. The audience is able to cope with it all – unlike the unfortunate characters – because they are cultured and know their *Hamlet* . . . (pp. 131–2) □

Sinfield suggests that Shakespeare was reinterpreted in the 1960s to fit an absurdist ideology and cites the critics Martin Esslin and Jan Kott, and the directors Peter Brook and Peter Hall, as exponents of this ideology which embodied 'a very strong sense of the futility of the human condition':

■ . . . absurdist productions of . . . *Rosencrantz and Guildenstern Are Dead* were actively working to keep Shakespeare going. The hegemonic culture cannot afford to rest complacently: it must reproduce itself actively and continually, responding to changing economic and political conditions and meeting the specific challenges of subordinate cultures. It must strive to sustain the authority of its cultural tokens and keep control of interpretation of them . . . (p. 132) □

Stoppard, says Sinfield, satisfied the desire of young people in the 1960s, a period of rapid social change, 'to invest in the idea of absurdist futility':

■ . . . Esslin, Kott, Brook, Hall and Stoppard demonstrated that the Shakespeare myth was equal to these developments.

Stoppard and the Shakespeare myth serve each other, for even as Stoppard updates the myth, he makes space for his own writing. In adjusting the Shakespeare text, Stoppard does not aspire to dislodge it from its cultural space, but to alter the configuration so that there is space for him too and for his kind of writing alongside Shakespeare. Like the sick people with Jesus, *Rosencrantz and Guildenstern Are Dead* touches the hem of Shakespeare's garment and some of his power is conducted into the new work. (p. 133) □

Sinfield assumes Stoppard works entirely within the 'hegemonic culture'. He makes an eloquent anti-absurdist case against an early play, but *Rosencrantz and Guildenstern Are Dead* is no longer fully representative of his work. Much water has since flowed under the bridge (or carried the vessel) of Stoppard's talent, producing a variety of plays, some with a more overt political content. Stoppard, in any case, has never accepted the classification of absurdist.

Stoppard poses a problem for left-wing critics. He became conscious in the 60s that his talent did not lead him in the direction of the dominant post-1968 left-wing politics of his contemporaries, and he has defended his own position with increasing composure. In one of the most important interviews he gave – to Roger Hudson, Catherine Itzin and Simon Trussler (*Theatre Quarterly* 4, no. 14, May 1974) – he confidently argues his case:

■ The great irony about Marx was that his impulses were deeply moral while his intellect insisted on a materialistic view of the world. His theory of capital, his theory of value, and his theory of revolution have all been refuted by modern economics and by history. In short he got it wrong, but he was a giant whose shadow still reaches us precisely for the reason that, wrong as he was in detail, the force he represented sprang from a sense of universal moral justice. He realised which way things would have to go, and then he put together a materialistic theory which was quite irrelevant, like sticking scaffolding on a moving train. It was only a matter of time before somebody – it turned out to be Bernstein in 1900 – somebody with the benefit of an extra fifty years hindsight, would actually point out that Marx had got it wrong, but that doesn't matter because social justice was going to come through other means. Bernstein reckoned that the class war wasn't the way, that human solidarity was a better bet than class solidarity. And this argument between 'hards' and 'softs' constitutes a great deal of radical argument today. It is not an argument about tactics – that's just surface dressing – it's an argument about philosophy. I mean Bernstein stuck his banner on the grave of Kant . . . (Trussler, pp. 66–7) □

Stoppard, too, sticks his banner on the grave of Bernstein, human solidarity, and Kant's famous 'categorical imperative'. It is understandable that a materialist school rejects his work. His view that standards of good and evil are not entirely created by cultural institutions makes him a target. He does not believe in Marxist ideas of historical progression, and argues (along with ex-Marxists like Arthur Koestler – see *The Yogi and the*

Commissar (1945)) that history proves him right. He does believe, however, in a different form of human progress and is not committed to the view that seeking explanations is futile.

The argument about modes of progression raises the question of the function of theatre and the contribution it makes to human progress. For Stoppard, it is important not to make his plays 'the end products of my ideas'. If that were so,

■ They'd have it all more pat, but a lot of the time I've ended up trying to work out the ultimate implications of what I've written. My plays have a lot to do with the fact that *I just don't know.* (Trussler, p. 67) □

Aware that this is a statement that can be used against him, he ends by saying 'I'm not going to rebut the things I have been saying just now. One thing I feel sure about is that a materialist view of history is an insult to the human race'. Stoppard is saying that plays should be an *exploration* of different moral and aesthetic positions, not an assertion of previously held beliefs, though these, of course, may subtly inform the play, as materialists will argue.

Stoppard's view of the political function of drama is contained in the same interview. He denied that art was impotent, having previously been quoted in *The Guardian* 'in 14 point bold' as commending Auden for saying that his poems had not saved a single Jew from the gas chambers:

■ . . . ever since then I've wanted to pay homage to Auden, or his shade, with the rider that I was making a point about the short-term, not the long-term. Briefly, art – Auden or Fugard or the entire cauldron – is important because it provides the moral matrix, the moral sensibility, from which we make our judgements about the world. (Delaney, p. 66) □

Fugard, he argued, could not have the powerful short-term effect of journalism – he cites an article by Adam Raphael who broke a story that raised the wages of underpaid native workers in 48 hours. But Stoppard claims that Fugard, in the long term, helped to create a climate of change. Stoppard went on to write *Night and Day* (1978) in which he compared a hard-bitten with an idealistic journalist, both of whom, and the photographer, too, were committed to shedding light on an appalling situation, thereby contributing to general awareness and the possibility of improvement. The play also shed light on union behaviour, particularly that of the print unions. This did not make him popular with hard-line unionists; neither did it make him a right-winger.

A dramatic dialogue consisting of assertion, counter-assertion, rebuttal and counter-rebuttal, which made demands on the audience but left it free to make its own decisions, was Stoppard's favoured mode. In 1989, he asserted:

■ One thing I can't stand is the sense that food has been cut up on the plate for the person who eats it. You've got to let the audience have their own knife and fork. Otherwise they're not doing anything. (Delaney, p. 228) □

It is an image that he uses again in the interview with David Gollob and David Roper (*Gambit* 10, no. 37, Summer 1981), where the interviewers raise the crucial question of the dramatic function of comedy.

■ *Gollob*: Somebody once said – I think Griffiths in *Comedians* – that comedy is essentially conservative, even reactionary.

Stoppard: What an extraordinary thing to say. Is it?

Roper: I think it is. Comedy is grounded in a kind of fellow-feeling, a sharing of feeling about society that reinforces those feelings and militates against change.

Stoppard: That's very bright.

Gollob: It needs to be pessimistic about the outcome of change or innovation.

Roper: It reinforces stasis, makes you feel secure in what you are.

Stoppard: Well, think of Tom Lehrer, does he reinforce shared values between performer and audience?

Roper: Well, perhaps there's . . .

Gollob: (*interrupting*) I think he does!

Roper: . . . a difference between comedy and strong satire.

Stoppard: Well, I think you've got your knife out again to cut your sausage to suit you. If I said to you (and if we hadn't had this conversation) that comedy is a radical force, it wouldn't strike you immediately as being nonsense, one could make a case for it as much as you could for being reactionary.

Roper: You could, but if you were trying to make a serious point, you'd embarrass your audience. You embarrass them by trying to make them laugh at Auschwitz.

Gollob: Which is what Barnes did.

Stoppard: But then, is it still comedy? . . . (Delaney, pp. 150–66) □

Gollob is right to point to Griffiths' *Comedians* (1974), but oversimplifies a play that, by showing six tyro performers in a working man's club, demonstrates the difference between the comedy which reinforces racial and sexual prejudices and a comedy which makes audiences uncomfortably aware of them. In Griffiths' play a third form of performance, based on Grock, becomes a direct parody of the audience's racist and sexist expectations, and nobody laughs.

There is, of course, a long tradition of comic theory, dating from the brief observations of Aristotle to the view of Sir Philip Sidney, in *A Defence of Poetry* (1595), that the purpose of comedy is the exposure of evil. The 'relief' theory of Freud sees laughter as a response of the unconscious, anarchic self (see *Jokes and the Unconscious*) and Henri Bergson (*Le Rire*, 1900) argues that laughter mocks the stereotypical individual who has become encrusted (fixated?) with habit, vice or obsession and needs to be mocked into life. Laughter is healthful, theorists agree, and whilst much laughter may reconcile audiences to their prejudices, satirists have traditionally used it to distance audiences from entrenched ideas. Brecht, of course, relates his distancing effects to the comic tradition: *'Ein altes Kunstmittel, bekannt aus der Komedie'* – 'a time-honoured comic technique'. To say that comedy is conservative or 'needs to be pessimistic' is a great simplification, as Stoppard quietly points out.

Stoppard seems not to want to make a strong case for the political value of comedy, but suggests a joke can be reactionary or radical depending on delivery and audience response as well as authorial intention. When Wilde originally uttered his *bon mot*, 'Work is the curse of the drinking classes', did one laugh at the working-class drinker? Or at the moralistic and probably middle-class utterer of temperance clichés? Or at ourselves, because we recognise our foolish dependence on language, reason and logic?

A theoretical analysis of the value of Stoppard's theatre needs to examine the function of comic play. All the arts play with the various patterns or 'languages', verbal, visual, musical or physical, which inform them. The motives behind such play are equally various – to experiment, to learn, to persuade, to dominate, to have fun, to protest, to protect the self, to fill in time, to entertain, to advance a career, to make money, etc. and a number of these may operate at once in the creation of theatre.

In an interview with Richard Mayne (broadcast on Radio Three, 10 November 1972), Stoppard discussed the question of comedy in *Artist Descending a Staircase*:

■ *Mayne*: Can I ask you a very simple question, is this play a comedy or a tragedy?

Stoppard: That's not a simple question at all, that's about as complicated a question as I've ever been asked. It's an extremely comic tragedy, and I think that everything I write is supposed to work, at least on one level, in a comic way and, as probably most writers hope, I hope that nothing I write is only funny. I think that I have a definite preoccupation with what I think of as being an obligation to make things funny. It's not an obligation imposed upon me, it's an internal one. It may be the expression of a certain insecurity. I've asked myself the question quite a lot in the past. I think that comedy is something I understand much more than tragedy ... (Delaney, p. 33) □

Many of the reactions to Stoppard are based on positive or negative views of the nature of jokes. Thus Ruby Cohn in her condensed and informed survey of Stoppard up to *Night and Day* (chapter 6 of *Contemporary English Drama*, 1981):

■ Stoppard's puns, parodies and performance *are* inventive but they serve no purpose except entertainment in the light drama that constitutes the bulk of his work. In his three major plays, ideological prose burdens his endearing, indomitable and doomed protagonists; their ideas seem comically quirky, but they prove to be quirkily conventional. Failing to achieve 'a perfect marriage between the play of ideas and farce and perhaps even high comedy' Stoppard belabours ideas – aesthetics, politics, philosophy – until they resemble funeral baked meats that coldly furnish forth the marriage tables of farce or perhaps even of high comedy. (p. 120) □

Ten years later, Stoppard had still not convinced Ruby Cohn, in her *Retreats from Realism in Recent English Drama* (1991), that he was writing the 'real thing':

■ No other playwright resorts so consistently to theatre in the theatre, dynamically inventive in the forms of his play. Yet Stoppard's essential centre – the real thing – remains a well-intentioned apolitical bumbler endowed with amusing logorrhea. (p. 127) □

Thus she classifies Inspector Hound, Henry Carr and Henry, the playwright of *The Real Thing*. And she contrasts Stoppard with the serious 'real thing' of Edward Bond's drama, which she defines as 'man's rational control of his destiny'.

It might be said that critics of Stoppard are divided into the categories that Northrop Frye defined as '*Iliad* critics and *Odyssey* critics'. The first group are concerned with how far the art work represents the 'real' world; the second group with art's creation of a play world that has never existed before and exists within the terms it sets up for itself. Art, like language, has both a moral and aesthetic function. It may be referential or musical or both, and the reconciliation of the two is difficult for both critics and artists.

'*Odyssey* critics' find their ancestry, if not in the late Victorian 'art for art's sakers', at least in the formalist school of the 1920s, which leads into the influential structuralism of the 1950s and 1960s. One of the first to apply structuralist principles to drama rather than to fiction was Keir Elam, in his *Semiotics of Theatre and Drama* (1980). His view of Stoppard was commented on in the chapter on *Dogg's Hamlet* and *Cahoot's Macbeth* (Bloom, p. 88). Stoppard's tortoise teaches us, said Elam, that the theatre 'is the privileged seat of pleasurably painful ambiguity'.

Stoppard would qualify Elam's emphasis on ambiguity. In a Tuesday lunchtime dialogue with the Reverend Joseph McCulloch in the church of St Mary-le-Bow on 20 March 1973, Stoppard suggested that

■ as long as one understands what a man means by a statement, what he really means, then his failure to put it into a precise capsule which has absolutely no ambiguity about it, in a sense, doesn't matter. If you and I both know what we mean by x, then it doesn't actually matter if we express it ambiguously. (Delaney, pp. 38–45) □

Ambiguity is not enough. Behind the patterns of language and beyond the comic ironies, Stoppard posits a meaning. He approves his professor in *Jumpers* who believes in the existence of absolute standards against which societies and actions can be measured.

This has final relevance to the vexed academic question of whether Stoppard is 'postmodern'. According to Peter Brooker's *A Concise Glossary of Cultural Theory* (1999):

■ Post-modernism is the conspicuous display of a formal self-consciousness, a borrowing from other texts and styles across genres in such a way that distinctions between high and low culture, Western and other cultures, or the past and present are broken down. The result is a self-ironic eclecticism and knowingness experienced by media-wise audiences and readers along with the post-modern artist, all well versed in the use of the key post-modernist devices of pastiche, parody, recycling and sampling. Post-modernism in this light is playful and allusive: its works are self-referential and intertextual metafictions exploiting a bank of past texts and diverse cultural forms made available in the here and now of a seeming 'perpetual present' by computerisation and media technologies. □

Much of this, especially the references to parody and pastiche, would seem to describe Stoppard's work, but there have been few attempts as yet to apply postmodernist definitions to Stoppard. The concept is more widely applied to fiction. Gérard Genette's work, for example, is based on Proust. Margaret Rose's recent broad survey: *Parody, Ancient, Modern, and Post-Modern* (1993) has no mention of Stoppard and there is little reference to twentieth-century theatre. There is room here for a critical article applauding or condemning Stoppard for being 'postmodern'. But one might also argue that if his work is only 'postmodern' then its value is diminished. Stoppard would probably welcome the application of the term to his work if it related only to the breaking down of a division between high and low cultures, but he would hope that his work is not only for the knowing and illuminated few. He may be a master of pastiche, parody and irony, but he has reservations about their limits. He uses a 'bank of past texts' and is master of a number of media, but his insistence on some universal moral values would take him out of the postmodern category. The question of values, and how his work itself has value, is at the centre of a continuing debate.

CHAPTER TWENTY-TWO

A Note on Character and Dialogue

THE CREATION of 'living' characters, it has been assumed, is a gift the dramatist and the actor must possess. Actors and writers who work in the naturalistic Stanislavsky tradition tend to assume that their characters are individual and whole. Ibsen, who established the naturalistic school, tells us he does not let his characters go until he has them 'to the last button'. But Stoppard has frequently said he was interested in ideas, not character, and that his characters, at least up to *Night and Day*, speak like himself. The question of characterisation in Stoppard (and drama generally) invites fuller comment.

The illusion of living character can be communicated in a number of ways – by the creation of thoughts through soliloquy or aside, by the sheer physicality of the actor's presence and facial and body language, by giving a character a habit of speech or gesture, by giving a character speech rhythms and modes of intellectual and emotional response. None of these means that characters are 'complete' and critics and dramatists have challenged the possibility of 'full' representation of character. Identity has been seen as a changeable social construct. In Brecht's *Mann ist Mann*, based on what Brecht had seen happening with the rise of Fascism in Weimar Germany, a character is taken apart and reconstructed. Pirandello's *Six Characters in Search of an Author* represented characters as a construct of multiple spectator viewpoints. Beckett created in *Waiting for Godot* stage personae which mock our attempts at interpretation. In *Hamlet* characters wear masks, go insane or pretend to be so. Hamlet acts in order to perform and performs in order to act. The acting process disguises identity, holds it together, or helps to create it.

Stoppard, of course, knows this. He places his characters in situations that threaten their identity and shows them, often comically, struggling to retain it. If a character is never complete, at least the struggle for completeness, in rehearsal or in life, is essential to dramatic interest. If characters in performance communicate a convincing humanity, this may consist in their desire to be whole or to their despair at not being so.

Sartre's definition in *Being and Nothingness* of human beings as *future-directed* – 'forever a not this' – is relevant to the portrayal of living, *because incomplete,* dramatic character.

If dramatists as diverse as Pirandello, Brecht and Beckett contest the idea of whole identity (and Stoppard, too, continually interrogates the *duality* of character), academics have done the same. Alan Sinfield in his challenging book *Faultlines* (1992), states his view as follows:

■ In my definition of character as continuous consciousness, I have not posited metaphysical coherence or "unity". For my argument, it is only necessary that a character manifest adequate continuity; as Dodd suggests [in an article in *Lingua e stile* 14 (1979), pp. 135–50], the reader [and one might add the actor] will fill this in as psychological density if he or she wishes. Unity is expected in essentialist humanism, and generally it is discovered through consideration of the characters of Shakespeare's plays. (p. 65) □

Here Sinfield could have cited Lionel Trilling, whose book *Beyond Culture* (1965) is a natural target for the cultural materialist. Trilling considers Shakespeare's heroes are all 'complete before they die' (*The Opposing Self*, p. 38). Sinfield goes on:

■ However, in my view this is a delusion: the effect attributed to unity derives from something else . . . the subjectivities that are admired in the plays do not actually depend upon the achievement of unity, coherence and full presence. Character criticism depends in actuality not on unity but superfluity – on the thwarting of the aspiration to realise unity in the face of material resistance. That is why "stereo-typical" characters, who do have a certain unity, are thought unsatisfactory, and why when characters gain an appearance of unity through closure at the end of a text they become suddenly uninterest-ing. And it is why there are so many essays on the characters of Hamlet and Macbeth: they resist any convenient coherence. Francis Barker, I have noted [in *The Tremulous Private Body*, Methuen, 1984, pp. 31, 35–8], finds Hamlet's interiority merely "gestural", not offering "the pleni-tude of an individual presence", having "nothing" at the centre. In my view that is not quite right: I see Hamlet producing subjectivity effects all the time in his dialogue, but some of them are provocatively dis-continuous, one with another. They construct a sequence of loosely linked interiorities, not a coherent identity . . .

What post-structuralist theory has not explained is the com-placency of essentialist-humanist critics, who have generally found Shakespearean characters very rewarding to speculate about . . . □

Traditional character interpretation, he goes on to say, is stimulated by discontinuity to search for a stabilising unity which does not exist: 'So interpretation disavows that which incites it' (p. 66).

As I have said, the idea of wholeness of character was challenged long ago by Pirandello. And Sartre in 1938 wrote *Nausea*, which shows a historian, Roquentin, who tries, and fails, to rediscover an eighteenth-century figure whose identity disintegrates as his researches progress. Beckett's characters deliberately invite differing interpretations and in any case the comic and tragic traditions have always made play with discontinuity of character in their emphasis on – say – duplicate twins, and the artificiality of fixated characters like misers, absent-minded professors, lovers and questors for some holy grail. Postmodernists and cultural materialists are right to question the search of 'liberal humanists' for unity and closure. The modes of drama may aspire to aesthetic closure, but the discontinuities that drama invites audiences to resolve are often the source of dramatic power.

Stoppard's view is already clear in the novel *Lord Malquist and Mr Moon* (1966). Mr Moon appears to be a bundle of conflicting moral prejudices. He is, like his namesake, sometimes crescent, sometimes half, only occasionally full. Nor does he see others as whole:

■ Hardly anyone behaves naturally any more, they all behave the way they are supposed to be, as if they'd read about themselves, or seen themselves at the pictures. The whole of life is like that now . . . opinion has been set up for you to read back . . . And yet faith in one's uniqueness dies hard. (p. 53) □

This disconcerting novel did not have the success Stoppard hoped for, perhaps because the discontinuities of character are not resolved into a humanity with which the reader can identify. (One character called O'Hara is Irish, black, Jewish and a cockney.) Defiance of the reader's need can defeat popularity.

In *Another Moon Called Earth*, the man who has just returned from the moon has 'made it all *random*' (p. 66). Seeing the earth from the moon is a shift of perspective that threatens confidence in causality and brings on a breakdown of identity and 'normal' behaviour. In the more conventional *Enter a Free Man* (1960), George Riley, the inventor and obsessional dreamer, is thought to change character between home and the pub: 'The point is', says his daughter, 'what's he like? I mean when we can't see him. He's got to be different . . . '. Already Stoppard is seeing characters (or having characters see characters) as, if not multiple, at least double. In *Travesties*, Lenin, Joyce and Tristan Tzara are seen in different ways through the unreliable eyes of Henry Carr, the narrator. Joyce is artist and Irishman, Lenin is revolutionary and lover of

Beethoven, Carr himself can't remember which Wilde character he played in Zurich. Names mingle, like that of the doubly named Hans or Jean Arp who comes from Alsace which is both French and German, or Hugo Ball who is 'unspherical'. Wilde's *The Importance of Being Earnest*, which *Travesties* travesties, insists, of course, that you can be Jack in town and Earnest in the country.

In life, people may be complex and sometimes break down. The aptly named Dottie in *Jumpers* is on the edge of doing so. But in general people do not wake up in the morning as somebody else, even if they sometimes think they do and Stoppard's characters progressively acquire fullness if not unity of identity. One of the problems he encountered in writing the more serious and naturalistic history play of the Polish Solidarity movement, *Squaring the Circle* (1982) was: who was General Jaruzelski? Was he Moscow's man? Patriot? Moderate? Wherein did the truth lie – in extraneous detail such as the colour of his car? Did it in fact lie in a correct psychological portrayal of the General?

For the time being, Stoppard shelved the question. No, he decided, 'truth' lay in the core question of the ideological conflict between Solidarity and the Polish Government – in the historical situation, not in character portrayal. It is a solution Brecht would have applauded. The situation and men's actions are more important than psychology. The uncertainty of character identity nevertheless continues to concern Stoppard. His solution in *Squaring the Circle*, as in *Travesties*, is to see his chameleon characters through the unreliable interpretations of a Narrator, thereby converting to dramatic use the literary methods of Henry James and Joseph Conrad. This blurred the political statement – or did more justice to its complexity – and continued to stimulate, without answering, questions about identity. Stoppard insisted, however, that neither the inscrutability of character nor the political situation was for him of central importance:

■ Actually it doesn't interest me to simulate life in some more plausible way. There are some writers who are far more fascinated by the differentiation of character, and I obviously have no interest in that. I'm only interested in the felicitous expression of ideas, and very often, when I'm rewriting, it doesn't matter who says something – if I need those lines elsewhere I'll give them to a different character. (Interview with Stephen Schiff, 1989; Delaney, p. 222) □

Dialogue is more important than character, this seems to say, and certainly the witty dialogue is crucial. Stoppard even suggests that dialogue takes the place of individualised character:

■ All my characters speak the same way, with the same cadences and

**sentence structures. They speak as I do. When I write an African presi-
dent into a play** [in *Night and Day*] **I have to contrive to make him the
only African President who speaks like me.** (Delaney, p. 132) □

One can hear Peter Hall saying that the clue to directing a playwright is
to listen to the writer's own voice, or Peter Barkworth insisting that an
actor must render the author's voice as well as the character's. But it is
well to qualify Stoppard's own assertion which implies that his dialogue
lacks variety. In the same interview with Mel Gussow (Delaney, p. 131),
he had already asserted: 'I write argument plays. I tend to write for two
people rather than for One Voice'. His plays have a characteristic rhythm,
but rhythm and style incorporate different discourses. He caricatures, for
example, the language of different jobs. In *Albert's Bridge*, Fitch speaks an
exaggerated 'accountantese' which contrasts with the speech of other
members of the committee. In *The Real Inspector Hound*, the clichés of
melodrama are mocked: 'The night is not yet over Simon Gascoyne'; 'So,
the madman has struck'; 'You're a damned attractive woman Cynthia',
or even: 'Well, I think I'll go and oil my guns'! *Dirty Linen* makes extensive use of French and Latin tags, and characters are prone to parapraxis
in the form of appalling malapropisms such as 'in and out of both
trousers of Parliament'. *The Dog It Was That Died* plays games with naval
terms, as does the adapted *Rough Crossing*, which mixes them up: 'A to K
the starboard davits – L to Z port beam amidships, – and don't crowd the
fences'. But the broadest experimentation with a variety of discourses
takes place in *Travesties*, which has Shakespearean sonnets, patriotic war
rhetoric, Wordsworth and Tennysonian references, Lenin's actual words,
the language of *Ulysses*, the rhythms of Oscar Wilde, popular song and
much else.

Languages are thus differentiated and so to a growing degree is individual dialogue. The distinction, for instance, between the witty and the
non-witty character is usually clear:

■ *Ivor*: **Well, as you know, I have a certain gift for, well, words, really.**
   Turai: **How would I know, since you have gone to such trouble to
   conceal it?** (*Rough Crossing*, p. 272) □

The different discourses do not always coincide with clearly differentiated
character, but their variety makes such differentiation less important.
Actors bring varied voices and regional accents to a role, which makes
apparent similarity of dialogue on the page less important than it might
seem. Even Shakespeare's script is less individualised than we think. Nor
should we forget that a single integrating general rhythm, as in Beckett
and Pinter, has a musical power against which a sudden change of pace,
vocabulary and syntax stands out very effectively. Lucky's long speech in

Waiting for Godot and Mick's interior decorating monologue in Pinter's *The Caretaker* are two examples. Fitch's accountancy language in *Albert's Bridge* is a similar device.

Stoppard's early dialogue has strong rhythmical echoes, not only of Beckett and Pinter, but of stand-up comedy, of Tommy Cooper or Morecambe and Wise. *Enter a Free Man* has this rhythm:

- **Just like that!**
  It's a small thing.
  Ho. Yes Yes Yes; a small thing. And so is the bath plug. Simple.
  Obvious. (p. 18) □

In the same play, Linda asks her mother, 'Do you ever think of yourself that there's a kind of sameness to your life?' 'It'd be a funny sort of life if there wasn't', her mother replies. One can hear Alf Garnett's long-suffering wife and sense the comic tradition that allows the down-to-earth reply to confound the questioner. The Fool beats the Wise Man in an exchange where the timing and the beat, not the individual voice, is what matters.

But Stoppard insists he is a playwright 'interested in ideas and forced to invent characters to express those ideas'. Unlike Pirandello, who listens to Six Characters in his head demanding to be expressed, Stoppard begins with an apparent abstraction. Stoppard's 'ideas', however, turn out to be pictures containing people. His phrase *'forced* to invent characters' does not seem fully appropriate. Characters are part of the picture – the idea of one man wanting to paint a bridge for eight years prompts the question: who is he? A non-recorded speaking clock prompts the thought: what does the speaker *feel*? Human voices naturally emerge.

Stoppard's ideas often involve juxtaposing a machine and a human being. This immediately refers us to a Bergsonian definition of comedy – the 'mechanical encrusted upon the living'. The famous formula suggests that laughter is at the expense of someone automatised. But in Stoppard's plays laughter does not anaesthetise sympathy. Within the comical idea lies a poignancy. Gladys, the speaking clock, has both a human and a mechanical voice. Albert's wife suffers from her husband's obsession with the bridge. Albert's need for a mechanical routine destroys the marriage and ironically the mechanical marching of workmen destroys Albert's bridge. Richard Corballis's book, *Stoppard: The Mystery and the Clockwork*, deals at length with this central dramatic tension. The mechanical predicates the need for a human voice.

The idea of an identity existing behind a discourse can create a dramatically powerful character. Thomas Whitaker (Stoppard's best critic according to Harold Bloom) discusses this in his book *Tom Stoppard*. He divides the dramatist's characters into different kinds of 'stylist' according to the way their personal anxieties and degrees of self-confidence prompt them to invent roles and discourses for themselves:

■ Who are Stoppard's stylists? Some of them – Lord Malquist, The Player in *Rosencrantz and Guildenstern Are Dead*, Sir Archibald Jumper in *Jumpers*, Tristan Tzara in *Travesties*, dazzle us with their panache. They are role-players who seem to have become the dandified roles on which they lavish their attention. Narcissists and often professed nihilists, they show few signs of anxiety, having dissolved that inconvenient emotion in the acids of style. Though hungering for an audience, they project images of sophisticated self-sufficiency. Certain others – George Riley in *Enter a Free Man*, Mr Moon, Rosencrantz and Guildenstern, Birdboot and Moon in *The Real Inspector Hound*, George Moore in *Jumpers*, Henry Carr in *Travesties* – are more appealing in their oddness and bumbling earnestness. No less concerned to elaborate a mask or invent a world, they have not known how to divorce themselves from the homely texture of our moral experience. Their ineptitude betrays the connections between a longing for style and an anxiety arising from loneliness, ineffectuality or loss of meaning. Yet others – Jane Moon in *Lord Malquist and Mr Moon*, Dorothy Moore in *Jumpers*, the musician Ivanov in *Every Good Boy Deserves Favour* – seem even less consciously in control of their own projects. Anxiety itself has overwhelmed their faculties, turning what might have once been persons into riddling images of what has not been faced. In their incoherence and exhibitionism we may hear strange cries for help. Even the most ordinary people in a Stoppard work tend to be at least unconscious stylists. (pp. 9–10) □

If this is true, and if the creation of an apparently 'live' character depends on the impression that he or she is choosing to shelter behind a style of discourse – or needs that style in order to create a secure identity – then Stoppard is a creator of living character as well as clever dialogue. The accusation that he is more style than substance becomes simplistic, even in the early plays. More recently, fewer people accuse him of this and Stoppard himself no longer admits to being uninterested in character. In a conversation with Mel Gussow in December 1994 (Gussow, p. 108), Gussow says: 'You used to say, and I never entirely believed it, that all your characters sounded like you'. Stoppard explains:

■ I used to say it because I used to think it was true and maybe it was true in those days. I think everybody in *Night and Day* sounds like me, for example. It's less true now. It's certainly not true in *Indian Ink* . . . I wouldn't say it nowadays. □

A sense of character, then, accompanies Stoppard's fascination with ideas. That sense is not only visual, it is multi-sensory. Thus, in *The Real Thing*, the opening stage directions suggest the physical *presence* of a character:

■ *Max doesn't have to be physically impressive, but you wouldn't want him as an enemy. Charlotte doesn't have to be especially attractive but you instantly want her as a friend.* □

Stoppard wants the actors to communicate a certain power. His apprehension of them is sensory. For a character to be convincing, author, actor and audience must sense this too, even if their modes of perception are not exactly the same. The process is mysterious and not fully subject to critical analysis – as Stoppard illustrates when he speaks of finding the right *name* for a character. Thus:

■ I never felt the person Mrs Swan married in *In the Native State* had the right name. And his name was – I've forgotten what his name was in the radio play. But I always felt there was something wrong with that name. When I was doing *Indian Ink* I realised his name was Eric. He's now Eric. (Gussow, p. 93) □

Stoppard fills out the story around the plot with characters whose names must be right. It reminds one of Chekhov peopling a world and creating a world around his people.

To venture a generalisation about Stoppard's work: there has been a progression from comically fragmented to seriously complex characterisation. But the mockery of stable identity gives way to a concern that the characters should bear names that represent the author's feeling about them. The audience's involvement with later characters, from Ruth, Wagner and Milne in *Night and Day* to Hapgood, Hannah, Valentine and Nightingale, Septimus and Thomasina in *Arcadia*, Mrs Swan and Flora in *Indian Ink*, Housman and A E H in *The Invention of Love*, grows with their rounded humanity – apparently rounded, Alan Sinfield might add. Even a flat supporting character who exists for the plot, like *Arcadia*'s Captain Brice, is given a mind: 'Rest assured Chater, I will let the air out of him', he says to the man who is to duel with Septimus five minutes before him. It takes a moment for Chater to spot the thought in Brice's head. But each character is given the capacity to think and grows more 'real' as a consequence.

The comparative slowness of such characters has a further function. They are what Henry James calls *repoussoirs* or 'contrasting colours' – they illuminate by contrast the lightning intellectual reactions, rapid cueing, and suave controlled demeanour of his Wits in the line of Congreve and Wilde. Such is Septimus; such is Turai in *Rough Crossing*. Across the growing individualism of Stoppard's characters, the general division between Wits and Non-wits still holds. The Wits are in the know and characters who know something that others do not are the staple of dramatic plotting – which has received a great deal of attention in previous chapters. The central argument of this chapter has been that Stoppard has interrogated the question of 'full' identity and created, through dialogue and situation, characters who appear able to reflect upon themselves and others. They give an impressive sense of being human in, or even owing to, their incompleteness or duality.

CHAPTER TWENTY-THREE

Conclusion

STOPPARD HAS not yet completed his work. The yield of the 1990s suggests there is much more to come, though Stoppard himself will no doubt insist he does not know what. So conclusions are premature and should be short. To look back on work so varied to see a clear pattern of evolution is tempting, but dangerous. Stoppard has always surprised his commentators and sheer chance seems to play a part in the ideas that strike his imagination at a particular time: 'You don't question the ideas that come up and hit you. You're just glad' (Gussow, p. 103).

Patterns provide a sense of security, but a dramatist worth his salt subverts such a feeling. Stoppard analyses, sympathises with and makes fun of our need for secure control of our lives and identities. In *Arcadia*, which many feel is his best play to date, Stoppard shows characters jumping to conclusions on insufficient evidence, and using false reasoning to reinforce their self-image or dominate their human situation. He shows other forms of response – 'gut reaction', intuition or imagination – which can either blind an individual or lead him to truth before reason can get there. In this there is comedy. It forges links, too, with the tragic tradition that goes back to that detective, Oedipus Rex, who tracks the light of knowledge and blinds himself when he discovers it. The detectives in *Arcadia* attempt to recover the past or track down universal laws that predict the behaviour of the infinitely large or the infinitely small. The modes of interrogation are particle physics and Newtonian physics. In the gap between them, says Stoppard, lies metaphysics.

In *Arcadia*, gifted but fallible human beings explore the natural world, examine history and predict the future. In doing so they both create myths and espy truths. In the final scene, twentieth-century retrievers of the past perform a momentary poignant dance alongside the nineteenth-century truth-seekers whose lives they research. The stage image remains with us. Past and present fuse in the instant, bringing the past alive again, or lending it new life. The process is reciprocal. The lives and work of the past invigorate Stoppard's plays in the present. Time is momentarily redeemed. The work of Eliot and Beckett and Shakespeare and Wilde and Housman and, yes, Agatha Christie and Morecambe and Wise mingle with the ideas of Wittgenstein and classical philology and Surrealism and Dada. 'You can't mix it backwards', says Thomasina of the jam in her rice pudding. The second law of thermodynamics prevails. But perhaps Stoppard has managed in art to mix it backwards, even if in life that is impossible. This does not prevent us awaiting the future Stoppard with some impatience. A book of poetry perhaps? There is promise of it. But we should be satisfied with the poetry already present in the plays.

SELECT BIBLIOGRAPHY

Plays

Stoppard's plays are available in five volumes in the Contemporary Classics series, Faber & Faber. Volumes for which page references are given in this book are marked with an asterisk.*

Plays 1: The Real Inspector Hound; After Magritte; Dirty Linen; New-Found-Land; Dogg's Hamlet and Cahoot's Macbeth, 1996.*

Plays 2: The Dissolution of Dominic Boot; 'M' is for Moon Among Other Things; If You're Glad I'll be Frank; Albert's Bridge; Where Are They Now?, 1996.

Plays 3: A Separate Peace; Teeth; Another Moon Called Earth; Neutral Ground; Professional Foul; Squaring the Circle, 1998.

Plays 4: Dalliance; Undiscovered Country; Rough Crossing; On the Razzle; The Seagull, 1999.*

Plays 5: Arcadia; Hapgood; Indian Ink; Night and Day; The Real Thing, 1999.

Other Faber & Faber collections are:

Stoppard: The Television Plays 1965–84, 1993 (reprinted as *Plays 3*).*

Stoppard: The Plays for Radio 1964–1991, 1990. (It contains *Plays 2,* together with *Artist Descending a Staircase; The Dog It Was That Died* and *In the Native State* (new edition, 1994).)*

Faber & Faber has published various editions of the following:

After Magritte (1971).

Albert's Bridge and *If You're Glad I'll be Frank* (1969).*

Arcadia (1993).*

Artist Descending a Staircase and *Where Are They Now?* (1973).

Dirty Linen and *New-Found-Land* (1976).

Dogg's Hamlet, Cahoot's Macbeth (Inter-action imprint, 1979).

The Dog it Was That Died and Other Plays (1983).

Enter a Free Man (1968).*

Every Good Boy Deserves Favour and *Professional Foul* (1978).

Hapgood (1988).*

Indian Ink (1995).*

In the Native State (1991).

The Invention of Love (1997).*

Jumpers (1972).*

Night and Day (1978).*

The Real Inspector Hound (1968).

The Real Thing (1982).*

Rosencrantz and Guildenstern Are Dead (1967).*

Squaring the Circle with *Every Good Boy Deserves Favour* and *Professional Foul* (1984).

Travesties (1975).*

Adaptations

Dalliance and Undiscovered Country (from *Liebelei* and *Das Weite Land*, both by Arthur Schnitzler). Faber & Faber, 1986.
Largo Desolato (by V. Havel). Grove Press, 1987.
Rough Crossing (by Ferenc Molnár) and *On the Razzle* (by Johann Nestroy). Faber & Faber, 1991.
Tango (by Slawomir Mrozek). Jonathan Cape, 1968, performed May 1960.
The House of Bernardo Alba (by Federico García Lorca). Performed May 1973.
Undiscovered Country (adapted from Schnitzler). Faber & Faber, 1980, performed June 1979.

Film Scripts

Brazil, directed by Terry Gilliam, 1985.
Empire of the Sun, directed by Steven Spielberg, 1987.
Despair (from 1932 novel by Vladimir Nabokov), directed by Rainer Fassbinder, 1977.
The Human Factor (from 1978 novel by Graham Greene), directed by Otto Preminger, 1979.
The Romantic Englishwoman (from Thomas Wiseman's 1972 novel), directed by Joseph Losey, 1975.
Rosencrantz and Guildenstern Are Dead: the Film, directed by Tom Stoppard, 1991.
Shakespeare in Love (with Marc Norman), directed by John Madden, 1999.

TV Adaptations

Three Men in a Boat (from Jerome K. Jerome's 1889 novel). BBC TV, 1975.

Fiction

Lord Malquist and Mr Moon. Anthony Blond, 1966; Faber & Faber, 1974, 1980.
'The Story', 'Reunion', 'Life, Times: Fragments', in *Introduction 2: Stories by New Writers*. Faber & Faber, 1964.

Interviews

Bareham, T. *Tom Stoppard: Rosencrantz and Guildenstern Are Dead, Jumpers and Travesties*. Macmillan, 1990. (Contains short extracts from Stoppard interviews.)
Delaney, Paul, ed. *Stoppard in Conversation*. University of Michigan Press, 1994. (Contains 39 interviews, selected from a full bibliography listed by year, of 215 interviews in print and, separately, 110 radio and TV interviews given between 1966 and 1994.)
Gussow, Mel. *Conversations with Stoppard*. Nick Hern Books, 1995. (Contains a series of interviews between Stoppard and the author between April 1972 and February 1995.)
Hayman, Ronald. *Tom Stoppard*. Heinemann, 1977, 3rd edn, 1979. (Contains two interviews with the author.)
Smith, Anthony. 'Tom Stoppard in conversation with Anthony Smith'. British Council audio-cassette, 1977 (recorded 17 December 1976).

Articles by Stoppard

Delaney lists 60 articles over a period of 20 years. Here is a selection, mostly available on *Times* microfilm in university libraries:

'Orghast'. Review of *Orghast* by Ted Hughes. *Times Literary Supplement*, 1 October 1971, p. 1174.
'Czech Human Rights'. Letter to the Editor. *The Times*, 7 February 1977, p. 15.
'Journalists' Closed Shop'. Letter to the Editor. *The Times*, 11 August 1977.
'Human Rights in Prague'. Letter to the Editor. *The Times*, 17 October 1977.
'Prague's Wall of Silence'. Open Letter to the President of Czechoslovakia. *The Times*, 18 November 1981.
'Lech's Troubles with Chuck, Bruce and Bob'. *The Times*, 31 May 1984, p. 14 (on *Squaring the Circle*).
'Some Quotes and Correspondence'. Letter about *Hapgood* to nuclear physicist J. D. Polkinghorne (with a reply). Aldwych Theatre programme, 8 March 1988.
'Going Back'. *The Independent Magazine*, 23 March 1991, pp. 24–30 (biographical account of returning to Darjeeling).
'The Uncut Jumpers'. Letter to the Editor, *Financial Times*, 22 April 1993, p. 22 (on Tynan's supposed cuts to the play).
'Another Country'. *Sunday Telegraph Magazine*, 10 October 1999, pp. 15–22 (long biographical article).

Selected Lectures by Stoppard

Stoppard has lectured widely in England and the United States. Delaney lists American lectures up to 1993.

'The Language of Theatre'. University of California, 14 January 1977. Partial transcript in Kenneth Tynan's *Show People: Profiles in Entertainment*, pp. 44–123. Simon & Schuster, 1979.
Lecture about political use of psychiatry in USSR, St Albans, winter 1978–9. See *Theatre News, 11*, no. 8, May 1979, pp. 20–2.
'The Text and the Event: From Writer to Actor' and 'The Text and the Event: From Writer to Critic'. Clark Lectures, Trinity College Cambridge, 8 and 15 February 1980. See *Textual Criticism and Literary Interpretation*, J. J. McGann, ed., University of Chicago Press, 1985, pp. 162–79.
'Direct Experience'. London P.E.N. Writer's Day, South Bank Centre, 23 March 1983, *National Sound Archive*.
'The Less than Sacred Text'. Darwin Lecture, Darwin College, Cambridge. Recording: Office of the Master, Darwin College. See also *Plays and Players* no. 386, February 1986, p. 6.
Lecture in support of Salman Rushdie, Stationer's Hall, London, 14 February 1992. Transmitted BBC 2. Edited version in *The Observer*, 16 February 1992, p. 22.
'Platform Performance'. National Theatre, London, 14 April 1993. See *The Independent*, 17 April 1993, p. 13.

Secondary Material

Books of general relevance mentioned in the text:

Auerbach, Erich. *Mimesis*. Princeton University Press, 1953.

Barkworth, Peter. *On Acting*. Secker & Warburg, 1973.

Bergman, Ingmar. *Bergman on Bergman*. Secker & Warburg, 1973.

Bergson, Henri. *Le Rire*. 1900; trs. as *Laughter*. Macmillan, 1911.

Booker, Peter. *A Concise Glossary of Cultural Theory*. Edward Arnold, 1999.

Brecht, Willett, ed. *Brecht on Theatre*. Hill & Wang, 1964; Methuen, 1964.

Davies, Paul. *The Cosmic Blueprint*. Heinemann, 1987.

Elam, Keir. *The Semiotics of Theatre and Drama*. Methuen, 1980.

Eliot, T. S. *Complete Poems and Plays*. Faber & Faber, 1969.

Esslin, Martin. *The Theatre of the Absurd*. Anchor, 1961; Pelican, 3rd edn, 1980.

Freud, Sigmund. *Jokes and the Unconscious*. Penguin, 1976.

Gleick, James. *Chaos*. Heinemann, 1988.

Henn, T. R. *The Harvest of Tragedy*. Methuen, 1956.

Huizinga, Johann. *Homo Ludens: A Study of the Play Element in Culture*. Routledge, 1949.

Ibsen, Henrik, ed. Sprinchorn. *Letters and Speeches*. Hill & Wang, 1964; Macgibbon and Kee, 1965.

Itzin, C. *Stages in the Revolution*. Eyre Methuen, 1980.

James, William. *Principles of Psychology*. 1890.

Kauffmann, Stanley. *Persons of the Drama*. Harper & Row, 1976.

Koestler, Arthur. *The Act of Creation*. Hutchinson, 1964.

Koestler, Arthur. *The Yogi and the Commissar*. Jonathan Cape, 1945.

Lukács, Georg. *The Meaning of Contemporary Realism*. Merlin Press, 1963.

Marowitz, Milne and Hale, eds. *New Theatre Voices of the Fifties and Sixties*. Eyre Methuen, 1965.

Olivier, Laurence. *On Acting*. Weidenfeld & Nicolson, 1986.

Rose, Margaret. *Parody: Ancient, Modern, and Post-Modern*. Cambridge University Press, 1993.

Saint-Denis, M. *Training for the Theatre*. Heinemann, 1982.

Sartre, Jean-Paul. *La Nausée*. Gallimard, 1938.

Sartre, Jean-Paul. *Sartre on Theatre*. Quartet, 1976.

Sidney, Sir Philip, ed. J. A. Dorsten. *A Defence of Poetry*. Oxford University Press, 1966.

Sinfield, Alan. *Faultlines*. Oxford University Press, 1992.

Stanislavski, K. *An Actor Prepares*. Methuen, 1981.

Trilling, Lionel. *Beyond Culture*. Secker & Warburg, 1966.

Trilling, Lionel, *The Opposing Self: Nine Essays in Criticism*. Secker & Warburg, 1955.

Trussler, Simon, ed. *New Theatre Voices of the Seventies*. Eyre Methuen, 1981.

Williams, Raymond. *Modern Tragedy*. Chatto & Windus, 1966.

Background Reading for Individual Plays

Stoppard reads 'three newspapers a day as a minimum, five on Sunday, because they educate and inform, even yet . . . ' (Gussow, p. 99). His considerable use of literature and philosophy is evident. A few relevant books are listed below:

After Magritte:
Gablik, Suzi. *Magritte*. Thames & Hudson, 1970.

Dogg's Hamlet; Cahoot's Macbeth:
Shakespeare. *Macbeth, Hamlet.*
Wittgenstein, Ludwig. *Philosophical Investigations,* 1953; trs. G. E. M. Anscombe.
  Macmillan, 1968.

Hapgood:
Gleick, James. *Chaos*. Vintage, 1998.
Gleick, James. *Richard Feynman on Modern Physics*. Little, Brown, 1992.

Indian Ink:
Forster, E. M. *A Passage to India.*
Seth, Vikram. *A Suitable Boy.*

The Invention of Love:
Horace. *Odes*
Housman, A. E. *Collected Poems and Selected Prose*. Penguin, 1988.

Jumpers:
Ayer, A. J. *Logical Positivism*. Glencoe, Ill., 1959.
Moore, George E. *Ethics,* 2nd edn. Oxford University Press, 1966.

Neutral Ground:
Eliot, T. S. *Collected Poems and Plays*. Faber & Faber, 1969.
Sophocles, *Philoctetes.*
Wilson, Edmund. *The Wound and the Bow*. W. H. Allen, 1941; Methuen, 1961.

Night and Day:
Waugh, Evelyn. *Scoop.*

The Real Thing:
Ford, John. *Tis Pity She's a Whore.*
Pirandello. *Six Characters in Search of an Author, Tonight we Improvise.*
Strindberg. *Miss Julie.*

Rosencrantz and Guildenstern Are Dead:
Beckett, Samuel. *Waiting for Godot.*
Shakespeare. *Hamlet.*

Shakespeare in Love:
Christie, Agatha. *The Mousetrap.*
Shakespeare. *Romeo and Juliet.*

Travesties:
Ellman, Richard. *James Joyce*. Oxford, 1966.
Motherwell, Robert. *The Dada Painters and Poets: an Anthology*. Wittenborn, 1951.
Ulam, Adam B. *Lenin and the Bolsheviks*. London, 1965.

Wilde, Oscar. *The Importance of Being Earnest.*
Wilson, Edmund. *To the Finland Station.* Macmillan, 1942, revised 1972.

Full-Length Critical Books on Stoppard

Bareham, T., ed. *Tom Stoppard: Rosencrantz and Guildenstern Are Dead, Jumpers and Travesties. Casebook Series.* Macmillan, 1990. (Contains critical studies of three plays, together with selected reviews and Stoppard's own comments.)

Bigsby, C. W. E. *Tom Stoppard.* Longman, 1976.

Bloom, Harold, ed. *Tom Stoppard.* Modern Critical Views. Chelsea House, 1986. (An excellent selection of 14 critical articles.)

Brassell, Tim. *Tom Stoppard: An Assessment.* Macmillan, 1985.

Cahn, Victor L. *Beyond Absurdity: The Plays of Tom Stoppard.* Rutherford: Fairleigh Dickinson University Press, 1979.

Corballis, Richard. *Stoppard: The Mystery and the Clockwork.* Amber Lane & Methuen, 1984.

Dean, Joan Fitzpatrick. *Tom Stoppard: Comedy as a Moral Matrix.* Missouri University Press, 1981.

Harty, John III, ed. *Tom Stoppard: A Casebook.* Garland, 1988. (A collection of 19 articles.)

Hayman, Ronald. *Tom Stoppard,* 3rd edn. Heinemann, 1979. (Has comments on the fiction as well as short appreciations of the plays up to *Dogg's Hamlet.*)

Hunter, Jim. *Tom Stoppard's Plays.* Faber & Faber, 1982. (Unusually arranged. Its chapter headings 'Playing', 'Staging', 'Laughing', 'Talking', 'Travestying', etc. assume a broad knowledge of the plays.)

Hunter, Jim. *Tom Stoppard.* Faber & Faber, 2000. (A student's guide to four plays: *Rosencrantz and Guildenstern Are Dead*; *Jumpers*; *Travesties*; *Arcadia.*)

Jenkins, Anthony. *The Theatre of Tom Stoppard.* Cambridge University Press, 1987; 2nd edn, 1989. (A useful commentary on the plays up to *Hapgood.*)

Jenkins, Anthony, ed. *Critical Essays on Tom Stoppard.* Hall, 1990.

Kelly, Katherine E. *Tom Stoppard and the Craft of Comedy, Medium and Genre at Play.* University of Michigan Press, 1991. (A valuable study containing a final chapter on 'Post-Modern Polyphony'.)

Londré, Felicia. *Tom Stoppard.* Frederick Ungar, 1981.

Nadel, Ira, *Tom Stoppard.* Vintage. A biography due to appear in 2002.

Page, M., ed. *File on Stoppard.* Methuen, 1986.

Sales, Roger. *Rosencrantz and Guildenstern Are Dead.* Penguin, 1988. (Contains sections on parody and 'Travesties and Metadrama' as well as a long commentary on *Rosencrantz and Guildenstern Are Dead, Hamlet* and *Waiting for Godot.*)

Whitaker, Thomas R. *Tom Stoppard.* Macmillan Modern Dramatists, 1983. (An attractive critical survey of plays up to *The Real Thing.*)

Wu, Stephen. *Tom Stoppard's Stagecraft.* Peter Lang, 1988.

General Books on Twentieth-Century Drama Containing Articles on Stoppard

Acheson, James, ed. *British and Irish Drama Since 1960*. Macmillan, 1993. (Contains 'Stoppard's Theatre of Unknowing', by Mary A. Doll, pp. 117–29.)

Bigsby, C. W. E. *Contemporary English Drama*. Edward Arnold, 1981. (Has 'Tom Stoppard: Light Drama and Dirges in Marriage', by Ruby Cohn.)

Bock, H. and Wertheim, A. *Essays on Contemporary British Drama*. Hueber, 1981. (Has two articles: 'Parody, Travesty and Politics in the Plays of Tom Stoppard', by Enoch Brater, pp. 117–30 and 'The Method of Madness: Tom Stoppard's Theatrum Logico-Philosophicum', by Dietrich Schwanitz, pp. 131–54.)

Boireau, Nicole, ed. *Drama on Drama: Dimensions of Theatricality on the Contemporary British Stage*. St Martins, 1997. (Contains 'Tom Stoppard's Metadrama: The Haunting Repetition', by Nicole Boireau, pp. 136–51.)

Brown, John Russell, ed. *Modern British Dramatists*. Prentice Hall, 1984. (Contains 'Tomfoolery: Stoppard's Theatrical Puns', by Hersh Zeifman, pp. 85–108.)

Cohn, Ruby. *Modern Shakespeare Offshoots*. Princeton University Press, 1976, pp. 211–17.

Cohn, Ruby. *Retreats from Realism in Recent English Drama*. Cambridge University Press, 1991. (Contains a number of challenging references to Stoppard.)

Dutton, Richard. *Modern Tragicomedy and the British Tradition*. Oklahoma University Press, 1986.

Hodgson, Terry. *Modern Drama from Ibsen to Fugard*. Batsford, 1992. (Has a chapter 'Freedom, Play and Rosencrantz and Guildenstern', pp. 182–92.)

Hokenson, Jan and Pearce, Howard D., eds. *Forms of the Fantastic*. Greenwood, 1986. (Contains articles on Stoppard by Gabrielle Robinson and Joseph Feeney.)

Innes, Christopher. *Modern British Drama 1890–1990*. Cambridge University Press. (Has a section by the author on 'Tom Stoppard: Theatricality and the Comedy of Ideas', pp. 325–48.)

Marowitz, Charles. *Confessions of a Counterfeit Critic: A London Theatre Notebook, 1958–1971*. Eyre Methuen, 1973, pp. 123–6.

Redmond, James. *Farce*. Cambridge University Press, 1988. (Contains 'The Stereotype betrayed: Tom Stoppard's Farce', by Gabrielle Robinson, pp. 237–50.)

Redmond, James, ed. *Drama and Philosophy*. Cambridge University Press, 1990. (Contains 'Drama as Philosophy: *Professional Foul* Breaks the Rules', by Michael Eldridge, pp. 199–208.)

Salmon, Eric. *Is the Theatre still Dying?* Greenwood, 1985.

Schlueter, June. *Metafictional Characters in Modern Drama*. Columbia University Press, 1979. (Has a section on Stoppard.)

Taylor, John Russell. *The Second Wave: British Drama for the Seventies*. Hill & Wang, 1971. (Contains a chapter on Stoppard.)

Tynan, Kenneth. *Show People*. Simon & Schuster, 1979, pp. 44–123.

Zeifman, H. and Zimmerman, C., eds. *Contemporary British Drama, 1970–90*. Macmillan, 1993. (Has Zeifman's article: 'Comedy of Ambush: Tom Stoppard's

The Real Thing', pp. 217–31; also 'The Optical Illusion: Perception and Form in Stoppard's *Travesties'*, by John Cooke, pp. 199–216 and 'After Magritte, after Carroll, after Wittgenstein. What Tom Stoppard's Tortoise Taught Us', by Keir Elam, pp. 184–98.)

Critical Articles

This list does not contain dissertation abstracts or articles in foreign languages. The titles of these and details of omitted articles in foreign journals are available on the very useful *MLA Bibliography* database. The journal *Modern Drama*, Downsview, Ontario, Canada, contains many articles on Stoppard.

Arnt, Susanne. '"We're All Free To Do as We're Told", Gender and Ideology in Tom Stoppard's *The Real Thing'*. *Modern Drama*, 40:4 (Winter 1997).

Astington, John H. 'The Clever Dog and the Problematic Hare', *Modern Drama*, 36:4 (1993).

Ayer, A.J. 'Love Among the Logical Positivists', *The Sunday Times*, 9 April 1972, p. 16.

Bailey, John A. '*Jumpers* by Tom Stoppard: The Ironist as Theistic Apologist', *Michigan Academician*, 11 (1979), pp. 237–50.

Berlin, Normand. '*Rosencrantz and Guildenstern Are Dead*: Theatre of Criticism', *Modern Drama*, 16 (1973), pp. 269–77.

Billman, Carol. 'The Art of History in Tom Stoppard's *Travesties'*, *Kansas Quarterly*, 12:4 (1980), pp. 47–52.

Brater, Enoch. 'Parody, Travesty and Politics in the Plays of Tom Stoppard', in *Essays on Contemporary British Drama*. Hueber, 1981, pp. 117–30.

Buhr, Richard J. 'Epistemology and Ethics in Tom Stoppard's *Professional Foul'*, *Comparative Literature*, Kalamazoo, 13 (1979), pp. 320–29.

Buhr, Richard J. 'The Philosophy Game in Stoppard's *Professional Foul'*, *Midwest Quarterly*, 22:4 (Summer 1981), pp. 407–15.

Camroux, David. 'Tom Stoppard: The Last of the Metaphysical Egocentrics', *Caliban*, Toulouse, 15 (1978), pp. 79–94.

Carlson, Marvin. 'Is There a Real Inspector Hound?', *Modern Drama*, 36:3 (September 1993).

Cobley, Evelyn. 'Catastrophe Theory in Tom Stoppard's *Professional Foul'*, *Contemporary Literature*, 25:1 (Spring 1984), pp. 53–65.

Cohn, Ruby. 'Tom Stoppard: Light Drama and Dirges in Marriage', in C. Bigsby, ed., *Contemporary English Drama*. Holmes & Meier, 1981, pp. 109–20.

Cooke, John William. 'The Optical Illusion: Perception and Form in Stoppard's *Travesties'*, *Modern Drama*, 24:4 (December 1981), pp. 525–39.

Corballis, Richard. 'Extending the Audience: The Structure of *Rosencrantz and Guildenstern Are Dead'*, *Ariel*, 11:2 (1980), pp. 65–79.

Corballis, Richard. 'Wilde/Joyce/O'Brien/Stoppard: Modernism and Post-modernism in *Travesties'*. Milwaukee James Joyce Conference. Delaware University Press, 1991, pp. 157–70.

Crossley, Brian M. 'An Investigation of Stoppard's *Hound* and *Foot*', *Modern Drama*, 20 (1977), pp.77–86.

Crump, G.B. 'The Universe as Murder Mystery: Tom Stoppard's *Jumpers*'. *Contemporary Literature*, 20 (1979), pp.354–68.

Darling, Robert. 'Tom Stoppard, Deconstruction, and the Question of Value'. *Bulletin of the West Virginia Association of College English Teachers*, 11 (Autumn 1989), pp.69–81.

Davidson, Mary. 'Historical Homonyms: A New Way of Naming in Tom Stoppard's *Jumpers*', *Modern Drama*, 22 (1979), pp.305–13.

Delaney, Paul. 'The Flesh and the Word in *Jumpers*', *Modern Language Quarterly* 4, 42 (December 1981), pp.369–88.

Delaney, Paul. 'Cricket Bats and Commitment: The Real Thing in Art and Life', *Critical Quarterly*, 27:1 (Spring 1985), pp.45–60.

Diamond, Elin. 'Stoppard's *Dogg's Hamlet*, *Cahoot's Macbeth*: The Uses of Shakespeare', *Modern Drama*, 29:4 (December 1986).

Donaldson, Ian. 'The Ledger of the Lost-and-Stolen-Office: Parody in Dramatic Comedy', *Southern Review,* 13:1 (March 1980), pp.41–52.

Duncan, Joseph E. 'Godot Comes: Rosencrantz and Guildenstern Are Dead', *Ariel*, 12:4 (October 1981), pp.57–70.

Durham, Weldon B. 'Symbolic Action in Tom Stoppard's *Jumpers*', *Theatre Journal,* 32 (1980), pp.169–79.

Egan, Robert. 'A Thin Beam of Light: The Purpose of Playing in *Rosencrantz and Guildenstern Are Dead*', *Theatre Journal*, 31 (1979), pp.59–69.

Elam, Keir. 'After Magritte, after Carroll, after Wittgenstein: What Stoppard's Tortoise Taught Us', *Modern Drama*, 27:4 (December 1984).

Ellman, Richard. 'The Zealots of Zurich', *Times Literary Supplement*, 12 July 1974, p.744.

Farish, Gillian. 'Into the Looking-Glass Bowl: An Instant of Grateful Terror', *University of Windsor Review*, 10:2 (1975), pp.14–29.

Freeman, John. 'Holding up the Mirror to Mind's Nature: Reading Rosencrantz "Beyond Absurdity"', *Modern Language Review*, 91:1 (January 1996).

Gabbard, Lucina P. 'Stoppard's *Jumpers*: A Mystery Play', *Modern Drama*, 20 (1977), pp.87–95.

Gabbard, Lucina P. 'The Roots of Uncertainty in Pinter and Stoppard', *Forum*, 16:3 (Summer/Autumn 1978), pp.53–60.

Giancaris, C.J. 'Absurdism Altered: *Rosencrantz and Guildenstern Are Dead*', *Drama Survey*, 7 (1969), pp.52–8.

Giancaris, C.J. 'Stoppard as Master Games Player: *Travesties* and After', *Perspectives on Contemporary Literature*, 6 (1980), pp.11–19.

Giancaris, C.J. 'Stoppard's Adaptations of Shakespeare: *Dogg's Hamlet*, *Cahoot's Macbeth*', *Comparative Drama*, 18:3 (Autumn 1984), pp.222–40.

Gitzen, Julian. 'Tom Stoppard: Chaos in perspective', *Southern Humanities Review*, 10 (1976), pp.143–52.

Gold, Margaret. 'Who Are the Dadas of *Travesties*?', *Modern Drama*, 21 (1978), pp.59–65.

Grant, Steve. Review of *Night and Day*, *Plays and Players* (January 1979), pp.18, 19.

Grüber, William E. "'Wheels within Wheels etc." Artistic Design in *Rosencrantz and Guildenstern Are Dead*', *Comparative Drama*, 15:4 (Winter 1981–2), pp. 291–310.

Guralnik, Elissa S. '*Artist Descending a Staircase*: Stoppard Captures the Radio Station – and Duchamp', *PMLA America*, 105:2 (March 1990).

Hardin, Nancy Shields. 'An Interview with Tom Stoppard', *Contemporary Literature*, 22 (1981), pp. 153–66.

Harris, Wendell V. 'Stoppard's *After Magritte*'. *Explicator*, Richmond, Virginia, 34 (1976), Item 40.

Harty, John. 'Stoppard's *Lord Malquist and Mr Moon*'. *Explicator*, Washington, 43:2 (Winter 1985).

Hinden, Michael. '*Jumpers*: Stoppard and the Theatre of Exhaustion'. *Twentieth Century Literature*, 27:1 (Spring 1981), pp. 1–15.

Hinden, Michael. 'After Beckett: The Plays of Pinter, Stoppard and Shepard', *Contemporary Literature*, 27:3 (Autumn 1986).

Howarth, William D. 'From Satire to Comedy of Ideas: The Examples of Anouilh and Stoppard'. *Franco-British Studies, Journal of the British Institute in Paris*, 3 (Spring 1987).

Hu, Stephen. 'Political Aesthetics and *Every Good Boy Deserves Favour*', *Theatre Annual: A Journal of Performance Studies*, 42 (1987).

James, Clive. 'Count Zero Splits the Infinitive: Tom Stoppard's Plays',*Encounter XLV* (November 1975), pp. 68–76.

Kahn, Coppelia. '*Travesties* and the Importance of Being Stoppard', *New York Literary Forum*, 1 (1978), pp. 187–97.

Kelly, Katherine E. 'Tom Stoppard's *Artist Descending a Staircase*: Outdoing the Dada Duchamp', *Comparative Drama*, 20:3 (Autumn 1986).

Kelly, Katherine E. 'Tom Stoppard Radioactive: A Sounding of the Radio Plays', *Modern Drama*, 32:3 (September 1989).

Kelly, Katherine E. 'Tom Stoppard Journalist: Through the Stage Door', *Modern Drama*, 33:3 (September 1990).

Kennedy, Andrew. 'Old and New in London Now', *Modern Drama*, 11 (1969), pp. 437–46.

Kennedy, Andrew. 'Natural, Mannered and Parodic Dialogue', *Yearbook of English Studies* 9 (1979), pp. 28–54.

Kennedy, Andrew. 'Tom Stoppard's Dissident Comedies', *Modern Drama*, 25:4 (December 1982), pp. 469–76.

Keyssar-Francke, Helene. 'The Strategy of *Rosencrantz and Guildenstern Are Dead*', *Educational Theatre Journal*, 27 (1975), pp. 85–97.

Krebs, Barbara. 'How Do We Know That We Know What We Know in Stoppard's *Jumpers*?', *Twentieth Century Literature*, 32:2 (Summer 1986).

Kruse, Axel. 'Tragicomedy and Tragic Burlesque: *Waiting for Godot* and *Rosencrantz and Guildenstern Are Dead*', *Sydney Studies in English*, 1 (1975–6), pp. 76–96.

Lenoff, Leslee. 'Life Within Limits: Stoppard on the HMS Hamlet', *Arizona Quarterly*, 38:1 (Spring 1982), pp. 44–61.

Leonard, Virginia E. 'Tom Stoppard's *Jumpers*: The Separation from Reality', *Bulletin of West Virginia Association of College Teachers*, 2:1 (1975), pp. 45–56.

Levenson, Jill. 'Views From A Revolving Door: Tom Stoppard's Canon to Date', *Queen's Quarterly*, 78 (1971), pp. 431–42.

Levenson, Jill. '*Hamlet* Andante/*Hamlet* Allegro: Tom Stoppard's Two Versions', *Shakespeare Survey*, 36 (1983), pp. 21–8.

Levy, B.S. 'Serious Propositions Compromised by Frivolity', *Critical Quarterly*, 22:3 (1980), pp. 79–85.

Londré, Felicia Hardison. 'Using Comic Devices to Answer the Ultimate Question: Tom Stoppard's *Jumpers* and Woody Allen's God', *Comparative Drama*, 14 (1980–1), pp. 346–54.

MacKenzie, Ian. 'Tom Stoppard and the Monological Imagination', *Modern Drama*, 32:4 (December 1989).

Meyer, Kinereth. 'It Is Written: Tom Stoppard and the Drama of the Intertext', *Comparative Drama*, 23:2 (Summer 1989).

Morwood, James. '*Jumpers* Revisited', *Agenda*, 19:4 (Winter/Spring 1981), pp. 135–41.

Nitzsche, J.C. 'McLuhan's Message and Stoppard's Medium in *Rosencrantz and Guildenstern Are Dead*', *Dutch Quarterly Review*, 10 (1980), pp. 32–40.

Pearce, Howard D. 'Stage as Mirror: Tom Stoppard's *Travesties*'. *MLN*, 94 (1979), pp. 1139–58.

Perlette, John M. 'Theatre at the Limit: *Rosencrantz and Guildenstern Are Dead*', *Modern Drama*, 28:4 (December 1985), pp. 659–69.

Prapassaree, Kramer Jeffrey. 'Stoppard's *Arcadia*: Research, Time, Loss', *Modern Drama*, 40:1 (Spring 1997).

Rabinowitz, Peter J. 'What's Hecuba to Us? The Audience's Experience of Literary Borrowing', in *The Reader in the Text, Essays on Audience and Interpretation*. Princeton University Press, 1980, pp. 241–63.

Robinson, Gabriele. 'Nothing Left But Parody: Friedrich Dürrenmatt and Tom Stoppard', *Theatre Journal*, 2 (1980), pp. 85–94.

Robinson, Gabriele Scott. 'Plays Without Plot: The Theatre of Tom Stoppard', *Educational Theatre Journal*, 29 (1977), pp. 37–48.

Rod, David K. 'Carr's Views on Art and Politics in Tom Stoppard's *Travesties*', *Modern Drama*, 26:4 (December 1983), pp. 536–42.

Rothstein, Bobbi. 'The Reappearance of Public Man: Stoppard's *Jumpers* and *Professional Foul*', *Kansas Quarterly*, 12:4 (1980), pp. 35–44.

Rusinko, Susan. 'The Last Romantic: Henry Boot, Alias Tom Stoppard', *World Literature Today*, 59:1 (Winter 1985).

Ruskin, Phyllis and Lutterbie, John H. 'Balancing the Equation', *Modern Drama*, 26:4 (December 1983), pp. 543–54.

Salmon, Eric. 'Faith in Tom Stoppard', *Queen's Quarterly 2*, 86 (Summer 1979), pp. 215–32.

Sammels, Neil. 'Earning Liberties: *Travesties* and *The Importance of Being Earnest*', *Modern Drama*, 29:3 (September 1986).

Sammels, Neil. 'Giggling at the Arts: Tom Stoppard and James Saunders', *Critical Quarterly*, 28:4 (Winter 1986).

Schwanitz, Dietrich. 'The Method of Madness. Tom Stoppard's Theatrum Logico-Philosophicum', in *Essays on Contemporary British Drama*. Hueber, 1981, pp. 131–54.

Schwartzman, Myron. 'Wilde about Joyce? Da! But My Art Belongs to Dada!', *James Joyce Quarterly*, 13 (1974), pp. 122–3.

Shiner, Roger A. 'Showing, Saying and Jumping', *Dialogue: Canadian Philosophical Review*, 21:4 (December 1982), pp. 625–46.

Simard, Rodney. 'The Logic of Unicorns: Beyond Absurdism in Stoppard', *Arizona Quarterly*, 38:1 (Spring 1982), pp. 37–44.

Sinfield, Alan. 'Making Space: Appropriation and Confrontation in Recent British Plays', in G. Holderness, ed., *The Shakespeare Myth*, 1988, pp. 128–44.

Stern, J.P. 'Anyone for Tennis, Anyone for Death: The Schnitzler/Stoppard *Undiscovered Country*', *Encounter* (October 1979).

Thomson, Leslie. 'The Sub-text of *The Real Thing*. It's "All Right"', *Modern Drama*, 30:4 (December 1987).

Thomson, Leslie. '"The Curve Itself" in *Jumpers*', *Modern Drama*, 33:4 (December 1990).

Treglown, Jeremy. 'Shakespeare's Macbeths: Davenant, Verdi, Stoppard and the Question of Theatrical Text', *English*, 29 (1980), pp. 95–113.

Varey, Simon. 'Nobody Special: On *Rosencrantz and Guildenstern Are Dead*', *Dutch Quarterly Review*, 10 (1980), pp. 20–31.

Weightman, John. 'Art Versus Life', *Encounter*, 43 (September), pp. 57–9.

Weightman, John. 'A Metaphysical Comedy', *Encounter*, 38 (April), pp. 44–6.

Werner, Craig. 'Stoppard's Critical Travesty, or, Who Vindicates Whom and Why', *Arizona Quarterly*, 35 (1979), pp. 228–36.

Wheeler, Elizabeth. 'Light It Up and Move It Around: *Rosencrantz and Guildenstern Are Dead*', *Shakespeare on Film Newsletter*, 16:1 (December 1991), p. 5.

Wilcher, Robert. 'Tom Stoppard and the Art of Communication', *Journal of Beckett Studies*, 8 (Autumn 1982), pp. 105–23.

Zeifman, Hersh. 'Tomfoolery: Stoppard's Theatrical Puns', *Yearbook of English Studies*, IX (1979), pp. 204–20.

Zeifman, Hersh. 'Comedy of Ambush: Tom Stoppard's *The Real Thing*', *Modern Drama*, 26:2 (June 1983).

Zinman, Toby Silverman. 'Blizintsy/Dvojniki Twins/Doubles Hapgood/Hapgood', *Modern Drama*, 34:2 (June 1991).

Zivanovic, Judith. 'Meeting Death Already There: The Failure to Choose in Stoppard's *Rosencrantz and Guildenstern Are Dead*', *Liberal and Fine Arts Review*, 1:1 (January 1981), pp. 44–56.

Bibliographies

Bratt, David. *Tom Stoppard: A Reference Guide*. G.K. Hall, 1982.

Carpenter, Charles A., comp. 'Bond, Shaffer, Stoppard, Storey: An International Checklist of Commentary'. *Modern Drama*, 24:4 (1981), pp. 546–56.

Kimball, King. *Twenty Modern British Dramatists: a Bibliography, 1956–1976*. Garland, 1977, pp. 217–30.

MLA Bibliography Database.

Ryan, Randolph. 'Theatre Checklist No. 2: Tom Stoppard', *Theatrefacts 2* (May–July 1974), pp. 2–9.

ACKNOWLEDGEMENTS

The editor and publisher wish to thank the following for their permission to reprint copyright material: Faber & Faber (for material quoted from Tom Stoppard's plays); University of Michigan Press (for material from *Stoppard in Conversation*); Nick Hern Books (for material from *Conversations with Stoppard*); Heinemann (for material from *Tom Stoppard*); Oxford University Press (for material from *Faultlines*); Methuen (for material from *New Theatre Voices of the Seventies* and *Stoppard: The Mystery and the Clockwork*); Chelsea House (for material from *Tom Stoppard*); Garland (for material from *Tom Stoppard: A Casebook*); Cambridge University Press (for material from *The Theatre of Tom Stoppard*); Macmillan (for material from *Tom Stoppard*); *Modern Drama* (for material from 'Comedy of Ambush: Tom Stoppard's *The Real Thing*').

There are instances where we have been unable to trace or contact copyright holders before our printing deadline. If notified, the publisher will be pleased to acknowledge the use of copyright material.

Grateful thanks must go to Sir Tom Stoppard for the immense enjoyment which study of the whole corpus of his plays has given the editor over the past year. He would also especially like to thank his colleague Nicolas Tredell for suggestions of material and for his and Duncan Heath's editorial help in the final stages of this book.

Terry Hodgson is Senior Lecturer in Literature and Drama at the University of Sussex, working in the Schools of European and English and American Studies and in Continuing Education. He has taught abroad in a Paris Lycée and was a lecturer in English Language and Literature at two universities in Turku, Finland. On returning to England he taught for Oxford University as Staff Tutor for the Extra-Mural Delegacy, and has frequently taught courses for Cambridge University Department of Continuing Education. Previous publications include *A Dictionary of Drama* and *Modern Drama* (both published by Batsford).

INDEX